The Sociopath's Playbook

The Quintessential Guide to Navigating the Sociopathically Adjusted Playing Field

50 Tactics Abusers Use and
50 Action Plans to Counter Them

Paul M. Conlon, MBA

PAGE PUBLISHING, INC.
New York, NY

First originally published by Page Publishing, Inc. 2019

ISBN 978-1-68456-047-9 (Paperback)
ISBN 978-1-68456-049-3 (Digital)

Printed in the United States of America

To my loving family, especially my late grandparents of incomparable character: Melba McNeil Moore, possibly the first female medical doctor to be born in Jackson County, Texas—an irreproachable and benevolent woman who so enthusiastically encouraged a small boy on a typewriter; my grandfather, Raymond Thomas Moore, health commissioner of the state of Texas and unrelenting advocate for the betterment of everyone's well-being; my grandfather, Silver Star recipient, John David Conlon, a medic whose nineteenth birthday was spent June 6, 1944, on Omaha Beach; and a woman whose sense of family and caring nature have always inspired me and taught me how to be a champion, my loving grandmother, Elizabeth Snyder Conlon. May the writing of a small boy born the day of your funeral be of assistance to many, many people. How I regret never meeting you.

Contents

Part 3: Epilogue

Prologue

You might be curious about why I chose to undertake this journey. I am afraid I cannot be absolutely certain. Beyond the obvious sentiment concerning feeling compelled to help others, something within urged me to keep going—like a figurative hunger, a need never silenced or satiated. It felt right. Thoughts were percolating within me in response to what I was researching that I wanted to share.

The project started, of all places, in a used bookstore. I came across a *Diagnostic and Statistical Manual of Mental Disorders*, fourth edition, text revision, for the first time—or as it is commonly referred to—a *DSM-IV-TR* (American Psychiatric Association, 2000). While flipping through its contents, I stumbled upon antisocial personality disorder. Upon reading its description, my sense of reality was rocked in a most groundbreaking manner.

Preceding that day, that moment—that experience—like so many, I just assumed everyone had a conscience, felt remorse, guilt, love, a need to self-actualize, and a desire to care about, and feel emotionally connected to, others. As I sat there on an old circular step stool, I began to perceive many lucid connections to the DSM descriptors—humbled by the complexities of the human mind. In the succeeding months, I felt this burning desire to learn everything I could access concerning the disorder, and then—somewhere along the way, something else happened—I felt this desire to begin writing about it.

A part of me felt like it was something I might be able to do—though it was never going to be easy to write about a subject without related course work or degrees. But I did have several wonderful teachers and professors who urged and encouraged lifelong learning—*especially* in areas in which one does not have any particular familiarity—and in that way, they were unconventionally wise, even pioneering.

Not all destructive sociopaths or psychopaths are readily identifiable as menaces, ne'er-do-wells, bullies, or outright criminals as some abusers operate undetected in the roles of educators, administrators, peers, friends, acquaintances, coaches, supervisors, bosses, coworkers, self-identified ministers, family members, and even complete strangers. Indeed, sociopaths and psychopaths come in all shapes and sizes, from all walks of life, and can occupy every conceivable profession—even expert psychotherapists specializing in treating personality disorders—or physically proficient law enforcement officers lacking the emotional and psychological capacities to truly qualify for their positions.

Everyone has a story. It would be dishonest of me to claim my life experience has remained bereft of encountering abusive sociopaths and psychopaths. In retrospect, perhaps things I have had the misfortune of experiencing have uniquely qualified me to endure, contemplate, and comment upon this subject matter compared to most individuals.

But others have had it and, sadly, do have it worse. *They* are who are on my mind. And my mind will not rest while they need people and resources to help them—just as much as they need people and resources to step up to the plate to address their abusers more effectively.

This work is not about me—it's about *us*. And it's not about ruminating or venting—it's about channeling energy positively, authentically empowering, and productively assisting. It's about helping others. It's about being proactive. It's about being there for others and giving a figurative hug and authentic intention of encouragement over the next seventy-five-thousand-plus words. And for every word in this book, it has been estimated, there is roughly one yet to be identified psychopath potentially operating abusively just in the United States alone. Not to mention, one in every twenty-five people you meet *just might be* a sociopath. Do you still see each word the same?

How can you begin to help? Consider the following premise for self-reflection: So you've made it this far in your life. Maybe you feel successful. Did you win the lottery? Not in the traditional sense of the word—but have you had a life with minimal encounters and interactions with those who are conscience-impaired and malicious? Have those in positions to promote you or protect you treated you with justice? Have you only ever felt so safe due to others that you never had trouble functioning around them?

If you find yourself thinking as much after careful consideration, congratulations, dear lottery winner—and please know, an *authentic* congratulations at that. But please remember—your understanding of conflict management, resolution, and avoidance does not necessarily apply to someone who was not quite as lucky as you, who was, or is, greatly impacted by the intentions and actions of abusive psychopaths and sociopaths. With this book, I encourage you—if you have not already—to take the chance to grasp others' misfortunate from another angle. An angle that does not necessarily presume others would be successful, if they only navigated life or interpersonal situations like you did to get wherever it is your success has brought you.

Perhaps you have already realized as much. And if so, thank you for your foresight, wisdom, and the consideration you have intended and currently show to your fellow members of the human race. And subsequently, thank you for what you do to help others, both non-abusively and genuinely. I am just one person, but I truly appreciate and thank you for using your position of strength to help others in need.

My proposals and opinions may be in many respects incomplete, superficial, or erroneous. It is too much to ask that the viewpoint of any one observer in so complex and confusing a matter be generally accepted as final. The whole field of psychiatry, by its very nature, abounds in questions still unanswered and about which diverse opinions naturally exist and arguments inevitably arise. If we cannot agree that the psychopath has anything like a "psychosis" or even a "mental disorder," can we not all agree that some means is urgently needed of dealing effectively with whatever it is that may be the matter with him?

—Hervey M. Cleckley, The Mask of Sanity (third edition), 1955

Part I

*The Beginning
of a Journey*

Introduction

Twenty Essential Questions

Though it is revolutionary, what if we actively taught children psychopathy exists—and what if we prepared them to identify and address it as it may affect their futures? What if we empowered them to recognize another's manipulation *before* they internalize the imagined inadequacies abusers have prepared for them? And what if we started right now?

Welcome, dear reader, and thank you for your time—not a detached, substanceless thank-you from a computer but from an actual human being, *me*. Whenever you read this, know that at a certain moment in time—though I do not necessarily know your name, where you are, or even when you might be experiencing this sentence—with appreciation I attempted to imagine you, mindful of your potential commitment to helping others.

With great limitation, I attempted to imagine your mind as it experiences these words—*you*—from a tremendous background, likely teeming with personal memories and countless thoughts and feelings percolating within. I intend sincerity with you and value your perspective. And further, with this writing, I intend positivity, love, and progression.

As a full disclaimer, though I hold several graduate degrees, they are not directly related to the discipline in this writing. I am not a psychologist, clinical health provider, or mental health professional. I believe in an environment where anyone can put his or her efforts toward learning and writing about a given academic endeavor. The sentiment that only "qualified" individuals should be allowed to share thoughts and advance innovation on a particular medically related subject matter feels incredibly restrictive to me. And further, the idea that innovation in a field can only come from self-identified experts or professional researchers is anathema to progress.

Researchers discrediting nonexperts' innovations on the grounds that such contributions represent noviceship engage in outmoded twentieth-century thinking. Did Aristotle have a doctoral degree in philosophy? And if so, did his predecessors who bestowed upon him his degree have predecessors who bestowed upon them doctoral degrees as well? And tracing that line backward, assuming extinct hominids did not grant one another PhD's, it becomes much easier to come to terms with the notion that even a formally educated adult scholar can learn something—*even* many things—from the minds of others with less formal education.

Additionally, I believe there can be strength in not being a certified "whatever" in the sharing, construction, and advancement of thoughts and ideas concerning sociopathy with others. I think back to a heavyweight, trailblazing contributor in the field of psychopathy like Hervey Cleckley, who, at one point in time, felt like a drowned-out voice in addressing how to make the world a better, healthier environment (as cited in Seabrook, 2008). And I ponder—what would he think about a nonexpert weighing in through written discourse?

I cannot help imagining his warm hospitality. With contentment, I find myself at peace in entering these deep waters, even if welcomed by few. Even without an established cure, many others, like he did, believe there exists value in advancing the discussion and promoting awareness of antisocial personality disorder and psychopathy in general. I seek to contribute to that value.

Before delving into the tactics and their commensurate action plans, chapters 1 and 2 provide relevant background information organized for convenience in a sequential question-and-answer format. But where should such a foundational background section begin? Perhaps no other place can serve as a more appropriate starting point than an attempt at defining one word in particular.

So what is a sociopath?

According to a *Merriam-Webster Dictionary* definition, a *sociopath* is "someone who behaves in a dangerous or violent way towards other people and does not feel guilty about such behavior," while a *psychopath* is "a person who is mentally ill, who does not care about other people, and who is usually dangerous or violent…affected with antisocial personality disorder" ("Sociopath," n.d.; "Psychopath," n.d.). Concurrently, Merriam-Webster defines antisocial personality disorder:

> [as] a personality disorder that is characterized by antisocial behavior exhibiting pervasive disregard for and violation of the rights, feelings, and safety of others…that is often marked by a lack of remorse for having hurt, mistreated, or stolen from others.…called also psychopathic personality disorder. ("Antisocial personality disorder," n.d.).

In essence, according to *Merriam-Webster*, the *antisocial personality disorder* definition links back to the term *psychopath*, just as the term *psychopath* indirectly mirrors the definition of the term *sociopath*—bringing all three terms full circle as inextricably linked and united to represent a related concept. Moreover, not only do the preceding terms mirror one another, the term *sociopath* actually stands alone as a one-word medical dictionary definition for the term, psychopath ("Sociopath," n.d.). Though—as will later be discussed—according to multiple experts, the words *sociopath* and *psychopath* may not truly prove synonymous.

The preceding definitions expose a semblance of unity among the various phrases. However, distinction between the terms presents itself for at least one glaring reason: the terms feature different dates of origin and induction into common vernacular. As evidence of this, the term *psychopath* has been around since the mid-1880s and precedes the word *sociopath,* which has only been known to be in use since the 1930s. But the youngest of the three terms, *antisocial personality disorder*, has only been circulated since the latter part of the twentieth century. Most recently, the term was defined by the American Psychological Association as

> the presence of a chronic and pervasive disposition to disregard and violate the rights of others. Manifestations include repeated violations of the law, exploitation of others, deceitfulness, impulsivity, aggressiveness, reckless disregard for the safety of self and others, and irresponsibility, accompanied by lack of guilt, remorse, and empathy. (2015, pp. 65–66)

And though the phrasing *antisocial personality disorder* may appear to suggest a relatively nascent concept, according to *Merriam-Webster*, *antisocial personality disorder* is synonymous with the much older term *psychopathic personality disorder*, which came into being during the 1920s. And approximately twenty-five years earlier, preceding the *disorder* component in the phrase *psychopathic personality disorder*, German psychiatrist Emil Kraeplin expounded on the meaning of the term *psychopathic personality* (as cited in Burton, 2012).

The term *psychopath* likely originated in the 1880s, but was not popularized until the 1940s, in large part due to the release of American psychiatrist Hervey Cleckley's seminal work on psychopathy, *The Mask of Sanity*. And around half of a century after the advent of the term *psychopath*—when it was first utilized in a professional context to describe immoral, shallow emotional affect—the word *sociopath* was monikered in the 1930s by psychologist G. E. Partridge. From there, the American Psychiatric Association evolved the diagnosis of "psychopathic personality" to "sociopathic personality disturbance" to its current phrasing: "antisocial personality disorder" (American Psychiatric Association, 1952, 1968, 2013a). And though the term *psychopath* outlasted the now antiquated phrases "mania without delirium," "moral derangement," "moral insanity," and "constitutional psychopathic inferiority"—one thing remains certain: within the last two-plus centuries, such phrases once circulated among the international mental health community, falling into and out of favor (Cleckley, 1941; Seabrook, 2008).

While new phrasing continues to be introduced, and definitions for antisocial personality disorder continue to be refined and evolve, the underlying concept has remained unadulterated and, if anything, is most clearly and elaborately defined in the present time period. However, multiple professionals currently express interest in divesting the labels *psychopath*, *sociopath*, and *antisocial personality disorder* to reflect hyperstringent, ever-evolving specific definitions for each individual term.

The word antisocial *seems simple enough to understand, but what does it really mean?*

In analyzing the term *antisocial personality disorder*—a murky and ambiguous word—*antisocial*, requires careful scrutiny. The word *antisocial* likely came into being near the beginning of the nineteenth century, but presents itself misleadingly. To many, *antisocial* is interpreted to mean an individual who is nonsocial, or, in effect, averse to being social.

This can be the case for the definition, but by no means is this interpretation all-encompassing. *Antisocial* can also mean "violent or harmful to people," according to *Merriam-Webster* ("Antisocial," n.d.). From this interpretation, it becomes much clearer how antisocial personality disorder refers to harming others, as opposed to being averse to interacting socially with others. To that end, sociopaths may frequently socialize with others, though—as will be later discussed—high-frequency social interaction does not necessarily equate to liking others genuinely or even forming and maintaining authentic interpersonal bonds with others.

Evidence seems to suggest that in various organizational publications, the American Psychiatric Association, *innocently enough*, grappled with and refined its intended meaning of the word *antisocial* for the phrase *antisocial personality*. For example, an earlier definition for antisocial personality disorder released in the 1960s featured the caveat, "This term is reserved for individuals who are basically unsocialized…incapable of significant loyalty to individuals, groups, or social values" (American Psychiatric Association, 1968, p. 43). And as would later, and more thoroughly, be addressed throughout the years, not only are some sociopaths abundantly networked interpersonally and masterfully proficient in social situations—some sociopaths do, indeed, exhibit loyalty. Though such loyalty arguably is never truly divorced from self-interest. Furthermore, it remains significant to recall that the action of exhibiting loyalty fails to constitute nonabusive behavior in every conceivable situation and circumstance.

Okay, the words can be synonymous, but come on—is a sociopath really the same as a psychopath?

Some experts believe the terms are interchangeable while others believe the psychopath may be more identifiably violent (Bonn, 2014). Some have suggested that psychopaths lack consciences altogether while sociopaths possess consciences that are very weak (Robinson, n.d.). Moreover, some believe a behavioral distinction may be made that identifies psychopaths as more subtly and cunningly manipulative, whereas a sociopath's behaviors and motives may display much more obvious and identifiable self-interest (Grohol, 2015).

Another distinction may be made through a common cultural perception of the word *psychopath* as reflective of an actual criminal, often a violent murderer, whereas a sociopath represents an individual with a dormant potential to engage in criminal activity. Still another distinction appears to modify the aforementioned one, which identifies the sociopath as criminally capable like a psychopath but perhaps dangerous to a lesser extent than the psychopath. And in regard to origin of the disorder, some believe sociopathy to be a learned behavior and psychopathy to be a matter of genetics or possibly brain dysfunction. Differences abound.

Again, while some experts draw distinctions, other experts feel the terms are interchangeable. By no means do I wish to discredit any researcher's substantial work or thoughts on such issues. Although it remains unresolved whether the terms possess no distinction, represent different diagnoses, or perhaps represent different spectrums of the same diagnosis, throughout this writing, the term *sociopath* is predominantly used to refer to individuals with antisocial personality disorder.

What is an empath?

An *empath*, a psychology neologism gaining momentum in academic discourse, is "a person who is able to experience the feelings, emotions, or thoughts of other people" (Songer as cited in *Merriam-Webster's Open Dictionary*, 2011). According to the *Oxford Dictionary*, an *empath* is "a person with the paranormal ability to apprehend the mental or emotional state of another individual" ("Empath," n.d.). While the idea of literally "feeling" another's emotions may seem irrational—as others' emotions are *their* emotions—it may help to think of the empath experience concept as being infected by others' feelings involuntarily. For the purposes of this writing, an empath generally refers to a nonsociopath individual with an ability to feel for and care about the feelings, desires, and needs of others.

What is empathy?

Empathy, a word of Greek origin that made its way into English by way of a rough translation from German around the turn of the twentieth century, is not a fully understood phenomenon. Evidence even suggests that it occurs among some other species, and is even believed by some to be partly attributable to natural selection during human evolution (Hanson, 2010). While terms such as *empath* and *empathy* feature various opinions and distinctions among experts, I concur with psychologist Mark Davis's interpersonal reactivity index, which serves as a classification system for the types of empathy humans experience (Center for Building a Culture of Empathy, n.d.; Davis, 1983).

Serving as a first—and most basic—stage in Davis's system, cognitive empathy, also known as perspective taking, implies that an individual possesses the intellectual capability to acknowledge others' emotional states. For instance, an adult with cognitive empathy might watch a story on the news about a recently mugged, badly bruised, elderly victim. The presence of cognitive empathy allows for the viewer to possess awareness that the elderly victim might feel any number of negative emotions. However, that comprehension does not necessarily emotionally affect the viewer.

The second stage of empathy in Davis's system, empathic concern, builds upon the mere acknowledgment of others' emotional states that are present in stage 1 by adding the element of an empathizer's emotional response. For instance, utilizing the same scenario, through empathic concern, a viewer might weakly "feel" an emotional response to external stimuli. Such a response suggests a basic emotional investment in the plight of the victim or a regret that the crime occurred.

Building upon "empathic concern" is a higher stage of empathy: *personal concern*. In this stage, an individual's emotional state may mirror the state of the sufferer. During this stage of empathy, an individual may become intensely emotionally affected. Often, individuals who experience the "personal concern" stage cannot help but experience emotion very deeply as a result of their external environments. A fitting example of this concept is when a moviegoer feels a deep connection to—and is subsequently affected by—the emotions portrayed by the actors on screen (Riggio, 2011).

If that seems far-fetched—to empathize with external stimuli that do not necessarily reflect reality, such as feeling an emotional connection to an actor's or musician's performed artistic expression—consider the following: empathic concern for others does not even necessarily require a logical, chronologically relevant timeframe. After all, according to *Merriam-Webster*'s medical definition, empathy consists of "vicariously experiencing the feelings, thoughts, and experience of another of either the past or present" ("Empathy," n.d.). In other words, an individual may experience genuine empathy for a perceived victim who has suffered, is suffering, or might suffer in the future.

Does higher-stage empathy exclusively link to nonabusive treatment of others?

Merriam-Webster's Medical Dictionary describes *empathy* as "vicariously experiencing the feelings, thoughts, and experience of another…without having the feelings, thoughts, and experience fully communicated in an objectively explicit manner" ("Empathy," n.d.). But the degree to which empathy is experienced for others is not represented by a universal absolute value among all *Homo sapiens*. And to make matters more complex, not only do individuals experience empathy at varying degrees, a high degree of empathy within an individual does not necessarily correlate with choosing to treat others in a nonabusive manner.

For example, according to psychiatrist Neel Burton, "Psychopaths with absolutely no sympathy for their victims can nonetheless make use of empathy to snare or torture them" (2015, para. 4). In effect, the idea that experiencing higher stage empathy for others can only occur among psychologically healthy individuals—and the idea that higher stage empathy practitioners solely choose healthy, nonabusive interpersonal behaviors toward those with whom they empathize *are* easily dispelled notions. Simply put, empathy *for* others does not necessarily imply caring *about* others.

What other implications can be made concerning sociopathy from the premise there are varying degrees for which individual humans may experience empathy?

At least five implications appear immediately evident. First, the question presents itself: do all humans equally "feel" for others and possess the capability to empathize with others? It is my belief that not all humans experience all types or stages of empathy. Second, an environment exists for individuals to play upon the popular misconception of empathy as a "You either have it or you don't" phenomenon. In other words, people incapable of fully experiencing all stages of empathy—such as those who only experience stage 1 "perspective taking" empathy—can deceptively and manipulatively contribute to the false argument that they experience empathy fully, which can put others in danger.

A third implication deducible from humans possessing divergent capacities for experiencing empathy is that some individuals who do not experience the "personal investment" stage—whereby they are subsequently not emotionally affected by others' experiences or feelings—may essentially operate unaffected by what occurs around them, also a potentially dangerous proposition. This leads to a fourth implication. In the event "personal investment" empathy is not an authentic, selfless emotional experience for every individual, it remains plausible that a given circle may not only tolerate feigned empathic expression but also expect such behavior from its members as a cultural norm.

A fifth implication evident from the premise that not all *Homo sapiens* experience empathy alike is that while individuals might exhibit different degrees of empathy for others—depending on their interpersonal "closeness" to others—for some individuals, such higher-stage empathy experiences may still lack authenticity. To preface this concept, the suffering of a close friend or loved one might affect a given individual more so than the suffering of a complete stranger. While this might be considered "normal," and even "healthy," the argument can be made that authentic "personal investment" stage empathy might possibly fail to occur for an empathy-disabled individual—apparently engaged in higher stage empathy—if he or she actually perceives select others not as separate entities but as extensions of him or herself.

To consider loved ones as one's self might, in some cases, reflect admirable selflessness. However, for clarification, the perception of others as "self" is intended, in this specific instance, to reflect an empathy-disabled individual's lack of awareness of—and consideration for—others as being animate, autonomous entities with valuable independent feelings, needs, and perspectives. After all, according to several experts in the field, the occurrence of an authentic empathy experience requires never "losing sight of whose feelings belong to whom" (Decety & Jackson, 2004, p. 71).

A point bears mention: though sociopaths might lack the capacity to experience authentic empathy for others, they *can* feel and experience emotions—though to what extent or degree remains difficult to determine and under-researched at present. However, to the credit of researchers, identifying the breadth and depth of an individual's capacity to experience emotion presents as a tremendously challenging endeavor. Nonetheless, the following instances reflect several specific examples within this writing of how an abusive individual might operate destructively in order to catalyze a self-gratifying emotional experience.

In tactic 12, an assertion is discussed in more detail that the abusive individual might feel exhilaration, pleasure, and empowerment through demeaning, emasculating, objectifying, dominating, dressing down, or—*in general*—embarrassing his or her victims; and further, it is offered that achieving such self-gratifying feelings may serve as motivation to engage in behavior considered emotionally and psychologically abusive. Moreover, in tactic 43, it is suggested that a possible motivating factor for an abuser to express rage and engage in temper tantrums is to feel a pleasurable sense of release and elation through discharging aggression—though obviously in an unhealthy manner and destructively at the expense of others.

Additionally, in tactic 39, a research study is indirectly referenced that addresses the reality that sociopathic individuals *can* feel the emotion of fear and may operate so as to avoid or challenge unpleasurable emotional stimuli. This is particularly relevant because a common misconception regarding the sociopath is that he or she is fearless. It is theoretically possible for a given individual to lack the capacity to experience a particular emotion—for instance, fear. But, to articulate this oft-misconstrued concept of fearlessness with greater clarification, perhaps the sociopath might simply possess an ability to disregard consequence or risk more effortlessly than most other individuals—thereby *merely appearing* fearless.

What is negative empathy?

The term *negative empathy* possesses unrelated definitions to various professionals. For instance, according to one psychology author, *negative empathy* is "a state of being so sensitive to other people's experiences that we become overwhelmed by their suffering, to the point where we begin to suffer ourselves" (Taylor, 2016, para. 4). For clarification, by no means do I desire to discredit any professional's research or authority to define *negative empathy*; nor do I desire to challenge the legitimacy of others' definitions for the term. Rather, I intend to comment upon a different meaning of negative empathy that was offered during a lecture by world-renowned primatologist, ethicist, and empathy researcher Frans de Waal—where negative empathy was insinuated to mean a construct to the effect of an individual possessing the capacity to empathize with another's feelings while simultaneously disregarding the well-being of the feeler.

The identity of an individual possessing a personal ability to experience a high degree of empathy is not necessarily antonymous with the identity of a psychopath or sociopath. For instance, a psychopath torturer might utilize negative empathy to identify the physical condition of a victim in order to prolong the pain experienced before death, or to keep a victim alive for future interrogation or suffering (F. de Waal, personal communication, October, 21, 2014). The point here is that the presence of empathy within an individual does not, within and of itself, constitute healthy actions, behaviors, or thought processes. Further, it is my belief that within a nonsociopath with sociopathic tendencies, the presence of empathy can be intentionally silenced, manipulated, or overridden solely by an individual's will.

Is there a difference between sociopathic personality disorder, psychopathic personality disorder, and antisocial personality disorder?

The three terms may have represented slightly different definitions as each came into being, but they currently—according to many scientists and medical practitioners the world over—are understood to be different names for the same condition. According to the American Psychological Association, the current consensus leans toward term unity, particularly among *sociopathic personality disorder*, *psychopathic personality disorder*, and *antisocial personality disorder* (2015). Furthermore, according to the National Institute of Health, *antisocial personality disorder* and *sociopathic personality disorder* serve as alternative, interchangeable terms for the same medical condition (as cited in Berger, Zieve, and Ogilvie, 2014).

Some experts adamantly refute the existence of a synonymous relationship between the terms in their present context. For instance, some view antisocial personality disorder and psychopathy—and even psychopathy and sociopathy—as separate conditions. And making matters more complex, the term *psychopathy* was, at one point in the past, an umbrella term for "any psychological disorder or mental disease," but now the word is regarded as a synonym for *antisocial personality disorder* (American Psychological Association, 2015, p. 861). Nonetheless, definitions refine and evolve as the global mental health community continues to chisel out the bones of the matter, excavating through ongoing research and collaborative discussion.

Is there a timing difference between the debut of the term antisocial personality disorder *and* sociopathic personality disorder?

The term *sociopathic personality disturbance* was utilized in the *DSM-I*, the first edition of the DSM project, originally published in 1952 (American Psychiatric Association, p. 38). Years later, with the release of the *DSM-II* in 1968, the term *antisocial personality disorder* began to appear. Thus, the phrasing, "sociopathic personality disorder" precedes the APA's current term of expert consensus and preference: *antisocial personality disorder*. However, while *sociopathic personality disorder* did not reflect the exact definitions of the DSM editions to succeed it, it still synonymously represents the currently in-vogue term, *antisocial personality disorder*.

What is dissocial personality disorder?

Dissocial personality disorder is an imperfectly equivalent diagnosis for antisocial personality disorder. While the phrasing *antisocial personality disorder* is prevalent within the United States, *dissocial personality disorder* is the internationally recognized name that is officially endorsed by the World Health Organization (WHO), a subsidiary component of the United Nations. The American Psychiatric Association represents the official authority for creating and maintaining diagnostic criteria for mental disorders within the United States and, in effect, naming and defining antisocial personality disorder. Similarly, the World Health Organization is a larger international effort associating roughly 190-plus countries around the world in charge of naming and defining dissocial personality disorder.

Upon close comparison, the two systems—the 1992 release of the WHO's *International Statistical Classification of Diseases and Related Health Problems*, tenth edition (*ICD-10*), and the 2013 release of the APA's *Diagnostic and Statistical Manual of Mental Disorders*, fifth edition (*DSM-V*)—represent similar theoretical frameworks to define sociopathic personality disorder. For the purposes of this writing, both organizations' criteria are at times utilized and occasionally woven together to analyze and comment upon real-world hypothetical examples of dissocial mind-sets, behaviors, beliefs, and actions. Such criteria from both systems provide a framework that serves as a foundation for this writing's suggested strategies to address the disorders—for the altruistic and constructive intentions of helping others and bringing awareness to the reality of the effects of underaddressed antisocial behavior. As one expert put it, "Mental disorders contribute more to global disability and disease burden than any other category of non-communicable disease… There's a huge need for services, and people are not getting them" (Reed as cited in Martin 2009, para. 4).

Dissocial personality disorder, also known by the *ICD-10* code, *F60.2*, represents one of roughly eight specific personality disorders recognized by the World Health Organization while antisocial personality disorder represents one of roughly ten specific personality disorders recognized by the American Psychiatric Association respectively. Within the APA's *Diagnostic and Statistical Manual of Mental Disorders*, fifth edition, antisocial personality disorder is often referred to as a "Cluster B" disorder. The Cluster B subcategory, in addition to antisocial personality disorder, includes borderline personality disorder, histrionic personality disorder, and narcissistic personality disorder. Serving as a connecting thematic phrasing within the Cluster B subcategory personality disorders are the potentially relevant adjectives for affected individuals: *dramatic, emotional,* and *erratic* (American Psychiatric Association, 2013, p. 646).

How does the World Health Organization recommend diagnosing dissocial personality disorder?

According to the World Health Organization, dissocial personality disorder requires at least three of the following criteria to be met:

> (1) [A] callous unconcern for the feelings of others. (2) [A] gross and persistent attitude of irresponsibility and disregard for social norms, rules, and obligations. (3) Incapacity to maintain enduring relationships, though having no difficulty to establish them. (4) [A] very low tolerance to frustration and a low threshold for discharge of aggression, including violence. (5) Incapacity to experience guilt, or to profit from adverse experience, particularly punishment. (6) [A] marked proneness to blame others, or to offer plausible rationalizations for behaviour [sic] bringing the subject into conflict with society (1992).

In addition to meeting three of the aforementioned criteria, dissocial personality disorder diagnosticians are encouraged to take into account sociocultural norms for each prospective case.

Furthermore, to diagnose dissocial personality disorder, evidence of preadulthood conduct disorder is not required, but may be a contributing factor. One reason why evidence of prior conduct disorder might prove particularly significant for dissocial personality disorder diagnosticians is that researchers have identified a link between a youth's incapacity for empathizing with others and exhibiting sociopathic behavior. For instance, according to several experts, "Certain developmental disorders…[inclusive of] conduct disorder…are marked by empathy deficits that likely influence [children's] antisocial responses to other's distress, albeit with aloof apathy or active aggression, respectively" (Decety & Meyer, 2008, p. 1053).

Moreover, the World Health Organization recommends that a diagnosis not occur as a result of one clinician-to-patient interaction. Additionally, the *ICD-10* encourages the diagnostic process to include thorough research into a patient's past history to form a more comprehensive case profile picture. This might include analyzing criminal or work records, and even interviewing those personally affected by the candidate for potential diagnosis.

Furthermore, according to the World Health Organization, dissocial personality disorder needs to meet several additional common criteria shared by all WHO-recognized specific personality disorders. Subsequently, a diagnosis for dissocial personality disorder should reflect possible deviations in a candidate's thinking, perceiving, moods, attitudes, feelings, impulse control, or even an unhealthy desire for personal gratification (1992). Additionally, such criteria must be accompanied by evidence of dysfunctional interpersonal relationships or interaction.

Moreover, for diagnosis, dysfunctional behavior needs to be *consistent* in its dysfunctionality, applicable to multiple interpersonal and intrapersonal situations, and internally distressful, or—if not internally distressful—at least negatively impactful on an individual's external environment. In other words, the dissocial individual might present as unaffected *by*, and indifferent *to*, the effects of his or her own destructive behavior on others. Additionally, in the WHO's *ICD-10* diagnostic framework, dissocial personality disorder can coexist with other diagnoses concerning a given patient; but it should be noted that physical trauma, injury, disease, or disorder, particularly concerning the brain, can actually negate an otherwise positive diagnosis.

How old does someone have to be to diagnose with antisocial personality disorder?

In multiple international jurisdictions utilizing the DSM and ICD frameworks, a preadult individual exhibiting antisocial behavior generally only classifies as exhibiting *conduct disorder* or *oppositional defiant disorder*. Whereas, the age at which an individual begins to be recognized medically as possessing a specific personality disorder—as opposed to diagnosis of a preadulthood emotional disturbance, conduct disorder, or oppositional defiant disorder—is often around or exactly eighteen. Obviously, this arbitrary age-limit concept raises several glaring issues. For instance, neuroscientist Sandra Aamodt has offered that due to the ongoing nature of human brain development, particularly in the prefrontal cortex, adulthood may truly begin for most individuals closer to twenty-five than eighteen (as cited in Cox, 2011). Nevertheless, in many legal environments, a juvenile can pass certain adjudicative competency measures that establish his or her ability to stand trial for a crime as an adult well before reaching an established age of majority.

Subsequently, the question remains: is it counterproductive to delay the diagnosis of antisocial personality disorder due to chrono-logical age? This presents a particularly loaded question that yet remains to be answered definitively. Nonetheless, in an effort to provide a less-than-elaborate yet contributive response—on the one hand—diagnosing sociopathy earlier could aid in the placing of pro-active and preventative measures in a given sociopath's environment for the benefit of others, and might well lead to more specialized treatment for the affected individual. After all, it may prove a spe-cious assumption to conclude that all preadult individuals with a remorseless disregard for ethical rules and the rights of others can rehabilitate without specialized diagnosis and intervention.

On the other hand, potential diagnosis in an individual's for-mative years poses challenges as well. Such a diagnosis might later prove erroneous if a younger mentally developing individual volun-tarily engaged in antisocial behavior due to external factors, such as destructively attempting to cope with feeling tremendous pain or distress in response to traumatic life events. Also, the argument can be made that diagnosing an adolescent for sociopathy before eighteen may impede the positive development of his or her own self-image. For example, preadult diagnosis within the mind of an adolescent patient might create the risk of a youth internalizing him or herself as being somehow perceived as a monster within his or her society. To that end, throughout this writing, it is the author's firm intention never to attack or stigmatize the individual affected by a disability or disorder but, rather, only to attack the harmful, premeditated choices of the individual—choices resultant from willfully and intentionally engaging in abusive antisocial behaviors and thought processes.

Can people who are diagnosed change?

Since at least the 1930s—and even into contemporary times—evidence indicates that multiple psychiatrists, psychologists, and physicians in general continue to express a frustrated *albeit* professional viewpoint that many observed psychopath patients historically exhibit a trend of continually disregarding potential consequence or punishment associated with engaging in illegal behavior, demonstrate a propensity to reengage in illegal behavior willingly, and lack any known curative solution (Keller as cited in Cleckley, 1941, p. 290; *Time*, 1937). From their collective perspectives, it becomes easier to face the daunting and unpleasant realization that communicating potential consequences and enforcing punishment alone cannot simply eradicate sociopathy or psychopathy.

Nevertheless, regardless of a criminal's apathy for, or outright dismissal of, such potential consequence or punishment, some professionals have emphatically asserted that the psychopath—though potentially lacking a medical capacity to care how his or her actions affect others—should be considered legally sane and held punitively liable for criminal activity. In other words, many medical professionals contend that the criminal psychopath logically possesses awareness that his or her actions may be illegal—or at least affect others abusively—and such awareness disqualifies a defense of insanity as actions still ultimately remain willed, intentional choices on part of the offender (Cleckley, 1955/2016). I concur with their assertion.

On a more encouraging note, some experts have reported major progress and improvement in the lives of patients who once exhibited significant antisocial behaviors (Lee, 2013). However, the individual affected by a specific personality disorder does not necessarily self-identify with a given diagnosis, internalize him or herself as affected, or desire to seek treatment. Moreover, avenues for counseling and psychotherapy for individuals with antisocial personality disorder face significant obstacles as destructive individuals with antisocial personality disorder may not desire to change. It should be noted, however, that some individuals with antisocial personality disorder may recognize feeling "numb" to the feelings of others, yet most heroically desire to learn how to modify behaviors so as not to be destructive toward others.

Is there any approved medication for it?

At present, no Food and Drug Administration–approved medicine exists to cure antisocial personality disorder specifically; however, existing, and even future, medications may alter brain chemistry productively as well as positively affect the disposition of participants. Moreover, future medical developments might present substantial opportunities. For instance, in the future, it might be possible to create a medicine, or engage in a surgical procedure, that allows certain individuals to experience having a conscience. Nonetheless, in the present, many researchers possess interest in working toward creating curative medicines to treat specific personality disorders, which many hope will work by isolating and influencing particular parts of the brain.

Does the DSM framework apply to only one country—and what entity endorses, defines, and serves as an authority to create a manual for diagnosing personality disorders?

The World Health Organization International Classification of Diseases (ICD) project features a storied history. And though its acronym now stands for the International Classification of Diseases, the letters once stood for the International Classification of Causes of Death. Over the course of a century, the purpose of the endeavor expanded beyond fatality and morbidity statistics to incorporate and categorize medical conditions (O'Malley, Cook, Price, Wildes, Hurdle, & Ashton, 2005, p. 1623).

In the late 1940s, the World Health Organization took on the task of authoring and publishing new editions for international consumption. And under the WHO's auspice, the *ICD-6* edition, released in 1949, was the first international disease classification system manual that actually attempted to classify mental disorders, as opposed to just recognize causes of death. Several years later, in 1952, the American Psychiatric Association released the first DSM, *DSM-I*. The WHO's ICD manual program is currently endorsed by the United Nations while the DSM program is endorsed by the American Psychiatric Association respectively. In both systems, only clinicians with specialized training are officially authorized to diagnose personality disorders.

The next WHO manual, the ICD, eleventh edition, has been loosely speculated for release as early as 2020, though no firm date has, as of this writing, been established. Meanwhile, the *DSM-VI* has no hard deadline for future publication. The *ICD-10*, published in 1992, serves more people internationally than does the *DSM-V*, released in 2013, which caters to medical practice in the United States. However, most recently, some American medical facilities previously operating under the jurisdiction of the DSM model have begun adopting and implementing *ICD-10* codes for patient billing and diagnostic purposes (ICD Codes, 2015).

The future of the two independent classification systems from a nosological perspective may come to an end. While there may be disagreement concerning naming and classifying any number of medical conditions by world experts, there also appears to be a sense of redundancy in having two programs. Perhaps the two manuals may merge at some future date.

The argument can be made that the two programs may feed off each other's developments and insights to make each manual stronger. To that end, a sense of proactive and congenial collegiality appears evident between the two entities. For example, within the *DSM-IV-TR*, the APA mentioned, "Those preparing *ICD-10* and *DSM-IV* have worked closely to coordinate their efforts, resulting in much mutual influence…[And] the many consultations…were enormously useful in increasing the congruence and reducing meaningless differences in wording between the two systems" (2000, p. xxix).

Is the etiology for this disorder biological, environmental, or psychosocial?

Some experts believe that psychopathy is attributable to genetic predisposition or physiological influence, such as neurological deformity or underdevelopment, while sociopathy may be due to psychosocial factors (Bonn, 2014). At present, no expert can answer with absolute certainty whether an individual "becomes" a sociopath or psychopath—as might be the case after experiencing brain trauma. However, some experts who believe genetic predisposition plays a role generally agree that heritability accounts, more or less, for half of the origin of sociopathy (Ferguson, 2010; Meyers, 2013; Stout, 2005). Moreover, research conducted on preadolescent twins further solidifies the contention that psychopathy is hereditary (Viding, Blair, Moffitt, & Plomin, 2005; Viding, Jones, Paul, Moffitt, & Plomin, 2007).

Furthermore, some research preliminarily suggests that psychopathy is, to some degree, due to physiological abnormalities in the human brain, and MRI scans have demonstrated differences in the amygdala, orbitofrontal cortex, and uncinate fasciculus (Nauert, 2009). Moreover, other specific areas affected by psychopathy are believed to include the "insula, anterior and posterior cingulate… parahippocampal gyrus…anterior superior temporal gyrus…and rostral, caudal, and posterior cingulate gyrus" (Kiehl, 2006, pp. 1, 27). Together, these aforementioned components constitute what neuroscientists refer to as the paralimbic system.

In regard to psychosocial and environmental factors, multiple experts have expressed an opinion that an absence of care for infants, particularly through a lack of receiving human touch, may create the parameters for interpersonal limitations regarding empathy. Still, others perceiving psychopathy and sociopathy as the same disorder establish no definite cause for the disorder, nor find a distinguishing etiological point of origin as its primary probable cause.

Moreover, what definitively causes the disorder—be it psycho-social, hereditary, or environmental, or some combination thereof—may be anyone's educated guess at this point in time. More research needs to be done, potentially for decades, or even centuries, to establish major answers to age-old questions. And assuming such answers will inevitably come with future research and scientific breakthroughs might prove overly optimistic.

How many people are sociopaths?

Identifying how many people in a given sample size, or population at large, are diagnosable with antisocial personality disorder remains nearly impossible. In addition to the human capital needed to conduct such testing and the tremendous financial burden required to engage in evaluation, other factors impede a full-on analysis of the human population. Specifically, social factors prohibit a testing effort—such as participants' willingness to be tested, a lack of protection and privacy initiatives for test takers concerning their results, communities' current lack of awareness of how testing may help others, and an international lack of understanding and consensus about how to perceive those affected with this specific personality disorder, to name but a few.

Nonetheless, according to some experts, around 3 percent of the population is considered to be diagnosable as having antisocial personality disorder (Grohol, 2015). World-renowned expert Martha Stout offered this number might approach 4 percent of a given population (2005). To put this 4 percent concept in context of the current world population—hovering around 7.6 billion people—it can be estimated that more than 300 million sociopaths reside on earth. In effect, it can be estimated that there are nearly as many sociopaths on earth as there are American citizens.

What has also been established is that men are, in general, more likely to test positively (Lenzenweger, Lane, Loranger, & Kessler, 2007). Factually, thus far, men have been diagnosed with antisocial personality disorder more frequently than have women (Burton, 2012). The *DSM-IV-TR* offered that, on average, 3 percent of men and 1 percent of women diagnose with antisocial personality disorder (2000, p. 704).

However, confounding any attempt at establishing the prevalence of antisocial personality disorder by biological orientation is the reality that not all individuals self-identify with their gender of birth. Also—in contrast with utilitarian philosophical ideology that might justify the reasoning, "The more of something, the more dangerous it may be," or "The less of something, the less dangerous it may be"—it remains important to remember that any sociopathic individual from any gender might possess the potential to be just as abusive and destructive as a sociopathic individual from another gender. Ergo, to reason—and ultimately conclude—that individuals from one identifiable gender are more or less abusive than the next is counterfactual.

Another factor that impedes an effort at diagnosis is the unresolved assumption among some within the scientific community concerning whether sociopathy, unlike psychopathy, is a learned and—even in some cases—culturally accepted lifestyle. From that vantage point, it becomes easier to envision how a positive diagnosis might identify an abusive individual functioning relatively "appropriately" in regard to his or her own societal or cultural norms. Still, others desire for psychopathy and antisocial personality disorder to be treated as separate, distinct conditions.

So is arguably the case with psychologist Robert Hare, world-renowned psychopathy expert and mastermind of the Hare Psychopathy Checklist testing concept—in use for multiple decades throughout many international locations (1993/1999). The current version for adults, the Psychopathy Checklist-revised (PCL-R) is widely considered the most credible assessment tool to diagnose psychopathy. Hare's diagnostic instrument is in part influenced by the contributions of psychiatrist heavyweight Hervey Cleckley, who released the groundbreaking book *The Mask of Sanity* in 1941—considered by some to the be the single greatest literary contribution to its field during the twentieth century. The concept of a "mask" serves as an allusion to the reality of a suspected—but concealed—neurological deviation among certain members of society at large who otherwise appear to function competently, yet ultimately prove conscience-impaired and potentially malicious (1941, 1955/2016).

The PCL-R examination consists of an interview component, as well as a qualified clinician's review of a participant's case file. Such information can be used to cross-check participants for dishonest statements and is often deemed particularly relevant in criminal proceedings. The Psychopathy Checklist-Youth Version (PCL-YV) also exists—and can be administered to juveniles, though it faces several noticeable challenges. For instance, in some environments, the PCL-YV might carry less weight as an evaluation instrument since testing participants are psychologically developing individuals whose behavior might be emphatically influenced by adverse external environments—and further consternating matters, consent by a guardian for the minor to undergo testing might be difficult for a test administrator to acquire.

A perfect psychopath-positive score on the PCL-R is 40 while a score of 30 or more establishes a diagnosis of psychopathy. In some clinical environments, 25 serves as the cutoff, not 30. Additionally, it remains possible for an individual to score a 0, implying no psychopathic traits, but even individuals who are not psychopaths often average a positive but negligible number. Ideally, more than one qualified clinician is encouraged to engage in rating independently, and the evaluators' scores should be averaged together afterward to increase the accuracy of the assessment (Hare, 2003).

For a testing participant to attain the cutoff value required for diagnosis as a psychopath on the PCL-R is considered by many to be much more difficult than it would be for that same individual to meet the APA's general diagnosis requirements for antisocial personality disorder. Hare has expressed interest in psychopathy being formally recognized as a separate diagnosis apart from antisocial personality disorder—perhaps, in part, to suggest this empirically observable difference in testing outcomes (Seabrook, 2008).

Also, sagely, Hare, as the test's creator, is of the professional opinion that only qualified, licensed clinicians should administer these examinations intended to test for psychopathy (2003). Moreover, the American Psychiatric Association's code of ethics offers a similar view on the importance of a credible diagnostic process through their Goldwater Rule—which essentially prohibits clinicians from disclosing unauthorized professional opinions and diagnoses concerning patients with whom they have not personally interacted and evaluated (American Psychiatric Association, 2013b). In other words, for the sake of psychopathy and personality disorder testing not being abused or manipulated, there exist incredibly stringent mechanisms in place for professionals to remain accountable and refrain from unduly engaging in public speculation.

Nonetheless, confounding the matter, an examination result for psychopathy—as well as for antisocial personality disorder—also incurs the chance of a test administrator's bias. In effect, an administrator may be required to make subjective decisions regarding many circumstances during the testing process. Such decisions may include, but are not limited to, deciding whether a testing participant truly experiences emotional detachment, possesses a conscience, cares about others, feels remorse, and even determining if a given participant is honestly participating with authentic responses. And on top of such factors, there remains the very real possibility that undisclosed external medicinal substances in a given case might influence past or present abusive, sociopathic behavior. The full medical definition from *Merriam-Webster* (n.d.) for antisocial personality disorder touches upon this notion, indicating that "drug addiction" and "substance abuse" can make antisocial personality disorder "difficult to diagnose."

Test administration challenges and undisclosed medicinal influences aside, prevalence rates understandably remain difficult to determine with exacting precision. For instance, assuming roughly four in every one hundred individuals *are* sociopaths might slightly overrepresent the proportion of the human population featuring antisocial personality disorder. But building on this estimated percentage, what are the chances that when two random individuals communicate, the "one in twenty-five" who is a sociopath might associate with another "one in twenty-five" who also happens to be a sociopath? Mathematically, the probability should only be .0016 percent—an astoundingly minute value.

But many strongly suspect it happens—abusive individuals find other abusive individuals with whom to interact, socialize, network, and even conspire. Indeed, an area that begs for ongoing research is identifying if—and how—sociopathic individuals identify like-minded individuals to corroborate in gray-area endeavors. And how might some find, recognize, and associate with others so effectively?

The implications are tremendous. Consider this: if an individual lacks a conscience and a capacity for meaningful interpersonal connection with others, it might even be convenient and preferable for him or her to communicate and socialize with others who do not require reciprocal emotional investment. In the same train of thought—though such an individual might not desire meaningful emotional connections with anyone—he or she might prefer the company of others who are also emotionally unavailable and who are also likely to exhibit shallow affect in interpersonal situations.

Additionally, abusive sociopaths, *identifying other abusive sociopaths*, might serve the specific purpose of enabling potentially illegal or destructive environments or group behaviors without concern of accomplices blowing a proverbial whistle. To this end, consider the toxic personality-hiring manager—unbeknownst to his or her good-intentioned employer—intentionally hiring another toxic personality to do the hiring manager's questionable bidding. Or consider the inert organizational culture operating in an unhealthy climate of distrust and bullying promulgated by a few abusers—just as the like-minded abusive, sociopathic individuals with leverage over subordinates might truly desire the work environment to remain. In all probability, something is going on, likely a yet-to-be identified phenomenon that aids individuals with antisocial personality disorder in finding, vetting, and corroborating with one another. And

.0016 percent just does not seem to do, for lack of a readily available term, *sociopath association theory* justice.

How many criminals are psychopaths?

Research suggests that approximately 15 percent of all prisoners incarcerated within the United States are psychopaths while psychopaths comprise approximately 1 percent of the population at large (Lipman, 2013). Research has also shown that released psychopath criminals are roughly twice as likely as nonpsychopath criminals to commit crimes again and around three times as likely to commit violent crimes following incarceration (Hare, 1993/1999). Moreover, one study estimated that more than a million male offenders in the United States criminal justice system classify as psychopaths (Kiehl & Hoffman, 2011).

Furthermore, studies have shown that females are diagnosed with psychopathy less frequently than males (Wynn, Høiseth, & Pettersen, 2012). Interestingly, evidence suggests that researchers have reached contrasting conclusions in determining if the prevalence rate of psychopathy among female prisoners is truly less than that of male prisoners. Nonetheless, a prevalence rate range of nine to nearly 18 percent appears likely for female prisoners while a prevalence rate of 15 to slightly more than 30 percent appears likely for male prisoners respectively (Warren et al., 2003; Grann as cited in Wynn et al., 2012).

Regarding crime, approximately one-third, give or take, of all violent crime in the United States can be traced to psychopathy, and the estimated financial cost of such crime exceeds two trillion dollars annually (Kiehl & Sinnott-Armstrong, 2013). And if that number seems staggering, consider this: such appraisals do not even include intangible costs related to affected victims' psychological suffering, emotional distress, lost productivity, and other lasting health effects. Perhaps for this reason, conscience-impaired criminals arguably possess the dubious distinction of being responsible for the most financially burdensome mental health issue affecting society.

Wait, detection and prevalence rates aside, *isn't this just common sense—if abusive individuals successfully "fake" emotions and "mimic" personas, wouldn't victims just easily be able to see through it all and identify the imperfection?*

No—contrary to the popular adage, "If it seems too good to be true, it probably is"—victims are often fooled when it comes to assessing abusers who *appear* to possess attractive, likeable, or even nearly flawless personal character. In effect, victims, through no fault or intellectual shortcoming of their own—when successfully manipulated—can assume the character, intentions, and actions of undetected abusive sociopaths or psychopaths to be exemplary. In certain situations, successful abusers may even rely on victims' presumptions regarding their false personas as a necessary prerequisite to gain enough of a victim's trust to cloak questionable intentions and behaviors effectively.

Evidence clearly indicates that writers have been observing and contemplating the paradox of individuals conning others by successfully misrepresenting virtues, which—in all actuality—such manipulators do not truly possess. For instance, in a commercially acclaimed mid-twentieth-century-novel-turned-stage-production *The Bad Seed*, author William March and playwright Maxwell Anderson alluded to the concept that effective manipulators can impersonate individuals possessing positive character attributes in such an attractively perfect and polished manner that deceived victims lose sight of how authentic virtue might more naturally manifest in more identifiably imperfect people (Anderson & March, 1955/1985; March, 1954/1997; see also Hare, 1993/1999).

To illustrate how imperfection might naturally manifest in real life, consider a loving parent who is willing to defend his or her children at any personal cost yet possesses a short attention span for listening to their needs and is also, at times, hostile and quick-tempered with them. In this example, both virtue and vice appear evident within the parent. However, the imperfect parent still authentically possesses the virtue of selflessness regarding sacrificing for the betterment of his or her children. In contrast, a manipulative sociopath mimicking the authentic parent's virtue—for instance, in a courtroom cross-examination after a crime may have been committed regarding child negligence or endangerment—might successfully lead jurors to conclude that he or she is nearly perfect in every category (i.e., patient with one's children, a good listener, attentive to children's needs, and selflessly devoted to their safety, etc.).

The Twelve Not-As-Essential-But-Still-Relevant Questions

In the event sociopaths or psychopaths are genuinely intellectually gifted, what implications can be drawn concerning entitlement mind-sets?

As mentioned previously in chapter one, some researchers identify any number of distinctions between the sociopath and psychopath—for example, some psychopaths are believed to be incredibly intellectually capable compared to their sociopath counterparts, as evinced through meticulous planning and effective manipulation. Another common line of reasoning holds to the viewpoint that sociopaths possess more developed consciences than psychopaths. And yet another distinction theorizes that one disorder might be learned whereas the other might be inherited.

Simultaneously, other researchers recognize no intellectual delineation that distinguishes sociopaths from psychopaths. And still others recognize no difference between the terms *sociopath* and *psychopath* in general. Nonetheless, a theoretically possible occurrence of superior intelligence in some *Homo sapiens* raises the question: if an individual with antisocial personality disorder exhibits particular intellectual competence, is he or she entitled to act abusively as he or she pleases?

There appears to be no shortage of individuals who dominate others based on a grandiose sense of self-entitlement. Often through such entitlement, these individuals feel qualified to determine who *is*, or *is not*, intelligent, as well as help themselves to assuming their own intellectual superiority over others. In such situations, entitlement, delusion, hubris, close-mindedness, and false pride might come into play. At times, though, such intellectual superiority appears to be "objectively" reinforced by some form or fashion of intelligence testing or peer affirmation. The case can be made, however, that a given sociopath's grandiose sense of intellectual superiority is based on false evidence and faulty premises and, dare it be written, incomprehensive testing.

IQ may or may not exist. But it is abstract and intangible—and the argument presents that we may not have the tests to rank this intangible construct accurately with paper and pencil, etc.—even if results are "normed." I think of it this way: we cannot visually see a high-definition "ultrasound" of our thoughts, at least at present, so how can we definitively claim that we can rank the quality of intelligence in others' thoughts?

Thus, from that angle, fault can be found within an individual's proclamation or endorsement of his or her own intellectual superiority—a common-enough occurrence in the realm of some personality disorders—for when someone labels others as intellectually inferior, in a most derogatory manner, it presupposes that an individual is especially equipped to measure that which is not necessarily even scientifically proven to be measurable. Moreover, what specific quality, proclivity, aptitude, capability, or potential an individual may appear to possess in a superior manner compared to his or her peers may be considered largely irrelevant. For instance, if an individual is outstanding at one particular endeavor—be it gymnastics, speaking multiple languages, or even mathematically comprehending the physics equations that identify the theory of general relativity, the question lingers onward—does one skill really reflect higher intelligence more so than another?

To attempt to provide an answer, there exists a famous quote, the origin of which is widely disputed and, very likely, never uttered by the twentieth century's most recognizable physicist (Pettigrew, 2013). It reads: "Everybody is a genius. But if you judge a fish by its ability to climb a tree, it will live its whole life believing that it is stupid." And though the quote—most probably—is not attributable to the late Albert Einstein, I find the sentiment within it to offer a valuable opportunity for meaningful reflection.

In effect, for us to presuppose intelligence is directly related to marketable skills for the twentieth or twenty-first century may prove a specious assumption. And worth mentioning, I would be remiss not to acknowledge Howard Gardner's work in this arena, the psychologist who first postulated multiple intelligence theory (1983). In effect, human intelligence may be exhibited by a diverse variety of human proclivities—very much unlike a timed, standardized test might lead one to believe.

Hypothetically, assuming a futuristic "ultrasound" machine existed that fully understood our minds' capabilities and potentials, and IQ could objectively be verified and holistically measured—*and* someone is "scientifically" proven as intellectually inferior to his or her peers—the counterpoint can still be presented, "So what? That does not define an individual's human dignity or worth." Moreover, the concept of intellectual superiority is relative: no one genius's ingenuity has singlehandedly cured everyone's illnesses, or modified his or her own telomeres in order to live indefinitely on earth—nor has any unaided individual, within a lifetime, taken raw materials and created modern, space-age circuit-board technology.

In effect, limitations are ubiquitous, and the relativity of human ingenuity is nothing to boast excessively about, let alone utilize as entitlement to abuse others. Some have become too comfortable with assigning an individual human's worth based on that individual's perceived level of intelligence. But consider the following scenario.

If you were not born to be seven feet tall, let alone even six, that does not mean you are worthless, right? Just the same as others might realize you are not exceptionally tall and not consider you worthless, it may remain your conviction not to abuse others by assessing their worth through valuing their innate, intangible attributes or limitations that are outside of the realm of their control. In other words, if I devalue another by calling him or her a derogatory name based on a subjective perception of that individual's "lack" of intelligence, in essence, I am no different than someone assuming I have less human worth because I did not grow to be seven feet tall. And on the flip side of that coin, for an individual to devalue me based on my limitations does not truly provide another individual authentic leverage to establish his or her own intellectual or human superiority. Thus, the argument can be advanced that intellectual elitism fails to justify devaluing, abusing, and taking advantage of others.

What might be some strategies to identify the presence of an abuser's self-appointed intellectual elitism?

Previously, I referenced an egocentric individual's potential self-identification as intellectually superior to his or her peers. But what might this look like in real life? Arguably, the presence of intellectual elitism can be observed in multiple communications and behaviors; however, two take center stage.

First, an individual might boast about his or her specific accomplishments that insinuate he or she deserves to be appraised as intellectually superior to others. For example, this might manifest through an individual who is, through impulsivity, all too eager to share with others how well he or she did on a popular standardized test—even years ago. For good measure, the individual might even mention how little he or she studied beforehand—as it to further imply a head-and-shoulders advantage over other humans. During this type of disclosure in which an individual brags about his or her untrue or even *possibly* true exploits, the self-proclaimed intellectual elitist ironically—and most counterproductively—demonstrates a lack of intellectual consideration for others' potential feelings of subsequent alienation while simultaneously desiring their adulation or submission.

Another way this behavior might manifest is among adult employees, where someone might boast to their peers about receiving an "A+" on an annual performance evaluation, when their peers never expressed any interest in knowing the grade of the unsolicited discloser in the first place. As if to imply, "We are in the same place at the same time. My grade is higher than yours. I am smarter than you. Don't forget it. And it feels good."

Obviously, this attitude—in addition to its delusional, erroneous reasoning—exhibits callousness toward others' feelings, blatant egocentrism, and even hostility, as manifested through the meanness of "rubbing it in." Additionally, if such an individual not only intentionally discloses but also demands to know from peers their evaluation results—to enjoy a self-gratifying comparison experience—it demonstrates impairment in personality functioning through a lack of respect for personal boundaries. After all, others' grades are *others'* personal information.

That stated, as a word of caution, someone who does not self-perceive him or herself as smarter than others might choose to disclose such information, like the stellar performance review, with the healthy intention of others altruistically sharing in his or her joy. After all, that individual might altruistically and authentically desire to root for his or her peers regarding their achievements and, from that same foundation of altruism for others, happily self-identify as a member of his or her peers' emotional support networks.

A second manner in which intellectual elitism appears observable is through an individual's propensity to gain advantages over others through an intentionally deceitful, manipulative persona. Such an individual, in turn, may rationalize gained advantages over others as evidence of his or her own intellectual superiority. In contrast, many nonsociopaths choose to live in what I refer to as a "shields down" honest and open manner. They share themselves—as well as their communications, intentions, and feelings—openly with others because doing so happens to be a preferred lifestyle decision. Moreover, living in this manner might actually improve their general happiness and well-being, reduce stress, and enhance the intimacy of their interpersonal connections.

Conversely, some abusive sociopathic individuals intentionally approach interpersonal relationships from deceitful angles. For example, they might feign interpersonal bonding with others, mimicking a genuine interest in friendship or others' feelings—or simply, even mimic possessing an interest in cordial, superficial dialogue with another—while making note of the more honest individual's thoughts, feelings, and intentions, all "fair game" to be exploited in the future. This might manifest through an abuser with a false persona asking a question to a "shields down" individual that is dressed up like an attempt to know another—*for the sake of knowing another*—when it truly serves to allow the abuser a window into a victim's mind to view for exploitable opportunities. For example, a manipulative coworker might seek exploitable information by asking, "How did you feel about the situation?" or, "What makes you upset about how things are going?"

Supposing that such a manipulator gains some advantage over a "shields down" individual by exploiting a victim's given disclosure, the manipulator may subsequently self-rationalize him or herself as intellectually superior, reinforced in his or her own mind by the advantage achieved. Of course, this represents flawed logic and delusion, which the egomaniacal individual often fails to recognize. It is akin to an individual playing hide-and-seek and declaring him or herself the winner when only that singular individual even desired to play the game in the first place. Analogously, others felt "too old" and "mature" to choose to play it anymore. Nonetheless, the manipulator might internalize "winning" the game as proof of his or her intellectual superiority.

Do any of the addressed behaviors or thought patterns within the fifty tactics apply to other personality disorders?

The behaviors and thought patterns addressed in each tactic may share similarities with other personality disorder criteria. For instance, narcissistic personality disorder, as well as antisocial personality disorder, may deal with an overexaggerated appraisal of self-importance and unhealthy egocentrism, to name just a few of the possible common characteristics between the disorders on a given case-by-case basis (American Psychiatric Association, 2012; 2013a). Moreover, the possibility of comorbidity exists (e.g., an individual diagnosing with multiple Cluster B personality disorders, such as both antisocial personality disorder and narcissistic personality disorder). Additionally, comorbidity might also manifest through any number of other mental disorders—such as an individual diagnosed with both antisocial personality disorder and pedophilic disorder.

In this work, narcissism, in particular, is hinted at throughout multiple tactics. However, the tactics addressed are meant specifically to identify real-world behaviors and mind-sets of sociopathic individuals. Furthermore, it is important to remember that any of the fifty tactics might apply to anyone outside the realm of clinical diagnosis as a sociopath. For example, individuals who do not officially diagnose as psychopaths or sociopaths might intentionally engage in abusive or destructive behaviors and thus engage in the tactics addressed. Lastly—to provide an example of comorbidity not at present officially recognized as a personality disorder by the American Psychiatric Association or World Health Organization—it remains possible for a clinician, under the legal authority of a given jurisdiction, to diagnose an individual with both psychopathy and antisocial personality disorder, *or* psychopathy and dissocial personality disorder, respectively.

The DSM and ICD criteria serve as descriptors for identifying sociopaths—but how do they relate to the fifty tactics?

The criteria within the APA's *Diagnostic and Statistical Manual of Mental Disorders* (*DSM-IV-TR*, 2000; *DSM-V*, 2013a) and the WHO's *International Statistical Classification of Diseases and Related Health Problems* (*ICD-10*, 1992) provide an outline for sociopathy. What the tactics do is fill in that outline to create a detailed picture of what antisocial personality disorder looks like as it can conceivably be manifested through *real* people in *real* life. The tactics supplement the DSM and WHO criteria by elaborating on—in what many cases merely remain—several words or phrases following a bullet point within their respective manuals.

Another way to look at the relationship between the manual criteria for diagnosing sociopaths and the fifty tactics would be to imagine the relationship between atoms and molecules. Atoms, individually, serve as subcomponents of molecules. In the case of a water molecule, or H2O, two hydrogen atoms are bound to one oxygen atom. Similarly, each particular trait, behavior, limitation, or thought process that represents a singular diagnostic criteria within the *DSM-IV-TR*, *DSM-V*, or *ICD-10* figuratively correlates to an atom, while the complex, often-abusive behaviors and mind-sets sociopathic individuals manifest figuratively correlate to a multidimensional molecule.

To simplify how this figurative molecule analogy concept can be put into action, consider the possibilities of someone who might not only be physically aggressive but also unable to feel remorse for his or her actions. In the preceding sentence, two criteria for diagnosis of antisocial personality disorder were featured: first, aggression, coupled with another criterion—the limitation of not being able to feel remorse. Together, these subcomponents might act like individual atoms that bond together and create a figurative molecule, so to speak, more complexly expressed as an individual with the potential to exhibit violent behavior with no remorse for his or her dangerous actions.

What is the value proposition of the tactics?

As previously mentioned, the tactics fill in the skeletal outlines of the DSM and ICD criteria, offering a detailed, creative picture of antisocial personality disorder in a particular way that has perhaps not been done before, especially in light of newly published *DSM-V* alternative model diagnostic criteria. Moreover, they allow researchers future opportunities to set up experiments and test hypotheses. To the world at large, the tactics promote awareness of antisocial personality disorder, create opportunities for discourse, and empower organizations, as well as individuals, to address abuse. For the victim—past, present, and future—mercilessly mistreated and abused at the hands of psychopaths and sociopaths, it is my personal hope that the action plans may provide even the slightest bit of help to even one person.

Does each tactic relate to one specific criterion from the DSM framework?

The tactics are not all-encompassing of every possibility, nor are they all exclusively linked to one criterion descriptor. They are like cocktails in that they are based off different diagnostic criteria from the *DSM-IV-TR*, *DSM-V*, and the WHO's *ICD-10*. Where a given manual might consider a particular trait, behavior, limitation, or thought process to reflect a specific diagnostic criterion for antisocial or dissocial personal disorder, this writing weaves and mixes together multiple subcomponent descriptors through each of its fifty tactics. In effect, the "fifty" really reflect combinations and mixtures of various subcomponent descriptors from the manuals, utilized for officially diagnosing sociopathy.

Additionally, serving as a key contribution to defining antisocial personality disorder in its present form, the American Psychiatric Association board of trustees approved and published the inclusion of an "Alternative *DSM-5* Model for Personality Disorders" (2013a, p. 761). Rather than competing with antisocial personality disorder diagnostic criteria material in use since publication of the *DSM-IV-TR*, the *DSM-V* alternative model offers a more elaborate and expansive definition of general criteria for specific personality disorders. Thus, to evaluate a patient for antisocial personality disorder, the current (i.e., traditional) model and the more expansive alternative model complement one another, and diagnosticians are encouraged to use both together synergistically (2013a).

The fifty tactics within this project are significantly influenced by contemplation of the recently published alternative model diagnostic criteria for antisocial personality disorder featured in the *DSM-V*. Thanks in large part to the contributions of others who worked to assemble this alternative model definition, the tactics herein benefit—as they are strengthened by its painstaking elaboration of criteria for antisocial personality disorder. Moreover, arguably *because* of the inclusion of the alternative model, the *DSM-V* possesses more detailed criteria for identifying and diagnosing sociopathy than either the *DSM-IV-TR* or *ICD-10* manuals.

Without exhaustively describing the updated criteria of the *DSM-V* alternative model for antisocial personality disorder, the improved definition within the alternative model urges diagnosticians to identify impairment in the following four areas of personality functioning: identity, self-direction, empathy, and capacity for intimacy. And in addition to identifying unhealthy personality functioning, the alternative model recommends that diagnosticians attempt to identify antagonism through the four pathological personality trait themes of manipulativeness, callousness, deceitfulness, and hostility, as well as attempt to identify disinhibition through the three pathological personality trait themes of risk taking, impulsivity, and irresponsibility (American Psychiatric Association, 2013a, pp. 761–765). At present, the World Health Organization has not officially endorsed a more elaborate diagnostic criteria framework to build upon its *ICD-10* definition for dissocial personality disorder in use since the early 1990s.

Why fifty tactics?

While the number of tactics represents an arbitrary value, considerable thought went into evaluating the DSM and WHO antisocial personality disorder and dissocial personality descriptors, and then creating and classifying the tactics in respect to their influence. These classification systems are often represented in this writing through a given tactic's implied, and sometimes explicitly stated, association with various diagnostic criteria from the different manuals. While an effort was made to trim down and combine like tactic subject matter—as well as to establish distinctions between unlike tactic subject matter—the associations between DSM and WHO descriptors and the tactics presented herein are augmented by readers' thoughtful input, reflection, and interpretation.

Are the fifty tactics all original concepts?

The tactics represent multiple constructs that, in some cases, might be completely original or, in other cases, attempt to offer and hopefully build upon what has been previously established; or, serving as another possibility, they might also reflect concepts many individuals might think about—or possess a subconscious awareness of—but that ultimately have yet to be addressed through the written word. And while some terms and concepts discussed in these tactics have already been established, this creative "field guide" playbook and action plan, "self-help" approach might represent the first published agglomeration of its kind, particularly due to its emphasis on *DSM-V* alternative model diagnostic criteria for antisocial personality disorder. Coupled with what has already been scientifically offered, the created intangible property within this qualitative writing seeks to complement and strengthen established discourse.

Concerning the tactics covered within this work—though terms may have been freshly monikered for concepts that have yet to be labeled, and though the tactics herein may feature original ideas that have yet to be presented—I, emphatically, do not possess any desire or intention to receive credit for others' contributions. Others' contributions are rightfully *theirs*. And with a spirit of unrelenting appreciation, I thank others for their good faith efforts in working toward corrective and curative solutions in sociopathy and psychopathy—past, present, and future.

Furthermore, the abusive behaviors and thought processes established and elaborated upon within this writing have, in some cases, benefited from others' research while, in other cases, they have merely been observed. Or—without observation—in some instances, they have been intrapersonally contemplated as realistic possibilities in which *Homo sapiens* might engage. Moreover, these tactics do not represent an exclusive list of every conceivable tool abusive individuals with antisocial personality disorder might possess in their arsenal.

Am I therefore assuming only sociopaths utilize these tactics? For the record, no, and—moreover—not all sociopaths willingly engage in abusive actions or behaviors. However, at some level, it appears that the proliferation of these tactics is infectious and can influence the nonsociopath into dysfunctional and abusive patterns of destructive behavior. This phenomenon, in many cases, is further consternated by pervasive, unhealthy, ongoing, improperly-addressed-and-accounted-for social acceptance of abusive sociopathic behavior.

Wait…by laying out and explaining tactics, aren't you encouraging sociopathic behavior by spelling them out for an abuser to emulate?

No—the abusive behaviors and consequences of the tactics would still be occurring, regardless of whether the tactics were described in detail by anyone. However, through describing the tactics and bringing them to conscious awareness, a reader might stand to gain exponentially. Whether or not readers agree with them, the tactics expose subtle, often-unspoken-for behavioral and cognitive occurrences that are in desperate need of readers' awareness, critical analyses, ideas, and intervention. With that in mind, the action plans are designed to empower and encourage victims of sociopathic abuse, as well as to assist past, current, and potential victims in their endeavors to create healthier life experiences.

Though each tactic does not necessarily relate to only one specific criterion within a respective manual, do the tactics cover every possible angle of sociopathic behavior?

While some of the tactics reflect back to one specific *DSM-IV-TR*, *DSM-V*, or *ICD-10* criterion, most of them link to multiple manual descriptors. Moreover, the tactics are not all-encompassing of every possible behavior or mind-set that a sociopathic individual might utilize to operate abusively. An argument can be made that a perfect, complete analysis on the subject of conceivable tactics utilizable by sociopathic individuals may be theoretically impossible to construct for at least two identifiable reasons.

First, at the current time, not enough is known, particularly concerning neuroscience, to address definitively all personality disorders. Second, like a cat-and-mouse chase, abusers evolve and modify thought processes utilized to control situations and victims. Therefore, what was written in the past may not adequately address what may come to pass in the future.

Is this subjective opinion or science?

Empirical evidence, repeatable and replicable in controlled experimental scenarios, exclusively constitutes that which is considered science. In effect, what is provable *is* science. Everything else, until it is provable, merely remains *possibly* science. Science is that which is known with factual, absolute certainty. That which is only known with relative certainty fails to be classified as science in its present state of mystery, though the process by which it is pursued in many cases is "science."

In science, what is known with absolute certainty holds superior weight to that which is merely known with relative certainty. A quintessential example of the phenomenon of relative certainty is an individual being asked to prove his or her own date of birth—after all, he or she likely does not remember it. As will be discussed in more detail later, the particularly cunning sociopath can twist a "lack of absolute certainty" argument to his or her own advantage, finagling victims through denouncing intentional misdeeds and destructive behaviors on the grounds that such abusive actions cannot be "true" when accusations lack the proof of absolute certainty.

While such an undertaking as this writing is, in part, subjective, creative, and interpretable, it provides strength to the field of study through representing the complex, real-life behaviors and thought patterns individuals exhibit—inclusive of individuals with antisocial personality disorder, as well as individuals who merely embrace and exhibit sociopathic tendencies. Whether or not the tactics are "science" depends on future empirical study, which the author encourages and welcomes. Though the tactics represent an individual qualitative analysis, they are intended to address issues with objectivity. Further, the tactics are never meant to imply an intention to attack any individual affected by a disability but, rather, if anything, to attack the intentional abusive behavior destructively affecting the individual personally and possibly others.

In attempting to acquire answers through accessing the research that has been established, a thought ardently occurred to me: it remains impossible for one individual to find and access all the research and resources concerning personality disorders; and subsequently, it remains impossible for one individual to touch upon everyone's valuable contributions. I apologize in advance for missing them. Any one work, such as this writing, on its own may fail in covering all angles. For instance, none of the tactics addressed herein directly deal with Robert Hare's valuable observation in the field of psychopathy concerning a manipulator's potential talent of engaging others with captivatingly mesmerizing, persuasively good-natured eye contact (Hare, 1993/1999; see also Seabrook, 2008).

By implication, even the most disingenuous person might possess a capability to exercise exemplary interpersonal communication skills. And, right or wrong, eye contact, in multiple cultures, symbolizes honesty—which, by the way, leads to the following question: are we really so sure that a lack of eye contact implies dishonesty? After all, some individuals who truly epitomize genuine interpersonal transparency might struggle from any number of biological or psychological disorders that inhibit a given individual's capacity to practice prolonged periods of eye contact. And if that is the case, is it ethical to take off points for a lack of eye contact on a child's grade school speech assignment, or to pass up the most qualified applicant because he or she exhibited awkwardness via poor eye contact in a job interview? But I digress. Before setting about the fifty tactics abusers utilize and their commensurate action plan sections, perhaps it would be an ideal moment to touch upon an obvious elephant in the room concerning their sequencing.

The tactics are designed to flow together, sometimes complementing and building upon previous chapters. But for the casual reader, jumping around is also a possibility and can also provide an opportunity for reflection and insight. With that kept in mind—just one last issue.

Okay, there are fifty tactics here; but if you had to identify and briefly describe three or four concepts helpful to identify someone as a potential sociopath abuser, what would they be?

The following four tips regard scouting sociopathic abusers based on specific actions and behaviors. In brief, they touch upon abusers' potential disregard for victims' dignity, feelings, and safety—often accompanied by a brutal, cold disposition and shallow affect. That coldness might be lacking, though. Remember, the warmth you might perceive directed toward you from an individual does not necessarily equate to others experiencing that individual similarly. Just think about it: has a friend experienced warmth from someone else particularly cold to you, and then tried to defend that person you tried so hard to be nice to? Sometimes it was never going to matter how hard you tried because, at the end of the day, that abuser did not identify anything to want or need from you as a resource, unlike your friend experiencing him or her differently—hence, the emotional unavailability, numbness, and lack of warmth directed toward you.

1) Assess your internal feelings with respect to your external environment

I would start by offering that sometimes you can feel it. You might be thinking, *Wait a second, feel it? Is this eluding to the paranormal?* Please don't drop the book. If you're not sure you are on board, don't worry. However, here is some food for thought: the *Oxford Dictionary* (n.d.) defines an empath as "a person with the paranormal ability to apprehend the mental or emotional state of another individual." And for an additional breather, though quite the *Star Wars* fan—rest assured, this book is not about to compare empathizing with others' undisclosed thoughts or feelings to using "the Force."

However, what I'm really getting at is that you can feel others by their actions. Have you ever walked into a room and felt tension? Rationally, you couldn't figure out why, but something did not seem welcoming, and the room did not feel comfortable to you, maybe for others as well. You do not equally feel comfortable in every room you enter. Why is that?

Homo sapiens can instinctively communicate with one another, very powerfully, in nonverbal language. With or without intention, our species can nonverbally express feelings connected to emotional concepts such as "welcome," "peace," "love," as well as "fear," "danger," "anger," and "suffering," to name but a few. So stay in-tune with your "gut," unrepressed, and be mindful of what you are feeling in response to your external environment.

> 2) When an individual comes across as brutally insensitive about another, as well as reckless to another's well-being

Perhaps you have heard people gossip and say vicious or spiteful things about someone else not present. To your perception, the message registers as hurtful, and you might catch yourself wondering if others ever really intended to communicate such destructive thoughts to the nonpresent victim directly. Perhaps you catch yourself feeling sorry for a victim, reasoning you wouldn't desire people to say something nasty like what you just heard about you or the people in your life.

When you hear, or even overhear as an unintended recipient, nasty, vicious, flat-out mean commentary about innocent victims who are not present, pay special attention to how things are said. It can be difficult to determine why they are said, but through paying attention to the circumstances surrounding how they are said, you can sometimes feel out a person's character.

Here is a specific example: suppose you overhear a conversation about a nonpresent victim in which an abuser discloses unverified, destructive, potentially confidential information and proceeds to berate and degrade the victim behind the victim's back. Perhaps you notice a smirk, accompanied with no sense of shame. And most boldly, you perceive the accuser to relish on the commentary about the victim, as if there is an authentic feeling of joy and sadistic pleasure derived from attacking another and reflecting upon his or her potential misfortune. And this is because—as the argument can be made—quite possibly, there is.

> 3) When an individual shows no value for your reputation

You wouldn't want to be shamed publicly, right? Especially for something you did not do. Your reputation—if you are a good-hearted, law-abiding citizen—is worth a lot to you. Sadly, your reputation can be worth nothing to a sociopath or psychopath abuser. Libel, slander, defamation, extortion, *fraud*—these are but a few of the strategies abusers utilize to control you and your insatiable, good-faith desire not to be falsely accused and ruined within a community.

Remain mindful for the attitude of "I reserve the right to determine other people's intentions for them, as well as to vilify and demonize others unjustly; and I reserve the right to make any convenient argument, as well as engage in any convenient action that I desire—for my benefit, regardless of how destructive and meritless my actions really are." To give an implication of how dangerous this can be, imagine if someone else appeared to take the time to listen to you and later intentionally misconstrued your message in order to harm you in some way. Abusers can twist the original intention of a message or idea to do their bidding. Additionally, this manipulative behavior applies to throwing others' character away wrongly as well.

Your reputation is valuable to you not merely because you likely wish not to have it ruined but because you have potentially spent a lifetime developing it. In just about any situation in professional life where you currently have better character but less power than a sociopath abuser leveraged above you, you are in serious danger. You are involuntarily "playing" on what I refer to throughout this writing as the sociopathically adjusted playing field.

4)   When an individual shows no value for your contribution

You possess talent and skills. You have likely heard you are uniquely *you*, and best at it. And do not worry—I am not here to disagree. However, perhaps you have picked up a vibe that others fail to appreciate you and, possibly, your contributions.

It goes without saying that individuals desire to feel valued in personal relationships, as well as in the work environment. To this end, some years ago in a qualitative analysis, I created an *optimal work happiness model* for workers, presenting and emphasizing a theory that worker happiness remains contingent upon the importance of the individual feeling valued—as well as feeling that others value his or her contributions.

	Worker feels valued, finds work meaningful, and enjoys work.	Worker does not feel valued, find work meaningful, or enjoy work.
Employers, coworkers, and customers value worker, and appreciate worker's contribution.	Optimal Work Happiness	Suboptimal Work Happiness
Employers, coworkers, and customers do not value worker, or appreciate worker's contribution.	Suboptimal Work Happiness	Minimal Work Happiness

Figure 1. Optimal Work Happiness Model by Paul Conlon (2012)

To some sociopath abusers, what you bring to the table can have no value and be worth nothing. Unless, of course, what you bring to the table benefits such abusers' interests in some form or fashion. This is a hard truth. But the silver lining is now you can reperceive destruction that you have endured previously. Part of antisocial personality disorder deals with an individual's potential incapacity. In other words, when others have made you to feel as if you have no value, now you know, others simply *lacked the ability to value you and your abilities.* Let your self-esteem soak that in. Hang in there—life can get better.

Remember, some individuals who lack a capacity to care about others know they cannot care—and this is different than choosing not to care. And some individuals, knowing they cannot care, try very hard to make decisions so as not to be destructive to others in a heroic manner. Think of it this way: if you were born with an inability to care about that which is external to you and yet you make every attempt not to be destructive, you can be one of the most selfless people of all.

Part II

Tactics and Action Plans

The "You Choose What You Feel" Tactic

The first tactic establishes a framework for an individual to abandon and disassociate from personal responsibility for his or her potentially abusive actions. In doing so, it serves as the foundation for many of the other tactics within this writing. The "You choose what you feel" premise provides several glaring fallacies. Such fallacies include, but are not limited to, the concepts that others possess complete control over their feelings and choose what, and even *how*, they feel.

In the first chapter, other issues were established that challenged the "You control what you feel" mind-set. For instance, during the process of experiencing human empathy, many *Homo sapiens* involuntarily become infected with the feelings they perceive in their external environments and, therefore, are at risk of being intentionally manipulated. Additionally, there exists the possibility that specific *Homo sapiens* who possess higher biological set-point—a genetic predisposition for experiencing happiness—may have more control over feeling "happy" in adverse circumstances. Moreover, the first chapter alluded to the possibility that an individual who lacks the ability to experience "personal investment" empathy might actually feel no emotion in response to the feelings of others—addressed as a dangerous proposition.

A common offshoot of the "You choose what you feel" argument can be phrased, "I'm not doing anything to you; you are doing it all yourself." From this phrasing, manipulation appears especially evident. Often, a sociopathic abuser will justify that what he or she does is not abusive; rather, from his or her perspective, it is the victim's fault for feeling a negative emotional response—and, moreover, that victim, according to the abuser, is not even perceivable as a victim.

Think of how out of touch this way of thinking is. Essentially, an abuser, in a very direct manner, could walk up to a victim and say, "I am cold, and I am taking your jacket," rip the jacket off the victim, and then proceed to justify blaming the victim for choosing to feel not only cheated but cold. Of course, at first glance, that example may sound outlandish and unrepresentative of how some individuals treat others, but is it really either? The hypothetical scenarios that describe this phenomenon of baseless rationalization appear innumerable.

Another version of this justification is closely related: "I am not doing anything to [insert victim] because I haven't even interacted with that person in so much time." To begin addressing what is inherently flawed about this reasoning, it should be mentioned that ostracism is a form of psychological and emotional abuse (American Psychological Association, 2015, p. 747). The absence of an individual from one's life can prove devastating to a victim, even if the individual who has exited a victim's life may be an abuser.

The feelings a victim experiences when an abuser intentionally shuns him or her have real and lasting effects. To illustrate, cunning sociopathic abusers can voluntarily ostracize individuals with whom they were once interpersonally close. An abuser then can justify that the absence of interpersonal interaction over a given amount of time with the ostracized victim vindicates the abuser from any responsibility for the condition of a victim after the victim is cut out of an abuser's life. While there are multiple incentives for an abuser to engage in exclusionary behavior and cut others out of his or life, a foundational motivation bears mention: in the realm of antisocial personality disorder, interpersonal relationships may merely serve as instruments for an abuser to obtain a desired end.

Others are staunchly opposed to the premise one cannot choose to be happy and alleviate his or her own suffering. Evidence, at first glance, seems to support this notion. For instance, there have been multiple cases in human history where individuals enduring extreme hardship and injustice have reported choosing to feel happy and subsequently reported becoming happy. I would offer that such individuals' feelings are authentic; however, they were likely born with an enhanced ability to experience much higher "biological set-point."

As previously mentioned, biological set-point refers to the propensity of an individual to experience happiness, largely contingent on genetic factors (Diener & Diener as cited in Golman, 1996). To that end, it appears possible that individuals who experience a particularly high biological set-point—and who are, in any number of ways, disadvantaged or disabled—may experience more happiness than individuals who enjoy what appear to be better life circumstances (Headey & Wearing, 1992; Lykken & Tellegen, 1996). Conversely, other researchers increasingly deemphasize the role of genetics and believe subjective well-being is environmentally influenced and, to some extent, within an individual's internal locus of control (Lucchini, Della Bella, & Crivelli as cited in Bruni & Porta, 2016; Lyubomirsky & Layous, 2013; Lyubomirsky, Sheldon, & Schkade, 2005).

Nonetheless, it would remain difficult to find a physician who openly agreed with and endorsed the notion that a clinically depressed individual with lower set-point and "better life circumstances" can receive treatment by being told to "Snap out of it." In brief, if feeling happiness can be willed, it requires genetic capabilities, which not every human being receives equally, let alone possesses. Thus, *Homo sapiens*, due in part to heritable factors, experience limitations in the pursuit of willfully changing emotions and feelings.

This brings the discussion to the contention that an individual can "rationalize" through his or her feelings to become happy. To that end, there has been no shortage of good-intentioned, wishful thinking on the subject of an individual possessing an internal locus of control to choose what he or she feels. For instance, some might offer a hypothetical scenario in its defense, such as the following.

A small child drops the rest of his or her candy on the ground, feels terrible, and begins to cry. However, after helping the child realize that the world is not coming to an end due to the loss of the candy, and that there will be more opportunity for candy in the near future, maybe in the next several minutes, the child then can begin rationalizing how he or she does not need to feel badly and can go back to feeling happy. It would then stand to reason from the preceding example that, at all times, people can learn to reprogram their feelings to become happy, like the small child. Yet, there is a major problem with that assumption.

Chiefly, that hypothetical scenario provided way too much influence for controlling and correcting the parameter that negatively affected the child (i.e., an opportunity and means to replace the child's candy). What's more, the scenario oversimplified what it means to satisfy human needs. Maslow's effectively constructed, "one-size-fits-most" hierarchy of needs comes to mind: in ascending order, starting from the most basic human needs first, Maslow offered "physiological" needs, "safety" needs, "love/belonging" needs, "esteem" needs, and finally "self-actualization" needs (1943). However, as a word of caution, the arguments can be made that not all humans have the same needs, nor experience the same intensity of desire to fulfill the needs they do possess—particularly regarding a potential need to be in control, as well as a potential lack of need for experiencing meaningful belongingness and "feeling" loved (considered in more detail in tactics 39 and 44 respectively).

The action of losing candy—while authentically psychologically devastating during the moment—reflects merely a physiological need for the child to eat, coupled with the want or luxury of choosing what shall be eaten. As humans, our needs—take "love" and "belonging," for example—are not easily compensated for when they are not met, unlike the need for biological nourishment. For instance, it is not feasible to meet the complex "love" and "belonging" needs of people who feel severely lonely by just creating a business for lonely individuals to have employees with whom customers socially interact, nor is it feasible to expect such interactions to cure loneliness. A particularly lonely person might find others compensated to interact socially with him or her—as well as any ensuing "social experience"—as lacking in substance, inauthentic, and unfulfilling. Human needs and desires are complex. They are not necessarily willable toward human happiness.

Some might counter that individuals can control their feelings with external substances, such as medications. While it is true that some medications modify the brain, the question remains: are individuals really happier, or is their experience somehow false? Moreover, the realm of modern medicine mirrors the field of psychiatry in its nascency. Much more information is needed than is available at this time to say definitively if medicine makes people happy. Nonetheless, this is a discussion that exceeds the scope of this writing, and I do not wish to discredit the tireless work of researchers addressing it. However, it simply helps underscore the point: if you are not in control of how you feel, who or what exactly is? And is it possible that what you feel may be influenced in part by "you" involuntarily, as well as by others?

Not to be in control of one's self yet for one's self to have control over you—seems a bit difficult to digest. After all, if you affect how you feel, how can you not control you? Perhaps the best way to answer is that you do control you, just not *all* of you. Do you consciously control the estimated thirty-seven trillion cells within your body (Bianconi et al., 2013)? Obviously not, but a healthy body seems to know what to do. So too does your mind, without your consent, affect how you feel. Sure, you can influence how you feel, but controlling how you feel—that is a different story.

To the skeptic absolutely sure of his or her own ability to exercise self-control over feelings, imagine the following scenario: you are in the zoo, next to the lion's cage. Not so bad, right? However, imagine that, for some reason, you found yourself in the lion's cage, standing mere feet from the lion, with no foreseeable exit plan, tranquilizer gun, or beef jerky to throw in the opposite direction. How would you feel?

Are you catching yourself rationalizing how you would will yourself not to feel any fear? By the way, it is nothing to be ashamed of, to feel fear. Fear may have saved you from entering a lion's domicile the last time you visited the zoo. If you are human and mentally aware of your external environment, it stands to reason that you would inevitably feel fear.

So why the emphasis on addressing what makes humans feel and on who controls what humans feel? The answer inevitably lies not in the action of experiencing emotions but in the operator catalyzing those emotional experiences. You see, if you cannot control how you feel and you are willing to concede that how you feel is contingent upon external variables, then you are forced to face the trepidatious possibility that *others* might play upon your inability to control your feelings—to control you. Enter the sociopath.

Action Plan

A sociopath abuser may play on your inability to control your feelings to achieve desired ends. Scan your internal feelings and external environment for the following three attitudes from others: "It's your fault—you choose what you feel," "I'm not doing anything to you, you're doing it all to yourself," and "I am not doing anything to you because I have not even interacted with you in so much time." Remember, these attitudes may be expressed verbally or even nonverbally with actions.

While these attitudes hint at possible psychological underdevelopment, people who exhibit these attitudes may be very clever and have learned such mind-sets can be acceptable behaviors in certain organizational cultures. In essence, these mind-sets can represent endorsed shortcuts to undervaluing others, thereby creating leverage for an abuser to take advantage of and manipulate others. While, to a skeptic, it may seem too calculated for anyone to act like this, it is not rocket science. Often, skilled abusers have had a lifetime of practice with eliciting particular emotional reactions they desire others to feel in response to a premeditated action—in a concerted effort to attempt to influence others' emotions. It is a rather remarkable feat, considering that the abuser who catalyzes the emotional response of a victim may not be able to experience what it may feel like to empathize involuntarily due to external variables as his or her victims might.

To help with identification, remember someone may attempt to influence another to feel—not just negatively but—positively, as in the case of the individual lecturing another on how he or she needs to reframe his or her attitude "to feel happy." The intention may be in good faith, but the advisor may lack an understanding of higher-stage empathy and even perhaps an ability to experience it. Also, as insensitive as it may sound, an out-of-touch individual telling a depressed person to "Snap out of it" might offer such words from a place of good intention, though he or she might be empathically disadvantaged and thus not understand what is wrong with saying as much. The point here, as throughout this whole work, is not to harp on or judge others negatively for their potential limitations. However, as with this instance, through identifying potential limitations preemptively, an individual is better prepared to understand an abuser and better equipped and protected in the event interpersonal communication with an abuser occurs at a future time.

Lastly, consider the following distinction: what an individual thinks, how an individual behaves, and even how an individual chooses are arguably within his or her control *whereas* choosing how he or she feels is not. For the health of all, consider bringing to the forefront of discussion how it may be dangerous to assume humans are in control of their own feelings and, also, how it may be dangerous to overlook the possibility that abusers take advantage of victims' inability to exercise complete self-control over feelings and emotions.

The "Judge of Facts and 'Creator' of Reality" Tactic

Have you ever felt like someone did not acknowledge the facts as they truly are? The case can be made that an individual may not care about the truth or how you feel, or *care* only to the extent that your feelings affect their interests. Possible reasons for this reality include an individual unable to experience higher-stage empathy or an individual perhaps lacking a developed conscience—or even a sense of consideration for others. Perhaps you have reasoned before, "You know, I really try to listen and behave considerately to some people, and they just don't seem to reciprocate that same sense of interpersonal connection." For some individuals, this is a telltale sign of a dysfunctional interpersonal relationship. And it should be.

Have you ever felt physical symptoms during a tense moment due to another person's overwhelming sense of willpower to subdue your perspective with which he or she did not happen to agree? Perhaps the antagonist attempted to talk over or discredit your logic. Perhaps he or she, in classless fashion, attempted to discredit your character. These very real instances that occur in tense interpersonal relationships and situations are so powerful that they not only wound and destroy empaths physically and psychologically, I believe they can even lead to illnesses such as clinical depression and post-traumatic stress disorder.

Perhaps within you, an example of this sort of situation has unpleasantly revisited your mind. These unfortunate situations are like flat tires. You know they have happened to you or others before, and you never know just when and where they will happen again. For the empath, these situations are devastating.

Imagine seeing, hearing, and perfectly witnessing a crime. You are called to trial to testify. Only you, an individual in right mind and of reasonably sound judgment knows what happened. Remember, you witnessed it. But perhaps nobody believes you—well, except you. Insecurities start running through your mind as the defense team drills you. They prod and push you, trying to find buttons to exploit. They may even know you are telling the truth. They may even know the criminal is guilty. But all that matters now for the defense is breaking you.

Forget about the fact you never asked to be in this situation. Forget about the fact that you would not go out of your way to put another person through what you are experiencing—let alone, you would never desire to commit the crime that was witnessed. You feel the pressure and an odd sense of blame throughout the entire courtroom, as if you did something wrong. Your testimony will affect the outcome of someone else's life. But again, you witnessed the crime. Your conscience will be vindicated with the peace derived from honest testimony. You know what is real because you experienced it. This pressure and attack upon you feels not only incredibly exhausting but disheartening.

However, the abusive sociopath does not necessarily really care. A defense lawyer who does care about what you are experiencing probably is not an abusive sociopath. Perhaps the defense team knows the accused is guilty, and so too they also feel guilt and remorse that they, in attempting to pressure and deconstruct your word, an innocent passerby who happened to be the key witness to the crime of the defendant, lead to your suffering.

The argument can be made that defense lawyers who are abusive sociopaths may even feel a sense of exhilaration while cross-examining you. For this moment, they get to legally play God. They are in a unique position to exploit what actually happened in the past, to create what legally was believed to happen in the past. This can be like being a kid in the candy store to an abusive sociopath on a mission of destruction. If they are successful, they can actually get a judge or jury to endorse their version of what happened in the past *legally*.

Empathic lawyers and innocent, well-intentioned key witnesses aside, such abusers may thrive on a sense of control in situations where the perspectives of others are subdued. Within their minds, not only are abusers experiencing a sort of personal ecstasy from conquering another, they, in their own way, may enjoy self-identifying as a superior being, as well as exercising an exclusive privilege as a "superior being," chiefly to establish facts and shape reality during conflict. Sociopathic abusers can be sat down in a room and explained to, over and over again, that being chief of determining what the facts and truth are, as well as suppressing others' perspectives, can lead to serious health conditions for others. Moreover, many can understand all the words coming out of the mouth of the explainer, but that is different than *actually* caring about another person's feelings. And furthermore, even if abusers do agree that there is a connection between their actions and another's feelings—that remains distinctly different from *actually* caring how victims are affected by abusers' actions.

Sure, they may reason, "Well, I wouldn't feel hurt by someone else's actions," which perhaps is commendable for honesty. But because many abusers do not operate like others and do not feel hurt themselves in many situations where nonsociopath empaths feel excruciating pain, they are liable to find what is explained to them as irrational and unnecessary, and subsequently refuse to accept empaths as genuinely hurt. Sadly, this dichotomy hints at an implication of an attitude of competitive natural selection: the abusive sociopath, while being perceived as empathically disabled by the nonsociopath, in turn, might perceive the nonsociopath as unfit to live in the world where reality is determined not by what actually occurs but by the individual most successful in lying about it. And for even the most psychologically healthy individual, this can lead to a tremendous sense of anxiety and stress.

Action Plan

Please understand that there exist unfair, nonnegotiable parameters when encountering individuals who judge others abusively and inaccurately for their own convenience. Such parameters include whether your intention is altruistic or rooted in goodwill—and whether you are innocent of any accusations made against you. While channels for recourse may prove difficult to identify, or perhaps, and most unfortunately, not even exist, understand your emotional responses can and will be used against you by abusers with malicious agendas.

To provide an illustration, if you are stood up for an interview and communicate your displeasure to the individual who does not take responsibility for his or her actions—every word you say can be used to claim that you are argumentative or combative. Please consider not giving an abuser any material to work with against your character. So often—as sociopathic behavior is so infrequently brought into discussion—victims default to attempting to create a "teachable" moment to persuade an abuser of his or her "inaccurate" thought processes. This is a trap. An abuser may know a victim is wrongly accused and, perhaps lacking a conscience, be content with making accusations. Moreover, any extra response by a victim further helps to build baseless accusations against the victim. Realize—abusers are counting on your emotional reaction to their inequitable treatment of you.

While such nonnegotiable parameters in any given situation are determined by an abusive sociopath—*for* the convenience of an abusive sociopath—the question presents itself: what can one do to scan the environment for individuals operating under the "judge of facts and creator of reality" tactic? Five opportunities for reflection present themselves that help in determining if an abuser engages in this tactic. First, ask, "Do I feel like this person's words or actions are communicating that he or she feels solely entitled to determine what the 'truth' is, even if he or she cannot be absolutely certain what the 'truth' actually is?"

Second, "Do I get the feeling that the character of others is 'for sale' with a given individual?" Third, "Do I feel pressured to go along with a 'judge of reality' abuser's judgment when it does not endorse the truth of a situation?" Fourth, "Do I feel intimidated and threatened that an abuser might judge others' character negatively if an abuser is challenged?" And fifth, "Does this individual ever concede to making mistakes—or is every contention within a dispute an opportunity for him or her to express dominance over others?"

In this instance, dominance is not meant to imply superior debating but, rather, a strategy utilized to appear "correct" on a substanceless surface level—as specifically manifested through refusing to take responsibility for inaccurate assertions. This behavior often accompanies individuals who help themselves to making accusations without evidence and refuse to take ownership when an inaccurate assumption has been made. Abusers who engage in this strategy are often mistaken; for though they may think that they appear dominant in successfully defending their contentions in a dispute, to the wrongly accused, the abuser appears dominant merely in the sense of being manipulatively controlling during discourse.

Moreover, through utilizing such behavior, the abuser does not appear dominant but rather incapable of listening to and processing the viewpoints of others, as well as appears to exhibit a lack of personal responsibility for one's inaccurate assertions. Additionally, this dominance mind-set exposes the abuser's destructive intention. For unbeknownst to the abuser, when a "judge of facts, creator of reality" individual thinks that he or she appeared dominant and "won" an argument through such a strategy, the only person who has been convinced of the abuser's superiority is often him or herself.

TACTIC 3

The "Statute of Limitations on How Long You May Feel Your Feelings" Tactic

In my experience, sociopathic personalities frequently utilize a tactic to evade culpability—a tactic so subtle yet that appears honest enough—a tactic that seems to play the "attacked and innocent victim card" all the way to the bank. It is a tactic so controlling and dominating—*and* manipulative—there is but little the empath can do except to learn to recognize the strategy, acknowledge a playing field is not even, step back, and disengage. What is this tactic the sociopathic individual utilizes? An abusive sociopath with no official paperwork or guidelines publicly released to others, with all due convenience, can selectively invalidate grievances brought to his or her attention based upon arbitrary guidelines that are usually made up or decided on the spot. Translation: the abuser imposes a statute of limitations on how long a victim may feel his or her feelings and communicate grievances.

One of the fundamental areas in need of acknowledgment, intervention, and reformation in conflict settings is the understanding that it takes a tremendous amount of courage—or at least exposure to personal vulnerability—to address present and past grievances. What does that imply exactly? Well, for example, sometimes employees are afraid to bring about issues of harassment or abuse. After all, it is frightening to victims that it is not necessarily what actually happened that wins the day but who may be most successful in lying about what actually happened.

And then there is the issue of expendability. Individuals in personal or professional settings under duress in hostile environments may experience any number of negative symptoms, such as feeling disposable, expendable, demoralized, undervalued, misunderstood, or belittled, to name a few. If an employee has been wronged and addresses an issue, it is possible that an administration operating with a sociopathic culture may dismiss the employee's grievance on deceptive grounds to avoid having to deal with firing other workers who may seem less disposable and expendable, more dangerous to bring suit against, or perhaps just more subjectively preferable.

The argument can be made that the rules and regulations establishing the statute of limitations guidelines for private firms and public courtrooms alike are perhaps too rigid, coming across as small windows of opportunities to file grievances. Moreover, the chronology problem often occurs during interpersonal communication between individuals. Addressing an issue between individuals equates to social taboo as personal, informally-adopted time periods subjectively dictate how long an individual may have to "file" a complaint with another individual.

For instance, how many times in your life have you heard someone say in response to another addressing an issue, "Well, you should have brought that up earlier"? This phenomenon does not require direct communication with an individual addressing conflict: the receiver of a grievance may communicate to a third party that an issue has been communicated in an "untimely manner" as a means to berate the individual bringing forth a grievance and, even so sociopathically, pronounce an issue's communicator as "mentally" unfit. In effect, the sociopath abuser digs his or her heels in and refuses to welcome another's feelings, not necessarily because he or she may be incapable of acknowledging, or empathizing with, others in the first place, but because it presents as more politically correct and convenient to blame another for not bringing something to the abuser's attention sooner. Sounds pretty childish, right?

Moreover, these situations occur in romantic relationships frequently. During conflict, mates may tell each other that they should not have held something "in" for so long, which may be innocent enough. For example, one empath mate might tell the other, "Don't hold something in because I care about you, and I don't want you to hurt. Whatever it is, even if it's an unpleasant issue about us, share it with me so we can heal."

The skilled sociopath has learned to mimic this logic, at least superficially. The difference, of course, is that the empath genuinely wants to help the other whereas the sociopath abuser might desire to use the logic to avoid dealing with something or someone else—which, of course, is ironic. After all, if you impose an impromptu statute of limitations on how long another person may have to tell you something that is troubling him or her and proceed to attack him or her for not bringing it up in an "appropriate" time limit, aren't you engaging in avoiding the issue yourself? Subsequently, some sociopathic individuals may utilize the statute-of-limitations tactic to manipulate and dominate empaths.

Action Plan

So you just might be wondering, *I have a solution—eureka! If only I address the issue within a reasonable period of time, even the first chance I get, I am safe, and my issue will be addressed.* But unfortunately, double standards apply here too. There is no guarantee that the sociopath will pardon your issue or make a special commitment to address the issue and be personally accountable in appreciation of your "timeliness." In effect, when an empath shares a troubling issue sooner than later with an abusive sociopath, the empath risks being attacked for addressing it all the same.

To test the intention of the receiver of a message who initially appears unwelcoming of your feelings on grounds they were not communicated in an "appropriate" amount of time, try this: explain the situation to him or her and ask for his or her understanding as to why you did not bring up the issue sooner. If the individual will not even let you explain and appears aggressive, then you have cause to suspect that he or she does not intend to take responsibility for any accusation that implies his or her own liability.

However, if the individual—who has found you to be in violation of his or her arbitrary statute of limitations for an amount of time to address an issue with him or her—does listen to your explanation but does not agree with it, try the following: say something to the effect of, "Thank you for listening to what I had to say and my reasons for why I felt I had to wait until now to address this. I understand you do not necessarily agree with my reasoning, but would you forgive me and discuss this issue at hand with me?"

If the individual does not appear in the slightest to desire offering forgiveness, directly or even indirectly, and refuses to address the actual substance of the issue hidden beyond the statute-of-limitations standoff—then I am sorry. You are likely in a lose-lose situation with an individual attempting to manipulate and control you, not treat you with respect and validate your feelings and worth. This is a particularly difficult situation for empaths who can have very strong emotional attachments to abusive individuals. But remember, if someone intentionally abuses you, he or she does not intend for you to do well and be well.

It is a common empath rationalization—or, as I choose to refer to it as a portmanteau word, "empathization"—to assume people who are not forced to interact with you but choose to do so, for whatever reason, desire for you to do well and be well. Moreover, another empathization applies to the situation: the presumption that someone with a track record of treating another right most of the time *truly* desires to treat another right *all* of the time. Subsequently, empaths often rationalize instances of the poor treatment they receive from others as less-dysfunctional occurrences than they actually are. Specifically, empaths often erroneously reach the conclusion that the poor treatment they have received from another lacked malicious, callous, or reckless intention because dysfunctional events seem like isolated occurrences. Finally, preceding these flawed thought patterns is a much more general, base-level empathization to contemplate: "People will intend to treat 'me' well because I intend to treat 'them' well."

The "You Disqualify as Being Tough-Enough to Work Here; I Don't" Tactic

What is toughness to you? Is it iron resolve of character to persevere in adverse circumstances? I would almost say yes. But—the ambiguity of "character" and "circumstances" leads to subjective interpretation. Too often, the idea of possessing tough character means making ruthless decisions that are dressed up as difficult ones. To appear tough is easy for many who can *easily* make ill-advised decisions, in some cases, affecting others. Authentic toughness of character precedes action. Toughness, to me, subjectively, is an iron resolve of character to stand for empathy in the face of circumstances adversely opposed to empathy's principles.

Perhaps you have found yourself in a situation where someone, perhaps a coworker or organizational superior, has said something borderline, or even outright, offensive about someone or something else. And then, as you automatically begin to show your contempt through facial expression alone, another coworker notices and responds, "Relax, you take things way too seriously. It's just a joke." Or maybe you have heard someone say something along the lines of, "Your skin is too thin," "You're too sensitive," or "It doesn't matter what that person said; just deal with it." The imperfect world manifests through the hostile work environment, often a by-product of an inert organizational culture.

In business school, hostile work environments within inert organizational cultures were very interesting to study. Though they make for interesting case studies, they are not particularly pleasurable to ponder, much like the cancer cases a doctor may deal with, who may genuinely love contributing to helping and healing others but—as an unintended by-product—involuntarily hurts from the displeasure of feeling the pain of terminally-ill patients and their loved ones.

Inert organizational cultures to me, and perhaps to you as well, are loathsome and unpleasant to ruminate about. Yet they are so readily present and egregiously offensive it is hard to sweep them under the rug of conscious awareness. So often, the inert culture informally defines toughness as an ability to do or observe wrongdoing with an iron resolve of character not to challenge it.

In a perfect world, why would a hostile work environment be tolerated? Sure, different people find different things offensive, and in turn, some things that some people find offensive are not found to be offensive by others. But ideally, intentionally destructive, abusive behaviors would not be welcome infringements on any worker. It is my belief that abusive, sociopathic culture attempts to inundate organizational culture like water rushing against makeshift plugs lining the hull of a sinking ship.

Take the following example: if a sociopathic individual with organizational power has not only an inclination but also an intention to disregard the feelings of others and lie, cheat, or even steal—would not it also stand to reason that the same individual would disregard the empathic identity of the culture in which he or she operates? Multiply the influence of multiple ill-intentioned sociopathic individuals with organizational power and discover the establishment of deleterious organizational norms. Subsequently, the sociopath can create, and even endorse, abusive work environments, rationalizing that individuals unwilling to tolerate "appropriate" organizational behavior classify as "bad fits," not "tough enough" for the job at hand.

Action Plan

First, it is important to take note that someone who says something along the lines of, "Your skin is too thin," or, "In order to work here, you're going to have to roll with the punches better," is not necessarily a sociopath. They can even be empaths who are trying to nurture you along the way for your own good. After all, you potentially need a job; maybe the one you have is your only or best choice to make ends meet. So these messages communicated to you by others may be just that—messages—not necessarily the emotional empath messengers' endorsed version of a utopic reality. Nonetheless, this speaks to the sadness of the situation when well-intentioned individuals feel compelled to subjugate themselves to demeaning practices in order to keep steady work in debilitating environments.

In regard to dealing with individuals who idealize dysfunctional environments as best practices, understand—some, ironically enough, might appear the best suited for "taking suggestions" and "talking" about positive work environments and the importance of every teammate. Or you might run across a candid unilateral decision-maker who, very openly, could not possibly care less that other people, not "paid" to make his or her decisions, can possess informed, well-established thought patterns. Either way, neither may welcome enduring a teachable moment concerning empathy and authenticity.

So what are you left with? First, through contemplating the irony that toughness of character has been historically misrepresented, you can help others understand how to identify the occurrence of substanceless toughness of character. Case in point, the argument can be made that the only power someone who is undeservedly considered of "tough character" might actually possess is the power not to have to care what others think or feel—and from that vantage point, the irony of what constitutes toughness appears especially evident.

This superficial toughness of character might, for example, manifest through inconsiderate decision-making, or through an individual with a high degree of egocentrism judging others' toughness as inferior based on his or her own self-gratifying perception of others' susceptibility to respond when their "buttons" are "pushed."

Coinciding with this notion, reflect on how egomaniacal it is for an individual to assume the role of sole arbiter in determining the correct amount of "thickness" for others' "skin." After all, if you experience the legendary "You're too sensitive" comment, dare to challenge the notion an individual is too sensitive with the notion most individuals are not sensitive enough.

The "Donating to One's Self Through Appearing to Donate to Others" Tactic

Many people choose to give to or serve others through financial contributions, donation of goods, volunteering, or some other form of charity work—even something small like offering to let another borrow an umbrella. You may have been ingrained with the notion that it is not your place to question, let alone wonder, why someone appears motivated to participate in giving because, as the viewpoint goes, essentially, there is something classless and selfish about assuming another human being may be doing something that appears to benefit others for his or her own gain—which is taboo. After all, no one goes up to a microphone and says, "Thank you to all of our volunteers who came out today. Obviously, many of you are here to pad your résumés with service experience, or because your company instructed you to attend."

Likewise, no one seems to respond after being thanked on a microphone, "Don't mention it. I really don't care about the organization. It makes me look good to be here, and I'll tell everyone I know I was here today—literally everyone. This will really be a nice little boost to bolster my image to others. And by the way, I'm really not a high-character person, so when I can get out to these types of activities, I know talking about them to everyone will help throw people off my trail in discovering what kind of character I actually have." Or perhaps another way this may manifest is an individual with sociopathic tendencies committing through a toy drive to buy a toy for an impoverished child and making a point to mention to others how much he or she will spend on the gift, while proactively reminding others of how the gift benefits a child in need. And to really "sell" the selflessness of the gesture, he or she might bring it up guised as a question to solicit others' opinions on what toy would be best to buy.

The skilled sociopath can be exceptionally tuned in to societal and cultural rules and values for charity. Sure, people perform charitable acts for any number of altruistic motivations. Yet count on some abusive individuals with sociopathic tendencies to know at least three main informal rules.

First, it is impolite and, frankly, perceived as classless to question why someone donates or volunteers. Second, most people feel pressure not to check volunteer service records; and if they do, they will rarely attempt to meticulously research the frequency and extent of another's involvement with a charitable organization. It is not that people—for example, hiring managers or employee supervisors—fail to wonder if an applicant or a subordinate really volunteers for a charity listed on one's résumé. And the argument can also be made that it is not that they do not wonder why an applicant or employee "really" volunteers—but more so, if you call up a nonprofit organization and ask them to take their time and use their resources to talk about a subordinate or job applicant's involvement with a charity, the inquiry may not stay confidential, and it may come back to make an employer look tacky and burdensome to a nonprofit, as well as perhaps even untrusting to a volunteer.

Third, people are taught to assume other people "give back" because they are good-natured—a classic empathization. Whenever possible, it is considered politically correct to give the benefit of the doubt to someone who seems moved to help others. So much so, the action itself of engaging in charitable work is often even perceived as a form of personal amends and character transformation for someone whom may have a particularly bad reputation or troubled past.

Action Plan

Empaths, be mindful. If you find yourself tempted to choose to believe someone is reformed from past transgressions through present charitable work, perhaps you are correct. However, make sure that your understanding of another's character is not merely a projection that you "charitably" assign onto another for appearing reformed—you know, through a sense of obligation to give the benefit of any doubt and credit another, a temptation resounding within your conscience like a bell that will not stop ringing.

For here lies another empathization: all people can change, and will change for the better. And why is this line of thinking derailing? Because there exist some highly skilled sociopaths who want you to feel called to the charitable act of projecting positive character attributes upon themselves. Then they can leverage your charity concerning their "charity" to manipulate you.

Recall the three informal social norms regarding donation: first, to question why one donates is taboo; second, due diligence performed to ascertain the truth about volunteers is rare and can be personally unpleasant for an investigator; and third, people assume others engage in charitable works to give back and help others in need, above any other reason, because everyone is inherently good-natured. With these three informal rules understood, coupled with an ability to warp the truth and not feel the effects of conscience, abusive sociopaths game the system—what system? Well, really, multiple ones—sociopaths game, day in and day out—but here in this writing, the system is generally referred to as the *sociopathically adjusted playing field.*

The "Fitting Square Pegs into Round Holes" Tactic

This tactic is all about an individual making one's way via the all-too-often socially accepted practice of invalidating the feelings of other people. Basically, in a nutshell, a victim's feelings are figuratively square-shaped pegs that are rationalized to fit into convenient round holes that comprise the perspective of an outsider. Here's an example: an employee works at a supermarket and is constantly being insulted and debased by another employee. Sometimes the two employees are supposed to work together as partners, sacking groceries and operating the cash register. The insults have gotten so out of hand that the victim now decides to complain to the employees' shared direct supervisor.

The supervisor converses with the employee allegedly responsible for the emotionally abusive treatment. The allegedly abusive employee tells the supervisor something to the effect of, "I really like my coworker. Sure, we joke around sometimes. I certainly didn't mean to hurt anyone's feelings. I'm sorry. I had no idea my coworker was feeling this way." Satisfied that the alleged abuse was not intentional, the supervisor ends the conversation, allowing the employee to return to the checkout area to work with the victim employee. The supervisor, trusting in the sincerity of the allegedly abusive employee, tells the victim employee nothing intentional happened and that there was nothing to take personally.

Though the abuser could have been fired several times over, the supervisor has created a version of "what may have happened" that is convenient. Reasoning there was no proof either way and possessing a generally positive impression of the alleged abuser, the supervisor sidesteps validating the victim employee's feelings. Several weeks go by, and the same employee continues to be verbally and emotionally abusive.

Now the supervisor is in a higher-stakes situation. The victim employee not only is claiming to have dates and times of hurtful remarks documented but is demanding not to have to partner any longer with the allegedly abusive coworker. The supervisor now fears his or her own job security—as not initially submitting the situation to upper management or human resources in a timely manner may have helped prevent a lawsuit and potential bad press for the grocery store.

These sorts of situations are very common. People dismiss other people's grievances a lot of the time because it is the easiest alternative. However, some people also dismiss other people's grievances because they are incapable of valuing the feelings of others.

In the preceding example, the supervisor attempts to "fit" the victim employee's square-pegged feelings into round-shaped holes, figuratively speaking. Here is a variant example of the phenomenon. Perhaps you have experienced a friend having told you, "You are upset with me because I became friends with someone whom you feel has hurt you in the past—which is ridiculous for you to feel that way because what happened to you was a long time ago, and you should just let it go, move on, and stop being so critical and melodramatic."

Another version of the preceding example could occur where your friend has no idea that you feel pain because of the new interpersonal bond that has transpired, and thus your friend may lack any intentionally negative thoughts toward you concerning the situation. Subsequently, it is possible that an individual with sociopathic tendencies, without even premeditating any malicious intent toward you—in other words, without even thinking to disregard your feelings—may simply overlook, or even frankly not perceive, how your feelings will be treated as square pegs to fit into round holes. Therefore, it is fair to say that such occurrences of insensitivity toward another's feelings can show limitations regarding empathy but are not always intentional. Moreover, it should be noted, disregard for others' grievances is not the only derivable outcome for an individual with sociopathic tendencies as other people's grievances can be registered within the mind of a sociopath, and even fought for when the sociopath perceives the person threatened, in some sense, as his or hers possessively.

Action Plan

Remain mindful for any individual who seems comfortable reasoning how you should be feeling "for you," comes across as mandating how you should be feeling, or even appears comfortable offering insight into what you should be doing differently to accommodate his or her perspective on what you should be feeling. But that is not all. The square-pegs-into-round-holes phenomenon does not just deal with invalidating others' feelings but also invalidating others' thought processes.

For instance, an abuser might be found rationalizing how others' thought processes disqualify them from receiving assistance. For example, remain mindful of the ever-so-famous one-liners, "I can't help you or others if I don't know what the problem is," and its close variant, "I can't help you unless you tell me what the problem is." Obviously, an individual in a position to help another does not necessarily "need" to be told what a problem is to identify it and subsequently help others. The conveniently flawed reasoning of the claim that others must communicate grievances or risk the certainty of not having them addressed represents a square peg, while the round hole is represented by the premise that only "properly" communicated grievances can be dealt with by the manipulative individual possessing some special authority to address them. This convenient line of reasoning by an abuser, posing as a conflict-resolution resource, creates an easy way to abdicate responsibility for addressing and dealing with problems via blaming the alleged "inaction" of less-powerful people often too afraid and intimidated to communicate grievances.

If you pick up on these indicators, be weary—you just might be dealing with an abusive sociopath. If your feelings are square-shaped pegs, they are square-shaped pegs, and don't let anyone tell you any differently. Additionally, what you can do for yourself right now is reflect on your interpersonal relationships and, upon finding any semblance of being considered a square peg incongruent to fit into a round hole, make an important decision to fight the abuse by sticking up for yourself. Maybe that means disengaging an individual or assertively saying one syllable that, trust me, is not a bad word— *no*. Don't get bent out of shape by allowing another to dictate what *shape* you should be.

The "Backhanded Compliment" Tactic

Have you ever been told that one day you might be a good husband or wife, parent, worker, friend, or person? You know, like someone saying to you, "Keep trying. You might get there eventually." Well, that seems thoughtful and supportive on the surface. But is it really either of those things? With regard to being thoughtful, yes, a backhanded comment can be very thoughtful. And with regard to being genuinely supportive, well, absolutely not. The comment is infused with such negativity that it appears more an insult than a compliment.

For clarification, though a backhanded compliment is not supportive, it is rather very thoughtful. How could that be? The comment, while not actually intended to be supportive, featured thought put into it by its giver.

Unfortunately, for the receiver of the compliment, that thought was not, shall we say, very positive to begin with, nor intended to offer genuine, uplifting support to the receiver. And to make identifying authentic supportiveness within a backhanded compliment even more complicated, sometimes what appears to be an intentional insult is really only a microaggression. A *microaggression*, a term introduced by psychiatrist Chester M. Pierce in 1970, is a statement that violates others but might actually lack an intention to offend or insult a recipient by its author (as cited in Fisher, 2015).

Backhanded compliments are not exclusively sociopathic behaviors but are commonly frequented by abusers with sociopathic tendencies. But why might they occur? To understand the psyche of backhanded compliments, it may help to trace the negativity to a potential point of origin.

While many theories exist, I perceive there to be three main plausible motivations behind these passive-aggressive insults of subterfuge: first, an individual's selfishness, as manifesting through jealousy and smallness of character, inhibiting an individual from selflessly engaging in the merited praise of another; second, an individual's callous lack of concern for others, as manifesting through apathy toward another's good fortune; and third, an individual's false misconception of a victim's motivation and thought processes, endorsed by some sociologists as the concept of fundamental attribution error. In effect, through attribution error, abusers erroneously assume they understand victims' motivations and lines of thinking, only to misinterpret and sell short victims' truly altruistic and innocent intentions.

To provide an example of false attribution, a man might walk into a bar and innocently say hello to a woman he made eye contact with to be polite, only for the woman to tell him, "Get lost." Perhaps the woman assumed the man was attempting to come on to her when the man may simply have desired to appear friendly and sociable to everyone with whom he might interact within the establishment. Maybe he woke up and said to himself, "I want to be a nicer person to everyone," or even, "I am open to developing new friendships with strangers, and I will start today."

The argument can be made that regardless of motivation behind a backhanded compliment—be such antagonism manifested by jealousy, or a self-centered disregard for others, or even misinterpreting what makes others do the things they do through attribution error—the device hints at humans feeling threatened by other humans for resources in a hypercompetitive environment. Such resources may merely remain intangible—for example, the high esteem and prestige individuals may choose to bestow on others.

Some people have developed their self-images around how others have defined their proclivities for them, so any perceived threat to "what they may be good at" may be met with negative thinking within themselves. And of course, there really is not anything wrong with people taking a little pride in the healthy things they do, especially in what they do well. Of particular note, though, in the recently released alternative model for diagnosing specific personality disorders, the American Psychiatric Association suggested that the self-esteem experience for antisocial personality disorder might represent dysfunctional personality functioning—as an affected individual might construct his or her self-esteem identity through power, pleasure, or personal gain (2012, 2013a). Therefore, in an unhealthy manner—for example—the self-esteem of a sociopath might be contingent upon self-assessing his or her own degree of influence and dominance over others, or self-assessing his or her own degree of gaining advantages over others via manipulation or deceitfulness in interpersonal situations.

Okay, so jealousy implies a perceived threat to one's self-image and coveted desires, while an inability to care genuinely about others implies a disinterest toward building others up for their own sake through sincere, uplifting praise. Moreover, misunderstanding individuals leads to assumptions within abusers concerning victims' true motivations and intentions, thereby leading to insulting the perceived false versions of others.

However, what about the anger and hostility so often underlying the backhanded compliment? The argument can be made that one does not have to be angry to give a backhanded compliment—nor does one necessarily have to be angry to lack the ability to care about someone else's welfare. Of course, anger within an abuser may directly result from a lack of being "better" than a victim at something, or simply even jealously for not being considered "better" than—well, everybody else, further fueling the backhanded compliment furnace fire.

Imagine the athletes who do not win but nonetheless compete in the Olympics. Imagine the roller coaster of emotions a world-class sprinter or swimmer must experience to be so great but only ever to be the fourth or fifth best on the planet. Often, they possess no world records or gold medals but still truly remain one of the very best athletes in the entire span of human history at doing what they do so extraordinarily well. How does that sound for an identity?

Sure, some individuals may find genuine happiness and be at peace with as much. But to be nearly the best yet not quite the best may create inner turmoil—and possibly lead to tremendous anger. Many psychologists would argue it is healthy for an athlete to desire to be the best as well as to feel disappointment with not being the best—but also, that it is just as healthy to channel that disappointment without providing hostility, anger, or destructiveness toward others. To that end, it appears that part of what healthy, sane individuals deal with in an ongoing manner is appreciating capabilities while making peace with limitations.

Action Plan

If you are deciphering if a communication was intended as a backhanded compliment, consider the following two criteria. I have noticed from firsthand experience that individuals who routinely give backhanded compliments often share and exhibit two similar characteristics: first, it is as if, with every fiber of their being, they lack an ability to value others' positive qualities while also, second, they appear to be lacking a certain "bigness" of character to say something nice to someone unprompted, without creating qualifiers.

Oftentimes, backhanded compliments seem so inappropriate, it is as if you have been given access to peer within the mind of an abuser's subconscious perception of reality. You can hear things come out of the mouth you would never want to come out of yours because you recognize how dangerous it is for an inconsiderate comment not only to be misinterpreted but, sometimes worse, *to be interpreted correctly.* Remain on the lookout for derivatives of the following examples.

"You are not smart enough, but you are getting better." "It would be nice of you if you would just leave." "You're not needed. Thanks, though." "I appreciate your willingness to respond, but I wish when I ask you a question, you would just answer it instead of giving me an entire long-winded story." "Thanks for contributing, but I don't care what you think." "Thanks for contributing, but *they* don't care what you think." "Well, thanks for your input, but your idea isn't very well-developed." "I wanted to pull you aside and tell you thank you for always being on time for work. I want you to work toward really trying to shine." "Listen, thank you for coming in and interviewing with us today. So why should we hire you?"

And, of course, the backhanded compliment occupies the realm of interpersonal communication outside of the work environment. Here are several examples: "You look good from a distance." "Wow, you smell good today." "You look pretty with your new haircut." "That dress makes you look beautiful."

Perhaps you've read those and thought, *Well, what's so wrong with them?* I will grant you that there is a lot to be said for people successfully navigating life's turbulent waters, attempting to interpret positivity through that which may or may not have been intended negatively—a worthy action plan strategy within and of itself. Some people, to their credit, have a knack for choosing not to pay any mind to the writing that may or may not be on the wall. And further to their credit, they probably live life at times more stress-free than others, though the risk remains—as the writing of negative intention may truly be on the wall.

Nonetheless, the preceding quotation examples are all intended to convey antagonism against the receiver. They all, in their own way, say, "I don't have to feel your feelings. Your feelings don't come across my mind, but I vaguely am aware of the cultural norms around here that encourage or require all of us to say positive things. So in my mind, I'm doing what I need to do to get paid or look good. So here, take this backhanded disingenuous compliment. I'm doing you a favor. Yes, take these positive comments I'm distributing to you—oh, and you're welcome."

Potential causes for why backhanded compliments occur have been addressed, but to have a greater sense of peace, reflect on the following concept: the abusive sociopath—particularly through jealousy, an inability to care independently about the welfare of another, or false attribution—remains detachedly uncommitted to condemning the effects of the backhanded compliment on his or her victim's emotions. In some cases, it is precisely the negative emotional experience within the victim receiving the backhanded compliment that the abuser has sought to achieve, perhaps to make a victim suffer psychological distress through toying with a victim's mind and feelings or to passively communicate disdain for a victim's good fortune or coveted recognition—or even to attack a victim's character that is erroneously understood by an abuser in an unfair, negative light.

Thus, the argument can be made that the backhanded compliment, at times, is designed to make one suffer, as evinced through its subtle but present callousness. It will do a victim well to remember that many people realize others might already be just as skilled as they are at something, if not better; and though they are initially afraid to admit so, they find peace with their limitations. For a particularly egocentric individual, processing this objective reality may incur tremendous internal frustration—possibly manifesting through the hostility fueling backhanded compliments to others. From that vantage point, a victim would also do well to recognize, a backhanded compliment might not deal in the slightest with a victim's alleged flaw but rather an abuser's own limitations in embracing his or her own shortcomings. In effect, the hostility within the insult does not necessarily correlate with the abuser's alleged identifiable flaw perceived in the victim but, rather, most accurately, may represent an abusive sociopath's lack of self-fulfillment in not being perceived as the "best" or most worthy for reward by others.

Okay, so you might be thinking, likely, the majority of humans who have ever spoken have probably dished out a backhanded compliment. While backhanded compliments are not exclusively sociopathic behaviors, remember that individuals who seem unable to offer genuine, selfless praise may be neurologically incapable of providing it. Be careful to remember—though it may be your boss, coworker, or loved one that you desire to appreciate you, first and foremost, do your self-esteem, self-image, and self-respect a favor: realize that some people cannot appreciate you, medically speaking, any better than if you tried to take off on a runway to fly to your next destination by sprinting. Do what you do so well for others with such positive energy and vigor that, ultimately, you will genuinely grow not to desire others' acknowledgment or appreciation because it will be enough for you that you can acknowledge and appreciate yourself.

The "Deconstructive, Constructive Criticism" Tactic

The sky usually appears blue; billions of people live on the planet; grass, by and large, appears green; north is not the same direction as south; and criticism should be constructive, not destructive, right? To the credit of human resources departments the world over, the insistence and emphasis on utilizing constructive criticism appears paramount. While in theory, constructive criticism leads to healthier relationships and, thus, healthier, happier people—in practice, perhaps the concept of what is "constructive" is a little more complicated.

Specifically, when a superior tells a subordinate a "constructive criticism," it may actually be a deconstructive criticism. And seeing as how there has not yet been created, at least from my research, an ICCCE, or international coalition on constructive criticism enforcement, just about anything goes. Hostility seeps through the "apparent goodwill" of some comments offered to "assist" others. Does this sound familiar?

Perhaps you have received a backhanded compliment like, "Today you really seemed to work hard," or on a more lighthearted note, a frequent passenger in your car tells you, "Your car smells really neutral with that new air freshener." A backhanded compliment essentially is a type of a deconstructive criticism. Both backhanded compliments and other deconstructive criticisms have at least three commonalities: they both give the appearance of constructive communication, they are disingenuous, and they may be offered to make the comment's giver look good and the comment's recipient look poorly.

However, all deconstructive criticisms are not necessarily backhanded compliments. This is due to the fact that deconstructive criticisms do not necessarily imply a superficial acknowledgement of another's positive attributes like backhanded compliments do. The backhanded compliment implies the appearance of construction with some form of a substance-lacking praise *whereas* the deconstructive criticism may not have any compliment associated with it. Simply put, the "deconstructive, constructive criticism" may not have any semblance of positive reinforcement in its context whatsoever.

For example, a subordinate might be told by a superior in the workplace, "You are just about the lousiest, inefficient, dumbest, incompetent entry-level investment broker this firm has ever had. You need to spend more time checking the ticker during the day and less time talking with others in the break room." Okay, from the preceding example, nothing within the context appears "positive." Arguably, the comment is verbally, psychologically, and emotionally abusive. However, the superior with sociopathic tendencies does not necessarily perceive that the comment classifies as abusive and reasons that by making this comment, the subordinate will better know his or her limitations, address them, and change into a better employee. The superior clearly utilizes deconstructive communication to address what appears to be at issue with the subordinate.

The subordinate, completely blindsided by the deconstructive criticism, will possibly experience the following thoughts and insecurities—such as but not limited to the following: "I don't want to work in a place where I am called lousy, inefficient, dumb, and incompetent." "They see me as lousy, inefficient, dumb, and incompetent. I now wonder if I am actually lousy, inefficient, dumb, or incompetent." "I wonder if I am no good at life." "I wonder what did I do wrong to make my superior so unhappy with me." "I wonder if there is anything I can fix about this situation." "I wonder if it will make any difference if I explain to my superior that in the break room, the others with more experience discuss the trade with me and mentor me—and I always actively listen, observe, and ask questions to become better." "I wonder if I should quit." "I wonder if I should complain about being verbally abused." "I wonder if complaining about being verbally abused will have repercussions or make me a target with others in the firm." "I wonder if I should hire a lawyer." "I wonder if I could even afford one, even if I had a winning case." "I wonder if I say anything about this—how I might be unofficially blacklisted from another employment opportunity that I might be interested in pursuing." "I wonder if I should start packing and quit right now—and if I do, I wonder how to explain this situation to anyone in the future."

Remember, the skilled sociopath can twist the truth and rationalize what seems hopelessly irrational. The superior, if asked, may rationalize that the criticism rendered to the subordinate was justified. You might be wondering, *You have got to be kidding me—how?* If you think of it like a little child trying to get out of trouble for losing his or her temper by constructing an alternate version of reality, it's rather simple.

First, the superior could say, "Everything I told the subordinate is true. Second, what I said needed to be said for business purposes. Third, talking tough is part of being an effective leader and bringing out the best in my employees. Fourth, I have observed the subordinate lounging in the break room on a number of occasions, and I have no idea what goes on in there." And for the grand finale, "Fifth, what I said to the subordinate was constructive because the subordinate is lucky someone communicated these issues—and quite frankly, the more the subordinate adheres to my criticisms, constructively speaking, the better of an employee the subordinate will become for the firm."

Essentially, the abusive sociopath created an alternative version of reality to abdicate any responsibility for abusive behavior—which, with such extraordinary deftness, allows the sociopath not only to relinquish *any and all* responsibility for the incident but simultaneously allows the sociopath an absolute, unrestricted free pass to exhibit *any and all* future behavioral abnormalities. It's a great setup.

Action Plan

Understand where the manipulator wants the victim—befuddled—left truly wondering, did this superior really say these things, truly believing in his or her own reasoning, possessing altruistic good intention for the subordinate to develop and become a stronger employee? The victim might think, *It seems so far from rational, but maybe I need to rethink how I perceive the situation and relinquish my view that the superior was emotionally abusive. Maybe he or she is hard on me because he or she cares about me as a person and wants me to be successful in life.* Game, set, match—through even considering such wording as "not abusive," the victim is already actively engaged in allowing him or herself to be manipulated.

Also, put yourself in the manipulator's shoes to see the logic behind the self-interest. An admission of responsibility translates into an admission of liability. And an admission of liability may lead to a loss of reputation, control, and freedom for the sociopath abuser.

Meanwhile, even if the subordinate is experiencing post-traumatic stress from the encounter, the superior—marching to the beat of a different drum, perfectly justified, at least in his or her own eyes—marches on, impervious to the destruction caused to others. In effect, the manipulator is not operating on the emotional wavelength of anguish that the subordinate experiences.

Stay strong, even when you are pressured to believe one person's abuse is another person's truth, just worded frankly and directly. And honestly, a combination of professional courtesy, kindness, and even empathy for others should inhibit someone from insensitively berating and debasing another like in the aforementioned example. Lastly, if a manipulator pressures you to find yourself at fault and deserving of emotional abuse, remember this: in line with the alternative model for diagnosing antisocial personality disorder offered by the American Psychiatric Association (2012, 2013a)—people frequently losing their tempers, as well as being mean-spirited and nasty to others, arguably exhibit sociopathic traits such as impulsivity, hostility, and a reckless disregard for the emotional welfare of others.

TACTIC 9

The "Insincere Apology" Tactic

You know how good it can feel when someone apologizes to you? Perhaps receiving a sought-after apology releases dopamine and serotonin. And both chemical neurotransmitters are proven to increase feelings of happiness (Inglehart & Klingemann as cited in Diener & Suh, 2000). A particularly skilled manipulator can tell you that he or she is sorry in a concerted effort to make you feel that sensation.

A reason that this can occur—without arousing warranted suspicion within the recipient of an insincere apology—is because a victim can erroneously believe that a potentially deceptive person would never have incentive to admit wrongdoing openly, especially if an apologizer would stand to lose face. On the contrary, the deceptive individual may be quick to apologize, not because he or she is genuinely sorry for anything but because, through doing so, he or she can further position a victim to be manipulated. And furthermore, apologizing for a past action is incredibly easy for some abusers because they are not necessarily emotionally connected to or invested in the past, let alone connected to the feelings of their victims in the present.

Okay, if you run a business, say an Internet business, and a customer calls the number on your website wanting to place an order for flowers to be shipped to a special someone, you don't want the customer's phone to ring forever, right? Wouldn't that be incredibly frustrating for the customer, figuring someone will eventually pick up to take the order for flowers, yet no one is on duty at the time? If you can't afford to staff personnel to answer telephones twenty-four hours a day, it makes sense that you would have some sort of voice mail messaging system. Here is a free bit of unsolicited advice concerning voice mails, if you want repeat business: make sure that you are doing everything in the voice mail to communicate that you value your customers. And to anyone who would argue the preceding statement is common sense, I wish to offer two rebuttals.

First, I concede that it probably is common sense to you, and some others, but I doubt any of us can say we've only ever received excellent customer service impressions from our collective communications experiences. Second—and this is a big second—did the wording "Make sure you are doing everything in the voice mail to communicate that you value your customers" leave you with an idea of exactly the type of behaviors you've observed other businesses utilizing, you know, to put on an act to communicate customer appreciation that may seem forced and insincere?

Polishing up a voice-mail system, even a website, or points of contact with customers does not make you a sociopath. And that's not where we're headed here. Though, it might make you guilty of having drive to increase revenue or profit margins, a case in which being guilty as charged isn't necessarily a bad thing. After all, maybe you have a bunch of kids who have a bunch of ideas about how they want to go to a bunch of colleges; and though you have a bunch of love for them, they are soon going to need a bunch of money. In other words, you may be a perfectly healthy human being if you are constantly asking yourself how you can improve your customers' experiences as well as become more profitable.

However, as the saying goes, where there is smoke, there may be fire. There is something about underwhelming customer service experiences that eerily resemble sociopathic characteristics, such as lack of responsibility, remorse, authenticity, and accountability, to name a few. Food for thought, did we consciously welcome this?

I don't know about you, but when I see the word *sincerely* preceding a company name, I don't necessarily feel sincerity inside. If you've ever written a letter to a company to notify them about a sub-par experience you have had—say when one of their employees was particularly unpleasant, rude, or went AWOL around you or your loved ones—you might have that same suspicion of sincerity when some veiled customer service agent thoughtfully writes back, "Sorry you had a bad experience from the team here at our company." Oh, did I use the verb *writes*? Excuse me, I meant the wording—you might have the same suspicion of sincerity when some veiled customer service agent *chooses* a prewritten apology script with the click of a mouse and sends you an automated e-mail, which, really, is like being apologized to by a computer.

But it doesn't stop there. Have you ever tried to unsubscribe from an e-mail list—you know, one of those specials, discounts, and promotions feeds you never asked for in the first place? Once you click unsubscribe at the bottom of the e-mail, your computer might redirect to a message such as, "Thank you from us here at our company. We are sorry you're leaving us and would be happy to serve you again anytime. All e-mail subscriptions have been cancelled." Yet the e-mails just seem to keep coming into the mailbox. It's as if no one has taken you off any e-mail list. In fairness, your e-mail address may have been removed from some component of the customer e-mail address database, but not the master database where it is repopulated, a trivial issue that is resolvable.

What should that tell you? Think of how far we can fly in space. As a species, we can even subdue all the other animals into captivity in what we call zoos; and yet, after unsubscribing from major corporate e-mail marketing, ten to fourteen business days later, we are still receiving e-mails from addresses that we previously unsubscribed from. Really, people, this is sincerity?

The point of all this is to acknowledge that there is an extremely inauthentic customer service culture that has become increasingly acceptable as the best choice for a customer service culture. Now, to my knowledge, there has not been a convention of Fortune 500 companies in Las Vegas where everyone, after hitting up the casinos, met in a conference room and agreed that inauthentic appreciation and apology was the best and most profitable route to appear concerned and caring for customers. But observe your surroundings. You are immersed in the lack of authenticity. It's like how your body is constantly coming into contact with radio waves—it's everywhere.

Maybe, along the way, skilled, abusive sociopaths figured people would rather be lied to and have a machine periodically tell customers, "Thank you for waiting" during holding on phone calls rather than actually telling customers what might be the truth—which is, to some abusers, they are just another little fish in an ocean with little threat to the ocean, unless they manage to organize the other fish to complain about the murky water and the sharks preying upon them.

When you find yourself in a situation where the apologies seem automated, the "Sincerely" and "Yours truly" closings have no one's name written after them—where robotic voices repeatedly say, "Thank you" and, "We are sorry" on telephone lines yet somehow manage to hang up on you long before you can actually talk to a human being—*hear, hear*. When you find yourself in a situation where automated e-mails (not useful order confirmations and receipt messages for your records, mind you) are utilized to thank you for being a valued customer, or passively resolve, even *actively resist* resolving, actual issues—*be on guard*. When you find yourself in a situation where you get the run-around just trying to address an issue—*be hesitant*. The most important issue the administration of that company might intend to deal with that day may be avoiding bad weather on the golf course.

Action Plan

Ask yourself, "Do I really want a verbal apology?" Because the apology you receive may be part of a trade. For example, you may receive the words, but in return, you may be informally obligated to forgo calling out another's ongoing abusive treatment of you or others. Instead of essentially asking someone to lie to you with two words, consider scanning another for genuine remorse and even a desire to make amends. Consider the genuine apology not as a set of particular words but as a demonstration of perpetual actions.

Remain on the lookout for qualifiers. The insincere apology also can present itself through the use of qualifying statements worded within apologies themselves. How many times in your life have you heard, "I am sorry" followed by the word *if*? For a particularly petty individual, this may be the closest he or she can come to a full-fledged ownership of previous wrongdoing. A case in point: "I am sorry if you thought you were less wrong than me." Also, the qualifier serves another purpose: it allows a manipulator an avenue to abdicate personal responsibility concerning whatever happened. Perhaps no example better illustrates this line of reasoning than the ever-so-famous phrase, "I am sorry if you were offended."

Understand, the insincere apologizer does not necessarily perceive the apology in the same manner as the individual seeking an apology. In effect, it does not necessarily register within the apologizer's mind as a mark against his or her character, a loss of face, or even a symbol of showing submission to another. The insincere apologizer's perception of reality, as well as his or her perception of what that apology symbolizes, remains entirely disconnected from the individual receiving an apology's perception of reality. In other words, the insincere apologizer does not necessarily even concede saying "sorry" as an admission of fault or wrongdoing. This phenomenon represents a common empathization: specifically, the assumption that all people claiming to be at fault self-perceive the action of apologizing as a genuine admission of culpability.

Similar to the formality paradox tactic, where a skillful manipulator can attempt to change the chemical balance of a victim with a feigned "I love you," "please," or "Thank you," the insincere apology assists an abuser in gaining leverage over a victim. Moreover, skilled abusers can learn the words and phrases that have the most powerful impact on specific victims, tailoring words to influence victims toward desired actions, behaviors, thoughts, and emotions. Simply put, skilled manipulators can learn to tailor messages that they believe victims internally desire to have communicated. As the old adage goes, "If it sounds too good to be true, it probably is." Be on guard for when it seems like others are telling you what they think you want to hear, especially when others may covet something you possess.

The "Oops! I 'Forgot' to Keep That a Secret" Tactic

Welcome to the time-honored but honorless classic—the "Oops, I forgot to keep that a secret" tactic. Perhaps better explained as, "However, if I were going to be completely honest with you, I might let you know that it is not that I forgot what you expected to remain in my confidence, it's just that, well, first, I don't really care about your feelings, personal boundaries, or that you wanted to keep *that* a secret. Second, I don't really understand why you valued keeping *that* a secret. Third, when I agreed to keep *that* a secret, I didn't think it was an important agreement because I didn't actually think it was a big deal, maybe even a joke. And fourth, it was different back then when I agreed because our relationship was different."

These preceding justifications, in part or in unison, feature many real-life derivatives and represent four common thought patterns—in effect, four common excuses—to abdicate responsibility for violating another's personal disclosure. While these four alternatives appear worded to represent a literal conversational breach of trust by a confidant, they may be manifested nonverbally through actions. For example, perhaps a friend whom you were once closer to "incidentally" posts an unfavorable picture of you through social media but "allegedly" for a different motive than to share something you wished to remain private.

This tactic involves abusing another's trust through abdicating responsibility toward confidants and subsequently engaging in intentional libel, slander, and character defamation based on distorting personal disclosures. But does the "truth" set the abuser free? Is the abuser always justified in sharing the truth—if what is shared *is* the truth?

The answer clearly remains *no*. Even the action of replicating the truth of a secret held in confidence can qualify as an abuse of the individual whose personal disclosure has been violated. For example, Kate, an abusive sociopath, wishes to embarrass and psychologically punish her former social alliance and "friend" Sue. So Kate divulges at the company party the secret that Sue confided in her six weeks ago that Sue likes John, whom Sue hardly knows, and thinks he would look good dressed as a groom.

Action Plan

First, regardless of the fact that the divulged, potentially fabricated information may have started to stew in the minds of others who have heard the "gossip"—and regardless of the fact that such information may have been maliciously spread with the intent to slander, libel, or destroy you—take a deep breath and a mental step back. And by the way, congratulations, you now pretty much know that you have identified a major sociopathic tendency in another individual. You might be thinking, *Yes, but that doesn't necessarily undo the words and actions that have already begun to unfold.*

And you are right. But the identification of a sociopathic tendency in your slanderer is a huge step one because now, before you take the bait and try to reason with him or her, or seek your moment to let the world know the truth, you can step back and focus—I mean really focus. What was said about you? How close to the actual wording can you get without tipping everyone off that you are looking into the alleged disclosure against you or showing others the situation has gotten a major rise out of you? And the rise may be the point—so the abuser can sadistically enjoy observing a victim suffer.

Notice, this does not mean going up to ask the abusive sociopath to own up to what he or she said. That's not going to necessarily be an honest verbal exchange, and it's likely going to identify you as a threat to the abusive sociopath now more than ever, which will exacerbate the situation. Besides, a skilled sociopath can even take such a potential exchange as an opportunity to manipulate you into tricking yourself into feeling guilty for forcing him or herself into defensiveness during a potentially tense, uncomfortable interaction. And that's not all—an extremely skilled sociopath can even manipulate you into convincing yourself that you are of low character and abusive even to have addressed an issue with him or her in the first place, regardless of whom may be due the blame.

Once you have gathered your best understanding of what was said, think about not just what was said but why it was said. Have you found at least one probable matching contention out of the four aforementioned excuses that may serve as a potential justification for the "I forgot to keep that a secret" alibi? Okay, remember, when an accuser slanders an innocent person, this likely occurs because a victim is perceived as a threat to the perpetrator for some reason.

If you are struggling with self-esteem after being put down what seems like countless times, find satisfaction in this thought: maybe some others have chosen not to like you because, deep inside, they perceive you as more attractive or more skilled than they themselves are at something. Not only are you perceived as a competitor, you are feared to be a true contender.

Now, with that reasoning in mind, think critically—no matter how irrational, even nonsensical your thoughts appear—and ask yourself, "Why am I perceived as a threat by this person?" This is your angle for resolution. If it is possible, I have found that communicating you are not a threat, perhaps in some sort of subtle, indirect way, may stop the individual's character defamation offensive.

Unfortunately, even if you are successful in accomplishing this, it may not change an abusive individual on a mission. And unfortunately, people who are of small-enough character to engage in character defamation of the innocent are not always willing to put words back into their mouths or vow to undo the damage they have done to others. In effect, unfortunately, the person who was small enough to throw you under the bus may not be big enough to own up to it, regardless of if he or she has misperceived you as a threat for whatever resource that was initially sought after or desired. People who unjustly slander others aren't always willing to walk their words back or attempt to make any amends—and let that serve as a significant indicator of a slanderer's intent to behave with a reckless disregard for others' psychological safety.

And moreover, unfortunately, you may never receive a genuine apology, let alone an apology of any sort. This phenomenon affects and impacts the arena of personal, as well as professional, relationships. For example, while it is arguably superficial, idealistic, and even naive to expect everyone else to put effort into understanding you and valuing your character fairly, when you are unfairly devalued by loose-lipped individuals in the workplace, you can even find yourself losing your job and the means to support yourself.

In summary, you might find the abuser's angle, but you will likely not find an abuser's apology or genuine remorse for his or her hurtful disclosure. Consider doing something positive with the pain by identifying a way to help victims who are ravaged by such destructive behavior. Consider talking to others to encourage awareness of abusive, sociopathic behavior, as well as to stress that it is not okay to use whatever power or status one has to go through life taking advantage of others or acting like a bully. Consider emphasizing to others the importance of working through conflict with consideration for others' feelings. Empower others.

The "Finger Pointing" Tactic

Once, while waiting to catch a flight in a terminal at a major airport, I overheard and observed a conversation near a boarding area that helped me, to my perception at least, understand sociopathy a little better than I ever had before. Near the gate, an executive in what appeared to be an expensive suit sitting close by made a phone call to a lower-rung business partner. The animated caller displayed a range of tones, which spanned from assertive diplomacy to aggressive bullying, during certain parts of the conversation.

In particular, at certain moments, the caller utilized what appeared to be an increased inflection for emphasis. The conversation was about control. A financial client, not a party on the phone call, was not yet on-board with the numbers, and the chance for a big deal was souring quickly. The seated caller—let's call him "Jerry"—so insensitively said something to the effect of, "I'll tell you what you can do—you can take that nice, fat raise you got three months ago and make the client accept the offer!"

From what was discernable, Jerry, a senior business partner, was telling a younger associate not just to close a deal but basically to make the other party in the deal no longer difficult to work with, a seemingly impossible task to everyone—except, well, for himself. Jerry, the senior partner, unsympathetically kept revisiting the issue that when clients come across as inflexible, he has his hands tied, and figuratively speaking, untying clients' hands is what his subordinate associate was being paid to do. Listening to Jerry in the airport, I remember the repeated mention of the recent pay raise for the subordinate he was conversing with, as well as a repeated mention of how the relationship with the client needed to be forced into control.

The two concepts—the subordinate's raise and getting the job controlled—obviously appeared to correlate within Jerry's mind in a very primordial manner. It was central to his logic. From what was discernable, the subordinate appeared to suggest that there was little he or she could do to modify the apparent stubbornness of the client in question, which made Jerry all the more animated and furious.

Jerry spoke condescendingly to the subordinate employee, as if to a child who enjoys the privilege of receiving an allowance but neglects keeping up with chores and responsibilities. Listening to Jerry go on and on was like listening to a bigger child blaming a littler child for a beverage they both had a hand in spilling. He did not seem willing to accept any shared responsibility. I remember Jerry throwing out how much money in the millions he himself brings in for the firm, at least twice. But one thing struck me that seemed so odd that I couldn't help but just watch, even stare.

Jerry had his pointer finger out away from his chest and was getting in a preflight workout. I did not remember recalling ever having observed someone pointing an index finger with so much emphasis at nothing but the air in front of himself like that before. It was as if the subordinate employee was right in front of Jerry, taking his verbal lashings; yet no one was directly in front of Jerry, not even me. Jerry sat in the foreground, amidst empty seats, the only animate impression inhibiting an expansive view of the windowpanes brimming with blue skies.

As Jerry's obliviousness to me struck me, I wondered, was Jerry aware his arm-and-pointer-finger exercise was visible to complete strangers? I wondered if Jerry would care. I wondered, does Jerry think pointing while speaking actually helps him make his points or, at a fundamental level, solidify his "rightness" in the minds of others? I wondered what his brain would look like with an MRI or CAT scan. What would a brain specialist say? Would neurons in a certain area, perhaps the prefrontal cortex or paralimbic system, be particularly active, firing on all cylinders, as his pointer finger reinforces the hostility and aggressiveness expressed in his voice? Can I definitely say Jerry was a sociopath? No, but it appeared reasonable to conclude he exhibited sociopathic tendencies.

Individuals encountering limitations in experiencing empathy for others might exhibit frustration when desiring others to simply perceive or think about something as they themselves do—or when desiring others simply to feel as they themselves feel, even if what they feel in a particular circumstance is equatable to something akin to a numbness or nothingness. And that experience with frustration is certainly understandable—still potentially interpersonally toxic to others but understandable. And in defense of the sociopath, even a healthy, particularly understanding individual would be hard-pressed not to remember a personal experience that featured a communication breakdown followed by a sender redelivering a message, perhaps with more assertive tone or louder volume, the second time around—in hopes, through forcefulness fueled by frustration, the empathetic receiver would magically receive the message as the sender desires him or her to do so.

So again, the point is never to harp on the individual suffering from a disability; but through understanding and utilizing empathy, the nonsociopath can better relate to and understand the frustration some individuals experience in attempting to persuade another who is not like-minded via a pointed finger or other aggressive physical gesture. From that vantage point, the following hypothesis can be offered: sociopaths probably finger point out of frustration during attempting to make others' minds understand, or at least comply, with their "rightness."

Additionally, for clarification, *finger-pointing*—a hyphenated compound word—is an officially recognized entry in major dictionaries and refers to the action of figuratively blaming others. However, the nonhyphenated term, *finger pointing*, utilized within this tactic, is meant to imply actual, physical pointing as a mechanism for an abuser to engage in various sociopathic objectives—such as intimidating, manipulating, pressuring, guilting, and even coercing victims. Additionally, literal finger pointing can also incorporate unethically blaming and shaming others, like the officially recognized term referenced previously.

Action Plan

Visionary entertainment industry tycoon, the late Walt Disney, was rumored to dislike utilizing the hand gesture of a singular pointed finger (Van Luling, 2015). Allegedly, one possibility holds that Disney himself might have ordered his employees, as well as theme park cast members, to point with never less than two fingers, especially when interacting with customers. Perhaps upon reading this, you might have received an impression of Disney as an extremely successful but meticulously demanding and detail-oriented perfectionist. I cannot say.

But assuming it is true that such a mandate was offered concerning finger pointing—what if there is a much simpler explanation? What if Walt Disney was attuned to finger pointing as being an innocent and culturally acceptable practice for some individuals but, nonetheless, also understood finger pointing as a sociopathic means for other individuals to convey hostility, righteousness, intimidation, and aggression? What if somewhere in his life experience, long before becoming an internationally recognized household name, he personally experienced what it felt like to be pointed at while receiving another's antagonism? And what if—ahead of his time—he thought to himself, *Not with me, and not with my business.* What action-plan insight can be gleaned from this?

Finger pointing while speaking to another is a polarizing issue. In some cultures, it is acceptable and not thought of as demeaning, condescending, or judgmental. However, within any given culture, there are specific individuals who might take offense to finger pointing. In multiple cultures, finger pointing is often perceived as a power move, an action that reinforces the notion of the dominance of the speaker. However, because pointing at another while speaking is so common the world over, many have learned not to take any offense necessarily when interacting with finger pointers.

So, first of all, be open to accepting finger pointing as another's culturally acceptable behavior, and be open to considering the behavior not intentionally offensive. However, when you observe finger pointing that appears especially malicious or hostile directed toward you, it's probably time to start preparing for the possibility someone might have antisocial personality disorder. What you want to do is make sure not to point your finger back at another when you speak. In other words, what you don't want to do is reason, "Well, if a person can point a finger at me, then that individual doesn't mean to dominate or judge me, so it will obviously be acceptable, as far as he or she is concerned, for me to point my finger toward him or her when it is my turn to talk." This faulty reasoning presumes a shared, mutual understanding and agreement of what constitutes appropriate behavioral reciprocity during interpersonal communication.

Additionally, victims might dangerously self-rationalize as acceptable the behavior of returning finger pointing to an instigator in order to gauge his or her perception of offensiveness upon receiving the gesture. And while this may seem logical as a nonverbal means to test another's potential construed offensiveness to receiving finger pointing, it is not wise. That individual may not even remember, let alone register, that he or she pointed at you in the first place. And to assume hostile finger pointers are knowledgeable that they pointed at you and pointed first is like making the faulty assumption that everyone internally considers their potential wrongness with as much effort as they consider their rationalized rightness.

Remember Jerry? He might remember the phone conversation with his subordinate like yesterday, but he might not remember how his index-finger behavior would have come across to the subordinate if the conversation occurred in person. Jerry may not even remember that he pointed his finger as he spoke in the airport that afternoon. Perhaps a neurologist might be able to prove that Jerry may not even remember pointing his finger at all because it may have essentially been a subconscious manifestation of his internal frustration, hostility, and desire to control—perhaps something similar to a toddler asked to remember whether or not he or she threw a tantrum last week.

Also, if you point back with your finger to a guy like Jerry, he just might think, *This person dares to point a finger at me? So that's how we are going to interact now? Well, I have a pointer finger as well. As a matter of fact, I have two!* See how destructive this can become? Needless to say, if you speak to and try to reason with the initial finger pointer using your own finger gestures, that individual is essentially missing your points—except for the point that you find it acceptable to use your pointer finger. Okay, play on words with the word *point* aside, I believe it will work tremendous wonders for you if, when you experience conflict from this day forward, you restrain yourself from pointing at another. Moreover, not pointing at others will help to remove doubt from the minds of any observers that you exhibit sociopathic tendencies.

The "Sentences Said to Size Someone Smaller" Tactic

When you were a child, you probably remember asking adults questions like, "Where do you live?" or, "Are you a giant?" Fair enough, right? But did you ever ask an adult, "Where do you work?" or, "What do you do?" As a child, you probably had a curiosity with the concept of work that just needed to be explored. Perhaps your experience included questions like, "Why do I live in a place away from other members of my extended family yet so close to neighbors that are strangers?" or, "Where do all the adults go every day?" or, "Why doesn't my mom or dad work with their family members at the same place?" Perhaps you even pondered in an innocent way, *I wonder what this or that specific adult does for work*. Maybe certain work fascinated you, so on an elevator or in a store, you just might ask random questions.

As you grow older and start to gather your own work experiences, perhaps you begin to understand and appreciate how hard getting an adult job might be and realize how difficult it may be to get promoted. As an adult, sometimes the last thing you might want to do is tell someone where you work when you feel some sort of threat to your job security. Perhaps there is downsizing and layoffs on the horizon, or maybe a new boss just really seems to have it in for you. So as an adult, you are likely cautious so as not to focus too much conversational energy in asking another adult where he or she works, fearing conversational reciprocation.

That said, there are some adults who love to mention where they work and what they do. Some associate their profession strongly with personal identity and may even genuinely not seek to compare what they do with the next person. They are proud in a healthy way. While it is not surprising people like to talk about themselves, I would go so far as to say people generally like to answer questions about themselves that allow others to understand their holistic identities.

Don't believe it? Ask a professional athlete, even a former one, what life is like when anywhere that person goes, the only questions people seem interested to bring forth deal with sports. I know, you just might be thinking that sounds like a nice problem to have. Anywhere most of us go, many people seem particularly disinterested in asking us any questions to get to know our holistic identities. And that is a shame because, dare I say, we, the people, are still a stronger knowledge repository than any Internet search engine.

And when people do ask us questions in interpersonal situations, we often proceed with the following assumption: *There is an unspoken cultural norm that suggests that asking other people questions about their own lives equates to both a considerate and positive social behavioral interaction; therefore, we are obligated to answer any and all questions to reciprocate the positive and considerate behavior shown to us.* Unfortunately, the lines become blurred when the questions asked do not seek to know or value the answerer genuinely but possess some sort of ulterior motive. Quick, how much money do you make a year? Uncomfortable, isn't it? Perhaps you learned at a young age it was impolite to ask others how much money they make.

On some level, there appears to exist an acceptance that certain questions convey negative intentions on the part of the asker. However, not answering a question may lead to an asker assuming an answerer intends a negative intention as well. In other words, there is a state of balance between the asker and answerer loaded with potential tension.

Particularly skilled sociopaths know how to utilize this tension to manipulate others into feeling obligated to respond to potentially inappropriate or off-putting questions. Now, am I arguing for a relativistic notion that people should only answer questions based on what is convenient for them? No—of course not—because, in that case, hypothetically, no one would have any ethical responsibility to admit to a crime, let alone any wrongdoing. I am specifically referencing the sociopathic tactic of asking others self-damaging questions. And here is a key distinction: questions are not only damaging to a potential answerer merely because of the content of a potential personal disclosure but also damaging to the answerer based on how they violate and abuse the person pressured to answer them.

Action Plan

When you hear someone say the phrases "Where do you work?" and "Where do you live?" understand these may be harmless questions rooted in another's curiosity. Perhaps you have, while walking, decided to take a slight detour to see what was around the corner. Sometimes you even know what buildings or trees you might see around the corner, but you desire to see them from an angle that maybe you have never had the chance to perceive and appreciate before. A lot of times, the questions people ask us are caused by wandering minds walking around, so to speak, trying to decipher and appreciate what they perceive from different angles—perhaps even to appreciate you better. In that case, as the saying goes, we can take the questions we are asked harmlessly "with a grain of salt."

But sometimes "Where do you work?" "Where do you live?" "What do you do?" "How much money do you make and how do you make it?" and even the "would you commit the following crime if…" hypothetical are extremely toxic prods utilized by sociopathic individuals to size up others and consider future repercussions against potential competitors. Through such questions, the abusive sociopath ranks your status, exploits your disclosures into memory (potentially to be twisted against you at a later moment), and determines how best to proceed in challenging or dismissing you accordingly.

So be ready if you sense tension, hostility, competitiveness, or even a belittling tone. Be on guard. Don't tip off what you are potentially on to in the moment but, also, don't feel obligated to provide information that you are uncomfortable disclosing. If you feel a sense of guilt that you are "not being nice" when someone asks you an inappropriate question, stop yourself right there. You have worth and good intention. Where does an individual get off treating you like you should be made to feel like a piece of disposable garbage for not answering an unwarranted, abusive question?

If you are being pressured to feel guilty for not answering a question that is not someone else's business, internally acknowledge that another may be attempting to manipulate you. You may feel that being polite and considerate by responding to any and all questions that have been asked of you is merely your responsibility in adhering to the unspoken cultural norm addressed earlier. But understand, when you may feel uncomfortable with disclosing personal information, the abusive sociopath will not give you points for effort. Understand that when you may feel uneasy and strained due to even having to decide what to disclose to another in a response to a question asked of you, the abusive sociopath does not care. And, if anything, do yourself a favor. Consider reading aloud and ingraining the following sentiment into your memory:

> Whatever I choose to say in response to a question that I am uncomfortable with answering, the potential action of my disclosure and the information I disclose are never going to be appreciated genuinely or valued as a personal favor by an abusive sociopath. Such a disclosure, on both ends, will not forge a greater interpersonal bond built on mutual respect for one another, no matter how badly I might like to build a level of interpersonal connection with someone pressuring me to answer an inappropriate question. My disclosure will not make another value me more, no matter if the individual swears it will—and

> it is possible I will be contributing to gossip yet
> to occur concerning myself once this individual
> determines he or she desires to abuse me in the
> future.

And consider this—instead of asking questions that involve people disclosing their social or financial status, ask people who they are and what they are passionate about.

An important caveat requires attention: belittling questions used for abusive purposes can serve to subdue victims through demeaning and debasing their self-identities; however, it remains important to note that the "sizing others smaller" tactic manifests not only through questions asked for abusive purposes but also through the shots abusers take at their victims. For instance, "sizing others smaller" appears evident through demeaning language concerning others' employment identity, gender, social status, employment status, and even victims' perceived intellectual limitations. And in regard to intentionally abusive gender debasement, objectification and emasculation take center stage.

But why do this as an abuser? What would be in it for you? Step into figurative shoes for a moment and imagine the delight of the delusion. After all, doing so might help you realize how meritless words chosen to label and crush victims truly are—and how such words truly serve the abuser's intention of feeling powerful and experiencing a state of ecstasy at another's expense.

Imagine the feeling of ecstasy an abuser might experience while verbally subduing a victim. Imagine, as an abuser, the exhilarating rush of satisfaction that might flood over you, temporarily intoxicating you with a transcendent feeling of euphoria. Imagine purposefully emasculating victims so as to have them feel inadequate for their gender—or purposefully demeaning victims' lower social statuses so as to derive enjoyment from having them suffer through feelings of worthlessness and irrelevance. Imagine purposely laughing in the face of or taunting lower-level employees to have them feel like they are valueless and incompetent so as to enjoy the bliss of feeling dominant and untouchable. As this abuser, imagine how powerful you might temporarily feel to, at will, tell others they are not as smart as you—as you chew on your words in your mind like a dog relishing the taste of meat lingering on a bone, as you entertain with the strength of a small child's imagination that you might be the smartest person you have ever met.

Cloud nine, figuratively speaking, takes on a whole new meaning. Many abusers look for these moments of bliss at every step and turn and genuinely enjoy walking among the clouds. Unfortunately, the pain inflicted upon victims goes uncared about and often even self-rationalized by abusers as "the truth" that victims "deserved." These sorts of "sentences said to size someone smaller" transgressions affect victims' self-images in a most unhealthy manner and even lead to real health complications, such as post-traumatic stress disorder. So the next time someone says, "Put your big boy pants on," and they are not a comedian, ask yourself, "Pants aside—who may be desiring to wear a tremendous feeling of euphoria at another's expense?"

The Classic "Well, I'm Sorry, I Just Don't Have the Time" Tactic

When people feed you this garbage, do yourself a favor: take one of your hands and just give yourself a pat on the back. Why? Because somebody needs to give you some credit. After all, at least you have the time, right? The problem with most people claiming that they don't have the time to deal with another's issue is that, uncannily enough, it is socially accepted as a legitimate justification for not dealing with something; yet it reflects words that are as untrue and insincere as many pop lyrics.

Let me ask you—regarding the person who tells you, "I'm sorry, I just don't have the time," do you get the feeling that they are even willing to want to address something with you? Or, perhaps, have you experienced when a person might seem to send mixed signals as to what they are willing to talk about with you and what is off the table? What is likely happening in these situations is that people are utilizing their formal or informal power to avoid having to discuss something with you that appears unappealing or self-damaging, at least from their end. Perhaps that topic of conversation involves relinquishing power or admitting fault for something that appears to have gone wrong due to their actions or behaviors.

Simply put, for the individual with sociopath tendencies, what appears not worth giving time to *is* not worth making time for. Victims may feel abused and want to address an issue whereas abusive sociopaths in positions of authority, viewing a situation differently, may avoid giving the time of day to an empath, or even another sociopath, to address a grievance. This can seem, pardon the play on words, like a *timeless saga* in which an abusive sociopath never intends to *make the time*. Ultimately, not giving the time to another who may be genuinely experiencing a legitimate grievance can be abusive.

Not only might such an action demoralize, disenfranchise, or ostracize another, it may cause severe psychological trauma within a victim repeatedly denied the time or opportunity to address grievances. Have you ever experienced this phenomenon? Perhaps you had a "friend" who would allow for status-quo social interaction hours, even years, on end but refused to open the floor to an issue you wished to address. Perhaps, no matter how assertive you were while attempting to open the floor to address an issue while showing respect to your "friend," he or she seemed just as assertive at shooting down your attempt to access that part of him or her. On a more openly condescending note, can you think of a time when you desired to tell someone about abusive behavior and were given every inclination that there was no time to deal with your "little issues"? Or perhaps you have had a boss who has said something to the effect of, "Don't act like I'm wasting your time—if anything, you're wasting mine."

Action Plan

First of all, if you find yourself in this situation, give yourself credit. You deserve it. In this instance, you are acting like a grown-up, ready and willing to work through tough moments. Consider the following two concepts to strengthen your peace of mind.

First, the very same people utilizing a tactic to avoid giving time to address an issue with you must also eat and sleep. Think about that for a second. People have time to sleep, but they don't have time to deal with another person's issue? Now, the excuse "Well, I don't have the time" sounds much more ridiculous, right? When we sleep, we are not consciously counting the seconds, planning and determining what we do or do not have time for when we next awake. So you mean to tell me that every human being who has ever used the "I'm sorry, I don't have the time" card regiments their time to sleep so efficiently that they cannot squeeze a minute or two into the day when they next awake to actually deal with another's legitimate grievance?

Second, now that you have given yourself credit, and hopefully derived peace of mind, realize that though you might not change others, you can influence others by being a consistent example to them through making time for their needs. This concept represents a distinction addressed in more detail in the next tactic: altruistically "making time" for others as opposed to "making time for others for one's own self-benefit."

The "Time as a Bartering Tool" Tactic

In the preceding tactic utilized to take advantage of victims via manipulation and deception, the "Well, I'm sorry, I just don't have the time" tactic, I advocated for making time to address what is important to others. I suggested that one make an effort not to utilize power or leverage to resist making the time to deal with another's feelings and grievances. However, you might have noticed, I didn't write "taking time" but rather "making time."

To be honest, making time is an awkward phrase. Do you make time? I don't. Time is already made. Maybe Einstein might disagree. But this book is not about quantum physics—rather, constructively identifying and addressing sociopathic behavior. If anything, we choose to take the time we already have to do something specific with that time, but we don't "make time" as if time were a batch of cookies.

Why any emphasis on distinguishing between making time and taking time? Well, when people utilize the phrasing "making time," sometimes we can read between the lines. In effect, when people say they are making time for others, they may not mean they are taking time for others, but they may mean something more to the effect of doing others a favor by "heroically" giving their time to others. Okay, so what?

Well, sometimes through "making time for others," individuals possess the intention, even expectation, of receiving some sort of reciprocated benefit—which brings us to the present tactic: "time as a bartering tool." Whereas the previous tactic dealt with abusers intentionally not making time for others, the present one deals with abusers claiming to make time for others but really taking others' resources while exploiting others' time—under the guise of sacrificing their time for others.

This may really come across as unsettling. It may rock your sense of reality, so bear with me. When you take time to tell someone else something that is troubling you, for instance, a personal problem, not only do some people not care how you feel—some people believe that because they listened to you with their time, you now owe them something. You might be thinking, *No way, nobody is that small.* But ask yourself, has someone ever directly stated or implied, "look, I made time to listen to you several times—not saying I don't want to listen to you or that I don't care, but…"?

And not only that, what you say that may cast yourself in a negative light while sharing a personal problem with such a person is fair game to some abusers to throw in your face later. Moreover, what you say while someone like this listens to you is often, in his or her estimation, fair game to use as ammunition for constructing an image of your character flaws to others. You may have noticed in your life that after you disclose your thoughts and feelings to people like this, you merely accomplished aiding them in manipulating you.

Here's an example: Julie is very distressed because her boyfriend, Howard—who most of the time seems like a great catch, worthy for consideration as marriage material—sometimes threatens to break up with her when she prods him for every detail about where he has been. Julie tells her friend Donna about the fights they have and confides in Donna that when Howard threatens to break up with her, she retaliates by threatening to date one of Howard's best guy friends.

Julie knows that her action was a power move, and she doesn't have any intention to follow through and date anyone else. If anything, she just wants to stay with Howard. Howard continues to threaten to break up with Julie, largely because he finds her "clingy" and never willing to trust him when he is out and about. The fights have gotten worse, and Julie tells Donna that she flirted with one of

Howard's best friends, Bo, intentionally, just to try to make Howard feel the pressure and know Julie means business.

Unfortunately, Howard's power move, threatening to break up with Julie, and Julie's power move, threatening to date one of Howard's best guy friends, do not actually lead either side to resolution. Okay, so the key here is Donna. Remember, Julie confided in Donna about her trust issues with Howard, even just that once, let's say for approximately thirty minutes.

Julie subconsciously sought validation from Donna that Julie is not an awful person and that her actions, considering the circumstances, though Julie is not proud of them, remain logical to keep Howard. Meanwhile, Donna—who, since meeting Julie, unbeknownst to Julie, has considered Julie at different times both an ally and a competitor—decides that Julie needs to pay her back for those thirty minutes. So a couple of days later, Donna has a horrible day and lost her keys and wallet. Without transportation, she asks Julie to offer a hand and help her run an important errand, and Julie—who happens to be slightly preoccupied at the time—comes across to Donna as unappreciative for Donna's making the time to listen to Julie about her relationship woes.

Donna, upset and angry with Julie, when asked by another friend Cheri what Julie is like, decides to tell Cheri that Julie is self-centered, needy, and flirts with different guys besides her boyfriend. Somehow word of this gets back around to Howard that Julie flirted with one his best guy friends Bo intentionally. But to make matters worse, Bo has now decided, behind Howard's back, to pursue Julie after her initial advance. This causes the fight that ultimately leads to Howard and Julie breaking off a serious relationship headed for marriage.

Though appearing salvageable, the trust and maturity issues in the relationship turned out to be irreconcilable. And as for Donna, when cognizant of the reasons for Julie's breakup (due to the information that she shared with Cheri), she continues to lack any feeling of guilt, liability, or remorse for what has transpired. Moreover, Donna finds out that Julie is angry with her for spilling the beans on Julie's alleged character flaws. So now Donna, reasoning Julie has some nerve to blame Donna for anything, decides to go out of her way, with all due intended vengeance, to make other people see Julie as "vulnerable," "manipulative," and a "flirt."

Action Plan

Sometimes it really makes us feel better to tell whom we think are just the right people at just the right times what seems to be troubling us. Sometimes we share personal disclosures with others in an attempt—through our own vulnerability and courage—to forge interpersonal bonds and become closer to others. And when you tell others your problems, it can feel as if a weight has been lifted off your shoulders. Especially when someone else takes the time to listen and, even nonverbally, appears to validate your feelings as legitimate and warranted.

It might be easy to project onto others a presumption that they care about you and your troubles and that they respect your feelings and privacy. Empaths very selectively feel for whom to make personal disclosures with, as well as when to make them. Unfortunately, many individuals are manipulated and deceived by others, as well as themselves, regarding who is worthy to be responsible with receiving their personal disclosures. Sometimes skilled sociopaths are so carefully guarded, going through every motion superficially, that they can seem, through nonverbal language, to communicate all the right things as empathetic, active listeners.

Also, remember, when you hear someone imply they are burdened by having to "make time" for something external to the self, it might be time to "make time" to be suspicious. Of course, many people choose to say "take time" and even "make time" with no agenda of expected reciprocation or personal benefit, just the same as many people, innocently enough, pronounce the word *tomato* differently. Nonetheless, regardless of phrasing, pay attention for individuals tipping off to you that they might reason you or others owe them something.

Remember, other people may see their time differently than you do, especially when it comes to putting others first. Prioritizing some time to put others first may come natural to you, but don't assume other people, just because they are adults, agree to give their time selflessly to others.

When you talk to others—just as you are on guard for when people yawn as you speak to alert you subconsciously that they are uninterested, bored, or incapable of caring about you—be on guard for someone who seems too eager to make time for you to divulge your innermost thoughts in your potential state of particular vulnerability. Such people may see nothing wrong with making the time with their time to listen to you because their calculated investment represents a future opportunity to exploit you down the road when they want something. As a matter of fact, count on running into people like that.

When That Which-eth Is Not Air-eth Hit-eth the Fan: The "Sabotaging to Create Mutual Disagreement" Tactic

When that which is not air hits the fan, individuals can become keenly aware of the transgressions against themselves from others possessing sociopathic tendencies. Somehow or another, victims seem to find out how abusers intended to treat them all along, and even what abusers really think about them. Unfortunately, people too often find they are tools, even objects, in the minds of others—even to those who may have been perceived and considered as true friends. When sociopathic individuals intentionally decide to cut ties with a victim or drastically change the dynamics of an interpersonal relationship, there may be no "saving grace" element to reverse the abuser's modification of a relationship, or even an abuser's full-on departure.

In the case of intentional modification, the relationship may be unilaterally transformed into something less than it was; or in regard to departure, ties are cut, and the abuser disappears from the victim's life. However, sometimes, quite carefully planned and executed, something else happens altogether: an abusive sociopath may, for selfish purposes, create the parameters to influence an interpersonal relationship termination as mutually agreed upon. For instance, through sabotage, an abuser may proceed to create the parameters for a future "agreed-upon" fissure by both parties—brought about by manipulation—and further justify engaging in abuse of a victim in the present.

The abuser can rationalize present abusive behavior as justifiable since he or she foresees that future termination is imminent. In effect, if one or both parties no longer desire connection, reflecting backward on how they got there, in the mind of an abuser, can become a moot point. It is a "means justify an end" phenomenon that exists in many abusive interpersonal relationships but does not receive adequate attention in psychological discourse.

The abusive sociopath can create parameters for another to reason that an interpersonal fissure is mutually agreed upon. What does that mean? In essence, a sociopath abuser finds it within his or her own self-interest to influence another individual into devaluing an interpersonal relationship.

For example, imagine a committed couple married for six years. One of the two partners is an abusive sociopath who treats his partner much better than he does others. One day, out of the blue, the sociopathic partner, unprovoked, decides he does not want the marriage to continue or to have to speak to his partner ever again. Realizing that his wife may not agree to separate or divorce, he begins trying to sabotage the relationship to initiate some sort of termination agreement.

So he decides to psychologically abuse his nonsociopath partner, as well as premeditates having a provable affair in an effort to convince her to mutually agree to divorce him for philandering. As a matter of fact, he tells many of his wife's friends and relatives. This may sound so unrealistic that such a fictional character would "shamelessly" pronounce to the world he cheated on his wife. But it has happened before in the course of human history.

What he wants is to get her, and her immediate support network, to become convinced that cutting ties with him is the best option for her future. Remember, he really does not care how they see him. After all, it's part of his sociopathic advantage—he does not necessarily have to care. Where the empath would cringe at being perceived as a no-good philandering dog of a man, the sociopath may be so disconnected to the opinions of others, he can just as easily start anew with another network of people and not feel any lonelier than he did before with his previous network of human relationships connected to his no-longer-wanted wife. To some abusers, that's just called moving.

Three things generally happen when an abusive, sociopathic individual—attempting to craft an image and save face—decides to cut ties or drastically change the dynamic of a no-longer-desired interpersonal relationship. The first is the action of sabotage. The second is what I call reclassifying unilateral intention to dissolve an interpersonal relationship as mutual intention—*for* the abuser's benefit. Think of the ever-so-famous line: "Look, neither of us are or ever were truly happy," as an argument to incentivize termination. The third is intentionally misremembering the past to justify the present. This line of thought is especially evident in "The present justifies the past" backward-looking conversation.

For example, the abusive ex-husband might say to a future romantic interest at a candlelit dinner: "It was all for the better. After six years, she and I did not want to be together anymore. That relationship needed to end. She and I were so unhappy. And now I'm here with you." I know, he is not even real, and he makes you just want to punch him.

Of course, minus his recent and deliberate sabotage and abuse of his ex-wife, she may have been very happy loving him, flaws and all, and a healthy influence on her former partner. And building on that notion, the ex-husband, before deciding to terminate the relationship, may have also felt satisfied with having the relationship with his ex-wife. Though, throughout the relationship, he may have struggled with authentic interpersonal connection and emotional intimacy.

In the preceding instance, one party possessed a desire to dissolve a relationship, sabotaged it, manipulated another party into agreeing to cut ties, and intentionally misremembered the course of events as mutually agreed upon by both parties during a convenient moment. In the previous example, where the abusive sociopathic husband successfully manipulated his wife, he can, over time, look back and convince himself that the termination of the relationship was never just his idea alone—that the ensuing mutual agreement to divorce supersedes and even justifies his past actions of sabotage—though his partner may have experienced an authentic happiness with their imperfect relationship.

Of course, this fictional character probably doesn't have to care how his ex-wife remembers him or their relationship. And because he does not necessarily have to feel guilt or emotional stress about that—and he does not have to feel connected to her ongoing sense of anguish, within his own mind, through reasoning that the inevitable relationship termination was mutually agreed upon—he at least can convince others, for his own benefit, that he is of higher character than, say, just some ex-husband who individually concocted the successful intentional sabotage of his otherwise healthy marriage. These sorts of convenient rationalizations for misremembering mutual disagreement in order to dissolve and terminate mutual bonds transcend romantic partnerships and affect all sorts of interpersonal relationships.

Action Plan

Establishing an individual's incentive to terminate an otherwise healthy interpersonal relationship may be nearly impossible. Nonetheless, pay close attention for the following three behavioral manifestations: sabotaging a relationship, reclassifying unilateral intention to dissolve an interpersonal relationship as mutual agreement, and intentionally misremembering the past to justify the present. Sabotage may be manifested through any number of more subtle behaviors such as emotionally distancing one's self from a victim, or an abuser pushing the perceived buttons of a victim to reach a desired relationship-termination objective. However, sabotage may also be manifested through "loud" actions such as the case of the intentional and demonstrably public affair.

Following sabotage, remain observant for the behavioral manifestation of reclassification. The reclassification of unilateral intention to mutual agreement action exhibits deception and manipulation on part of the abuser. In a very slimy way, crafting mutual agreement allows the abuser an opportunity to use the words or actions concerning the victim's dissatisfaction with his or her treatment during relationship sabotage as a justification for the abuser's relationship abandonment.

And lastly, the justification phase enables the conscience-impaired individual an opportunity to rationalize his or her actions toward victims as both harmless and in all parties' best interest. The justification component may be accompanied by observable cues such as an abuser's current expressed lack of emotional investment in an abandoned close companion, as well as in the previously shared relationship with that companion—similar to a half-hearted apology in that the level of emotional investment lacks substance and authenticity.

Ask yourself, do you believe that a hallmark of people attempting to be nonabusive is that they make every effort to leave others as well as or better off than they found them—not abandoned, wounded, taken advantage of, broken, or in some form, destroyed? To that end, this tactic, in a similar way to the "mini-death tactic," is intended to address the strategizing of the abusive individual who takes and takes from others, leaving individuals abandoned and worse off than when a relationship commenced. It touches upon an unhealthy, destructive repeating cycle of abusing victims with whom one comes into interpersonal contact through sabotaging commitment, crafting mutual disagreement, and finally justifying having abandoned victims through intentionally twisted logic. Ultimately, ask yourself, "Do I, or someone I know, deserve to be treated like this and be made to experience this?"

Unfortunately, victims changing abusers' mind-sets may not be realistic. And if successful in persuading an abuser to stick around, some might desire not to leave for reasons unhealthy to the victims experiencing pain at the thought of an abuser exiting. Though perhaps uncomfortable, consider reflecting on the unpleasant notion that not everyone perceives interpersonal connection or emotional intimacy as an end worthy in and of itself. With identifying the three aforementioned behavioral manifestation components of the "sabotaging to create mutual disagreement" tactic, it might become slightly easier to identify what is occurring as an abuser intentionally crosses and burns bridges.

TACTIC 16

The "I Know You're Wrong, But What Am I? Right!" Tactic

Sometimes people attempt to dominate and subdue another's will or perspective. When a disagreement or dispute comes to light, a common tactic utilized by an abusive sociopathic individual is to refocus an argument on how one person is right and the other is wrong. Can you guess which person is the "right" one? True, nonsociopaths may engage in this tactic commonly enough, as is often the case with psychologically developing individuals.

However, most developed individuals have learned that this tactic is a two-edged sword. On the one hand, if wielded effectively, the tactic may allow person 1 to influence person 2 to step down from a tenable, justifiable position; while, on the other hand, the tactic may reinforce person 2's perception of person 1 as an individual with an inability to compromise or appear self-responsible. In effect, refocusing the argument on how one person is right and the other is wrong is high-risk, high-reward.

Subsequently, the tactic is phased out of one's repertoire of interpersonal communication skills for most developed individuals because it does not influence person 2's mind about anything—except, of course, for reinforcing negative perceptions of person 1's irresponsible, self-righteous, stubborn character. Regardless, in my personal experience, I have found that abusive, sociopathic adults continue to utilize this tactic when they calculate, in a given situation, that they possess enough leverage to suppress opposition; whereas, the empathic individual, possessing the leverage to do the same, likely will decline the opportunity.

That's not to say that good-intentioned empaths will always decline the opportunity—particularly when they are being actively manipulated to let their negative emotions get the better of them by an abuser during a dispute concerning who is "right." But empaths likely envision the action of subduing another as destructive with negative consequences for others. And empaths may decline strong-arming another's perspective on grounds that the action will not sit well within one's own conscience.

Moreover, to subdue an individual with less leverage's legitimate point of view, especially when such a less-powerful individual holds a tenable position, may foster resentment within the less-powerful disputant. Empaths fear utilizing this tactic. For they know dominating conflicts when one has the leverage to dominate leads to unforeseen, inharmonious consequences in the future—a conclusion intuitively reached by many empaths after having felt the emotional repercussions of being dominated themselves.

Action Plan

Ask the following question: is there an established motive? Imagine a situation where what is being disputed allegorically represents splitting hairs. If there is nothing that seems worth arguing about, what does the dominator really gain by attempting to dominate? It may be a sense of self-pride that may influence the dominator not to acquiesce during a dispute. To many, pride not to "lose" but to "win" when speaking with others is an irrational journey that self-validates the identity of an abuser as being someone and something superior to other humans—in the mind's eye of the abuser, of course. Also, look for emotional manifestations through word choice and inflection, such as animosity, hostility, cruelty, and a sense of reckless disregard for others.

Abusers attempting to dominate may help themselves to attacking the disputant's position by attacking not only the disputant's perspective but also the disputant him or herself. For example, an abusive sociopath intending to dominate another may claim his or her victim-disputant is late for a meeting because he or she is "loose." To a rational, nonabusive human being, where would an assertion like that ever come across as an acceptable, helpful, healthy, caring, constructive, and positive contribution? Such a snap judgment may allow the abuser an opportunity to relish in the destruction of a victim's alleged character—perhaps even physically manifested with a genuine smile or smirk. Nonetheless, while it may seem most boldly obvious, the abuser does not only use leverage for gaining an upper hand on an issue but also for gaining an upper hand on a victim.

But what may not appear so obvious provides another possibility that establishes a motive for "I know you're wrong, but what am I? Right!" domination altogether—even preceding the intentions of coercion and manipulation that so often accompany an abuser's agenda. Even more fundamentally than intention to abuse, what may not appear obvious is that some individuals are likely *neurologically disabled* and thus prevented from understanding and valuing others' perspectives. They dominate others out of a false sense of "correct" judgment.

They really think they are right—and some believe so—all the time, no matter what decision they make. To grasp this concept more clearly, imagine an instance of experiencing difficulty with making a hard decision due to unknown information and complicated variables. Now, imagine an inverse image of that process where other individuals, with ease and haste, feel 100 percent correct in the decisions they make based on what nonetheless remain difficult and unknown variables. In their minds alone, they may deem their judgments correct, even when such judgments are erroneous.

But providing hope to address this issue, an opportunity to reflect on an empathization presents itself. Chiefly, some empaths erroneously rationalize and assume that everyone has difficulty making hard decisions due to a sense of fairness and consideration for others. In effect, challenge that assumption and subsequently be better prepared to help and work with other people.

Once you have identified that there is a high probability that a disputant intends on being abusive and dominating, it is time to come to terms with what may actually be accomplished in the moment. I would like to offer the following advice. A woman named Nan was a lovely, sweet lady who infected everyone around her with kindness and her large heart.

Nan was a single parent who was scraping to get by and make ends meet. She did not have too much job security and struggled to find more secure employment. To provide for her children, whom she dearly loved, she endured psychological abuse in the work environment. Constantly, her bosses would demean her character, blame her for others' faults, and accuse her, a hard-worker, of not working nearly hard enough.

She, for all intents and purposes, was, in a most cruel way, her bosses' emotional punching bag. She was the butt of their jokes and the coveted target to dominate and bully. To them, though they would never admit it publicly, she was like a walking television channel, always providing an avenue for their own crass entertainment.

Nan sought help. She eventually found a good-hearted attorney who helped her establish a trail of documentation that irrefutably proved the intentional and reckless abuse she endured in a hostile work environment. Moreover, Nan, with the help of other good-hearted people, found a new, better job. Over the course of the eight years she worked for that company, often as a custodian, she never once told her three children of what she endured on a daily basis. She, in a most selfless way, did not want them to know what she went through to provide for them. Whether or not you agree with Nan not telling her children, the point I wish to make is one of encouragement.

Nan was heroic in her character and actions. She realized there was nothing to gain by arguing with abusive dominators in an environment where everything she might choose to say or do could be construed against her by dishonest, malicious characters. And likewise, she knew she really did not "lose" her character, no matter what baseless viciousness they spewed in her direction. She did not wait too long to address the issue. Sadly, it really took that much time for her to find an honest, good-hearted lawyer who willingly took her case knowing that it might never prove lucrative.

Nan, even in her own agony, selflessly did what she could to provide a healthy, positive environment for her children. She loved them so much and feared the pain it would bring them to worry about her. When they became adults, she let them know what she endured, prefacing the disclosure by reassuring them she is now in a better place. So what a victim can do, while fighting for advocacy, is to learn from Nan's example. Even in what seemed her most defeated moments, she never allowed her self-worth to be defeated. She never allowed her self-identity and character to be established by individuals truly lacking the ability to appraise them. She marched forward, pressing onward with a resolute strength to remain a positive, impactful influence on others.

A word of warning—though Nan is in a better place, it is imperative not to assume that the abusive sociopaths who did this to Nan, even after being brought to justice, magically care about the emotional stress Nan endured, and perhaps even still endures. Even assuming that those who bullied her within her old job faced criminal charges and the company lost business through damage to its reputation or litigation costs, the presumption should not be made that the abusers now *do* care how Nan's children would feel or be affected by knowing how their mother was treated. The abusers may even rationalize and blame Nan for her "inferiority" in not being like them and rolling with the punches better.

Of course, some scientists might even claim that Nan may possess a greater capacity to internalize and experience emotion, empathy, and interpersonal connection than her abusers. However, it is faulty reasoning to presume her abusers care about Nan and her feelings. They very likely do not feel remorseful and perhaps do not really think or feel they did anything wrong. In the "I know you're wrong, but what am I? Right!" tactic, the teachable moment does not present itself in how to "fix" the abuser but remains within the tools for the victim to identify the abuser, strategize through the ordeal, (if possible) bring the abuser to justice, and live a healthier, happier life.

The "Point A to Point B Fallacy" Tactic

Remember in the preceding tactic how the possibility exists that some individuals have no problem making decisions and perhaps, through something equatable to involuntary delusion, can feel like every decision they make is flawless? I have observed something similarly out of touch to occur with some individuals in regard to persuading others of their reasoning. Specifically, some people really believe that when they communicate their message—whatever that message may entail—other people are, by default, going to agree with their "superior" perspective.

While such a phenomenon may be rooted in arrogance, egocentrism, or even delusion, I would even go further to suggest that this is exclusively how some people understand how to communicate with others—essentially believing that what they have to tell others constitutes a two-way reciprocal understanding and mutual endorsement of the message being delivered. And how soon might such people believe this "mutual understanding" begins to occur? It seems as though it is expected to begin immediately at the end of the transmission—a remarkably short journey.

The shortest distance between two points is a straight line, right? Physicists, bear with me. I know you might raise an objection to the preceding sentence, especially since we know so little about wormholes. And I do not mean to get anyone started about the wave-particle duality of the yet-to-be understood movements of subatomic particles.

But the "shortest" distance avoids the longer journey of going through the motions of listening to others, or beating around the bush, to take what is desired from others or, in general, to get others to do one's bidding. In the realm of sociopathy, both long roads and short roads are utilized. Hence, it behooves victims to remember that intentional manipulation and deception do not always imply a journey on a longer road, with confusing detours designed to shake the victim off an abuser's true destination.

Paralleling the concept that the shortest distance between two points is a straight line, I have observed that some individuals theoretically choose to emit what they think (point A) to a receiver and, further, reach the conclusion that communication progress has, by default, occurred upon the receiver's acknowledgment of the sender's "superior" perspective (point B). To some individuals, I am afraid, this is what communication is—all of it. In other words, a receiver's expected compliance and submission with the sender's perspective registers to an abuser as a legitimate instance of reciprocal communication. In effect, the message made its way from point A, the sender, and was received and assumed as automatically endorsed by the receiver, point B—hence the "point A to point B fallacy" tactic.

So how is communication—in effect, the process of sending and receiving messages—supposed to occur? Eerily, to some individuals, the "point A to point B fallacy" tactic constitutes the process of healthy communication. Whereas, conversely, an empath might reason, "Emitting what I think [point A] leads to receiving a response from a receiver [point A, substop 1], which leads to reevaluating and reconsidering what I now think [point A, substop 2], which further leads to the receiver reevaluating and reconsidering what he or she now thinks in respect to what I have last transmitted [point A, substop 3]—in hopes of harmoniously reaching agreement or at least understanding of the specific message being communicated [drumroll, please—point B]."

Is this to say people who expect for victims to accept their persuasion like clockwork are unaware of the reality of their external environments? Not necessarily—perhaps the sender expecting the receiver to accept a given message is aware of others' ability to engage in independent, critical analysis. And again, perhaps the sender does not care what others think or feel. To that end, the sender may even have a strategy of surrounding him or herself with individuals willing to remain submissive to his or her unilateral instruction (see the "I'm surrounded, now everyone else put your hands up!" tactic).

While an individual may possess an ability to overvalue his or her communications to others for multiple reasons, it characteristically represents a personal limitation. Perhaps an evolutionary biologist might possibly associate this form of unilateral one-sided decision-making in interpersonal communication as connected to alpha primate behavior. For example, even preceding human history, various instances of a pack leader—who did not necessarily have to acquiesce to the concerns of his or her subordinate peers—ruled in multiple species of animals. A given scientist might even go further to suggest such behavior may represent under-evolved individual *Homo sapiens*. Of course, identifying if the ability to engage in high-functioning empathy for others is a matter of human genetics remains an unanswered, ongoing scientific endeavor.

Action Plan

While this all may seem far-fetched, consider this: have you ever had the feeling someone was telling you what you need to think or how you need to feel? Have you ever felt like someone was not listening to what you had to communicate concerning your perspective, rather, only inundating you with theirs? And what is at least one tremendously important reason this line of reasoning could conceivably occur? Ah yes, because some individuals really do not care what others—external to themselves—think or feel.

Dominating someone else through a reasoning fallacy does not have to imply an argument between two sides, or even an open dialogue for two-way communication. Scan the sender for endorsing a smoke screen on one-way monologue dressed up as two-way communication. Also, without any assistance on your end to communicate a given stance, you might find another, with all due hostility, from perhaps out of nowhere, combatively debasing your good intention and even mitigating your feelings—even while such an individual adamantly postures as willing to listen to and empathize with you. In such an instance, recognize the deception. When you identify this attitude, recognize that, at least in that moment, you are in a lose-lose scenario on the sociopathically adjusted playing field.

Complete avoidance from future interaction with abusive individuals is not realistic for every individual, especially in the workplace. In one study, researchers found that more than 90 percent of survey participants reported working with a toxic personality at some point in their careers while more than 60 percent reported working with a toxic personality during their present state of employment (Kusy & Holloway, 2009). Unfortunately, in life, in all likelihood, people will face dealing with many communication-process offenders stubbornly committed to self-centered and self-serving agendas, staunchly opposed to differing perspectives.

Nonetheless, look for the following implied attitudes: "I tell you what you need to do and what you need to think, period. Everything else is a waste of my time." "Effective communication is achieved when you, whom I do not care about, listen to me and immediately do as I instruct." "Effective communication does not involve getting to know somebody. It involves telling somebody, whom you do not care about, what they need to do and them doing it."

And for the inert organizational culture, point A to point B might be found in the following mind-set: "Though I know admitting this would be taboo, effective communication is steamrolling subordinates through one-way communication e-mails and text messages posing as two-way dialogue that intimidate, threaten, devalue, and violate victims." On that note, unfortunately, social media has allowed abusers a special, easier-than-ever-before means to throw victims away through the cowardice of one-sided, self-serving communications. In a most convenient manner, the abuser, unlike face-to-face communication of old, can enjoy the luxury of not having to witness—or even face acknowledging—his or her digitally communicated dealings as they injure specific victims, making for quite the out-of-sight, out-of-mind ideal abuser setup.

In the moment, recognize that a teachable moment for an offender may only appear to exist precisely because the offender may not be willing to accept responsibility for his or her behavior. Also, pay attention for an individual trying to accuse you of a one-way communication agenda when your intentions are altruistic and equitable. In effect, someone with significant cognitive experience utilizing one-way communication dressed as dialogue may attempt to manipulate your feelings to guilt you into giving into an abusive one-sided demand.

Lastly, remember "man's best friend." I once heard a great piece of wisdom from someone who said something to the effect of, "I would not even treat a dog the way some people talk to others." There is so much loaded, positive, powerful context to extract from that statement, but think about this: humans communicate with animals and even tell beloved animals what furniture is off-limits to be chewed on as well as where *and where not* to relieve themselves. But is that the same as dominating and treating an animal like it is a worthless thing? The action of communicating an instruction to another is not at issue with the "point A to point B fallacy" tactic. Rather, what is at issue is the value for—*and goodwill toward*—the receiver that the sender may not truly possess.

The "Smirk" Tactic

One telltale physiological sign of sociopathic behavior—in my estimation, at least—is an individual's propensity to smirk or even offer a full-on smile during certain off-putting interpersonal moments. In certain situations, these facial gestures reflect a lack of concern for the feelings and welfare of others, especially when a ruthless message from a sender may elicit feelings of emotional devastation within the receiver. Moreover, the smirk of the sender while delivering the message possibly reflects what might be best described as the sensation of deriving a sick sense of pleasure, satisfaction, or humor from the ensuing numbness or awkwardness.

Here's an example: a husband with a secret romantic life away from his spouse, due to recent developments, realizes he cannot keep up the appearances of his affair and is in the process of communicating to his partner that he cheated and destroyed the fidelity of their "monogamous" relationship. Perhaps while he looks at his spouse and delivers the message, dead in the eyes, the muscles around his mouth curl upward as if he is fighting off the urge to smile. Even in less formally serious relationships, smirks accompany quite a few of the classic lines. For example, some psychologically underdeveloped people can only say things while smirking such as, "Listen, I think we should break up," or, "Yeah, here's the thing—I know we've known each other for seven months now, but I really just want to get to know one of your friends," or even, "I think we should just be friends, but we can't hang out—I mean, I don't really have the time for casual conversations, at least at this time."

Another example of smirking is evident when an individual criticizes or engages in condescending tone with a coworker or subordinate. For example, a middle manager might consistently show up late to work and fear subordinate employees who might blow the whistle to upper management on the tardy manager. This middle manager might single out a particular subordinate who might be particularly knowledgeable of the superior's absenteeism. Let's say, in all honestly, the middle manager does not truly appreciate his or her employment opportunity and is not interested in learning what the victim—a good-hearted subordinate knowledgeable about the boss's lack of attendance—is doing to be a hard worker, who is invested in doing his or her best. The middle manager singles out the employee, smirks, and brutally declares, "I really am put off by how you have mailed it in and do not work hard. I really expected so much more. Your job security is in question."

The middle manager knows that authentic substance behind such a message is nonexistent but nonetheless intends to hold the employee to the undeserved threat and smirks through the message's delivery. The smirk, at first glance, appears only physiological; but as evinced through the previous scenario, it becomes clear how the abuser can utilize the smirk as a tactic to communicate nonverbally to a victim that he or she stands to be judged unjustly and made to live in fear. It is as if the abuser is communicating, "I know you know my claim is bogus. But I put myself first. I am not fair. I don't care about you, and I might be crazy. And if I so much as think you will go against me, you will be destroyed."

Another example of the smirk phenomenon outside of work or romance is found in the consumer experience. Have you ever tried on a pair of shoes that did not fit too well and communicated as much to a salesperson when he or she offered from out of nowhere, "Well, I think they look good on you, and you should buy two pairs of those today," followed by a smirk and possibly a chuckle of what sounds like nervous laughter?

Perhaps a salesperson refused to listen to your communication that the shoes did not fit but seemed persistent to pressure you into buying them, even purchasing more than one pair of the very shoes that you found to be rather uncomfortable. As if the salesperson somehow—in some sort of petty, misaligned mind-set—believed that by directly bringing attention to a customer spending more money, the customer would be inclined to spend more money. When in actuality, offended customers would be inclined to spend no money. In this instance, the salesperson perceived the customer as an object to increase the value of his or her commission, not as a person to be valued.

Action Plan

When you experience the "smirk," ask yourself, "Do I really want to give others my business or my heart? Should I trust someone who looks like they are smiling and about to laugh when they deliver bad news at another's expense?"

Also, imagine how it might feel not just as a receiver but as a sender when someone really seems disconnected from understanding how his or her criticisms or hurtful words come across, and from understanding how devastating such communications may be for victims. The abusive individual might even experience an awareness of creating tension through intentional deceit or insensitivity directed to another—accompanied by the smirk or outright smile—but lacks an authentic connection to caring about a receiver's emotional response and experience.

Furthermore, remember the "deconstructive, constructive criticism" tactic. Sometimes people deliver deconstructive criticism, and the victim even senses the criticism is not intended to make him or her better but merely to judge and criticize through unbridled negativity. Oftentimes, this ugly type of debilitating communication is manifested while an abuser smirks.

The abusive individual exhibiting sociopathic tendencies, though most likely numb to others' feelings, may or may not understand on some level that what is being communicated in a face-to-face disclosure, accompanied by an abuser's smirk, most accurately represents an action of interpersonal destruction. But regardless of how aware or unaware an abuser might be, the argument can be made that he or she delivers cheap shots with absolutely no objective intention to improve treatment of a victim or even change opinions about the quality of a victim's character or performance, regardless of a victim's positive, corrective, can-do attitude. So, victims, take solace. You are not necessarily what you are accused of lacking, and your emotional response to an attack is very real—though possibly foreign to the potential neurological limitations of your accuser.

The "Conflict-Solver Double Standard and Entitlement" Tactic

Some individuals pride themselves on concocting solutions for the conflicts of others. Well, what's wrong with that? To be candid, nothing is, necessarily. Conflict resolution, as a field of study and as a practice, persists as an important, meaningful, and respectable profession that is much needed. However, some individuals within the field bring about destruction, not construction.

So is the case with some "qualified" human resources department workers. Because some individuals are trained and authorized to offer resolution for conflict, some begin to believe that the policies they render are fair and representative to all parties involved. Yet ask every hardworking, innocent individual who has ever received a "letter" from human resources if the department took every reasonable step to gather the facts concerning any allegations and to discern objectively any judgment rendered against the individual in a given situation.

When individuals assume the identity of conflict solvers, there remains the chance that they judge situations self-servingly and even buy in to the notion that the conflict solutions they author are the most superior, equitable, and free of bias. And by no means does an individual need to work in the profession to claim competency in this arena or to self-identify as "superior" in resolving others' conflicts—again, perhaps blazing a trail of destruction, not construction, all along the way.

Tragically, the result of such actions is that people lose their livelihoods and often have no means for recourse when those called to judge them may be about as qualified as newborn infants to perform open-heart surgery. Let that soak in—and let that lift you up when a conflict-resolution expert wrongly convicts you. And moreover, the environment, at work and even away from work, along with the accompanying fear and tension that this creates for victims, can be deleterious to physical health.

Action Plan

In the moment, be on your guard. Claiming to be a conflict resolver during conflict with others may represent not only an attempt to save face for an abuser but an intentional sociopathic tactic designed to dominate others and operate above established rules. Even the emotionally abusive spouse can attempt to be judge, jury, and prosecutor—defining the conflict, assigning blame, and abdicating responsibility for his or her actions that contribute to conflict. From this perspective, it is much easier to understand how people who are "breakers" deceitfully and so manipulatively reframe their images as "fixers."

Utilizing one's leverage as a conflict-resolution specialist can be a favored sociopathic tactic because it endorses the notion of limited personal liability—*and even immunity*—for an individual based on his or her "lack of contribution to a conflict," at least in his or her own eyes. For the conflict agitator, this rationalization creates a convenient getaway vehicle to escape acknowledgement of how one's own actions have violated others. Think of it this way: how would you feel if someone who was violating you repeatedly went off track from exhibiting self-responsibility in conversations to reassure you of his or her role as a conflict-resolution specialist?

That would be like an individual with a lost temper going up to someone else and screaming at the top of his or her lungs, "You are lucky I am being so nice to you because I am certified to teach anger management courses!" It just doesn't add up. Nonetheless, assuming the identity of conflict solver and all the position's subsequent entitlements is a reality among some irresponsible individuals—a reality even reinforced by paychecks.

Perhaps you are wondering, *What should I look for?* It is helpful to be on the lookout for any awkward mention or action an individual offers in endorsing one's self as a conflict solver, even passively, especially while such an individual destructively initiates or contributes to conflict with you or others. And again, claiming to be a conflict-resolution specialist is not necessarily sociopathic. However, claiming to be a conflict-resolution specialist while deliberately engaging in interpersonally abusive behavior should raise flags within your mind.

When you observe abuse, pay close attention for an abuser to verbalize the following thought patterns: "What I do well is solve others' conflicts," "Not to mention—did I mention I professionally solve conflicts?" or, "My role is to solve disputes," or even, "Part of what I do is try different things—they don't always work out, but it's what needs to be done for things to work and conflicts to be resolved." Derivatives of all these should serve as indicators to you that someone's hands might possibly not be clean in contributing to conflict resolution, and that such individuals might be resolving—if anything—to avoid incurring judgment for their role in contributing to any conflict.

Indeed, what may be transpiring is not conflict resolution but a *personal resolution* to avoid *personal* responsibility for contributing to conflict. And when such an individual desires to be seen as a conflict-resolution specialist and yet contributes to conflict—ironically, such an individual hypocritically engages in conflict-resolution avoidance. After all, how can a conflict-resolution specialist contribute fully to conflict resolution if he or she avoids accepting responsibility for contributing to a conflict in the first place? Subsequently, if you experience another's hypocrisy *during* conflict, take comfort in knowing that at least one of you grasps that the "conflict specialist" can contribute to conflict by constantly attempting, somehow, to be more above conflict than his or her victims.

The "Watch How Cunning I Think I Am with Three Words: 'Agree to Disagree'" Tactic

Okay, for the certifiably uptight critic just looking for a bone to pick, no, I am not claiming to have created conflict-resolution specialists' second favorite chic catchphrase, "agree to disagree," nestled right behind the ever-so-popular (and powerful when authentic) adage "win-win." But I am ready to attack it. Do you know what "agree to disagree" accomplishes? No, seriously, I'm waiting for an answer. As a matter of fact, I have desired to know for years. Sure, I can tell you what I think the three words accomplish, and it's not up there with "I love you." It's right down there with "I don't care" and "You don't matter."

Nearly without exception, the phrase encapsulates an aura of negativity, condescension, and dysfunction. Why do I write nearly without exception? Well, you and a friend can "agree to disagree" on who the best jazz pianist in the world *is* or what is the best-tasting beverage, but it doesn't necessarily mean you devalue your friend's subjective evaluation as less worthy than your own.

As a matter of fact, it is this misguided, feel-good, Scout's-honor notion that you are not actually devaluing anyone's thoughts or feelings utilizing the "agree to disagree" expression that is largely to blame for the phrase's oversaturation on the contemporary conflict-resolution discourse market. Truth be told, "agree to disagree" a lot of the time means, "I don't care what you think. What you think doesn't matter to me. I don't have to care what you think, and I don't have to care what it makes you feel like when I invalidate your perspective. I have no intention of working through or resolving something that appears out of my way and unnecessary. And by the way, you now owe me for the time that I made to listen to you speak about such utter nonsense you obviously do not understand correctly."

Of course, in interpersonal communication, "agree to disagree," though appearing to clean up messes like a masterful product on a television infomercial demonstration, is more like cleaning a white linoleum floor with a mop covered in mud. "Agree to disagree" does not necessarily bring parties closer together, but it may bring them further apart. The party with less authority or pull may feel intimidated by hearing these three words and may come to form the impression that the more-powerful party does not value a differing perspective. For the party with more authority or pull, no longer hearing about an issue after issuing an "agree to disagree" to a less-powerful party may lead to the presumption that the issue is moot, null, or water under the bridge.

A lot of intractable conflicts arise because of power moves by more powerful parties to subdue the opinions and perspectives of less-powerful ones, as can be the case with the "agree to disagree" tactic, a tactic that—while in the short term appears to silence opposition and conflict—leads to long-term consequences such as hard feelings and irreconcilable differences down the road. Why the road reference? Because with "agree to disagree," you passively contribute that your attitude is "my way or the highway."

Action Plan

When you hear these three words, if you are at all like me, your stomach cringes. You realize that someone else may be there, yet not really *be there*. In other words, someone may be right in front of you, appearing to listen and consider what you think, yet so distant from actually being willing to work with you to any desired mutual end. You might feel objectified and perhaps even intimidated.

To give credit where due, the abusive sociopath, when uttering "agree to disagree," is likely being about as honest as you can expect anyone to be. For all intents and purposes, they really mean it: they disagree with you and possibly do not care what you think. Of course, understanding what is wrong with saying those three words is something that may be incredibly difficult for an individual with antisocial personality disorder to internalize.

So what can you do? Well, you can't necessarily change that another chooses to disagree with you or may be ignorant to what the three-word saying communicates. However, you can choose not to pull this tactic on others. You can set an example and keep the bar high. And here's the meat of it—if they tell you "agree to disagree," you can politely tell them, "Well, I'm sorry, but I wouldn't dismiss your feelings like that." No matter what they do or say, the high road you took should get the best of the situation—so much so that they may take such umbrage, that they even start becoming a chameleon on the spot, magically transforming into someone who never has been accused of dismissing anyone's feelings, ever. And in that case, enjoy the show.

But don't say these three words to get the best of someone else because you will not. Say these three words to be the best *you* can be for yourself—and for everyone else—when disagreeing about something trivial, like your favorite flavor of ice cream. That's a critical point. If you disagree with someone else about something, that is okay. Disagreement is natural and can be handled in a respectful, empathetic manner. The dominating "agree to disagree" wording wounds others and destroys interpersonal trust, and quite frankly, it does not make anyone sound smarter or any more like they should be cast for *Law & Order*. Forgive the onslaught of clichés, but "agree to disagree" is just not always a win-win.

Not Just an Ad Hominem Attack: "The Ad Hominem Identity" Tactic

Call me crazy, but I really think something frequently occurs in the mind of a sly, abusive sociopath trying to subdue a competitor. Something to the effect of this: *Hmm, I wonder what angles will work effectively to draw attention to—or even manufacture—another's apparent character flaws so people won't catch on to me avoiding this competitor's innocence, goodwill, honorable intentions, and legitimate issues, as I lie, cheat, or steal from him or her?* It would be difficult to prove that this sort of thinking occurs as getting someone to give you a backstage pass into the mind to see what's going on behind the curtains as the "show" plays on is asking a lot.

And of course, the ad hominem concept—discrediting the character of the victim to avoid addressing and crediting the substance of the victim's argument—is nothing new. What may be new, however, might be a collective awakening to the realization that though we are technologically advanced compared to preceding eras, we, collectively—like preceding eras—lack effective initiatives and awareness to challenge the acceptance of mass construction of others' ad hominem identities. Some might argue that we live on an under-civilized playing field, where everyone whom anyone becomes even slightly aware of, let alone meets, is fair game to be fitted with false character—and who one is perceived as, for better or for worse, trumps who one actually is.

The phrase *ad hominem*, Latin for "to the person," features a storied legacy in contentious interpersonal exchanges throughout human history. But I wouldn't stop there. The "ad hominem identity" tactic implies not merely discrediting another's character in the heat of the moment or with regard to some specific circumstance, but discrediting another's character in perpetuity, based on little to no authentic effort by an abuser to assess a victim's actual character.

Thus, the "ad hominem identity" tactic represents a means by which abusers can figuratively throw away the character of victims without ever making an attempt to know victims directly, or even ascertain facts about victims indirectly. To provide an example, imagine the abuser who offers, "I don't want to know you, and I don't need to know you." The preceding concept seems to invoke a sense of intended ignorance by an abuser but also implies and hints at a destructive rationalization mechanism utilized by an abuser to justify disavowing a victim of his or her potentially authentic and honorable character.

Action Plan

In a nutshell, many claim to value sincerity of character yet find themselves in environments where an individual's character attributes are often recognized by others for every reason under the sun, except for the fact they may actually be warranted. Don't believe it? Ask a businessperson if he or she has never felt the slightest bit of fear of receiving an intentional low-blow character assessment by another competitor.

It is what it is, but how do we deal with it? Well, we are not all the same. Some people desire for their actual character attributes to be recognized by others, and some people desire for the false character attributes they fancy but do not deserve to be associated with their own self-identities. And at times, the latter fares far better than the former.

With the mass acceptance of engaging in ad hominem identity construction of others' character, who one is perceived to be often overpowers who one truly is, at least in the minds of other humans. In effect, often people construct not who you are but who you will be, for all intents and purposes, advertised as. This is absolutely devastating for certain people. Call me biased, but the people who are most devastated internally by abusers' ad hominem constructions of their character are the people most admirably trying to live lives of integrity and selflessness. To the critic nauseated at the mention of integrity and selflessness, which represent superficial buzzwords, I earnestly contend that the concepts serve as tenets in many individuals' journeys toward a fulfilling and happy life. And to the reader, I share my opinion about whom this tactic most affects to offer you a perspective that may help you find for yourself the gifts of solace and encouragement.

In effect, if you feel devastated by false testimony or character assassination against your person—not merely because of what you stand to lose in a competitive environment as a consequence but because, as your own authentic character expert, you know the attacks do not truly represent your character—chances are, you are a good person, selfless enough, and trying to make your way with integrity. And for that, I, for one, hope you can pat yourself on the back and know that people like you inspire me to be writing this sentence instead of watching television. I tip my cap to you, you wonderful person. Hang in there. As much as it hurts, do yourself a favor for once. Start with ice cream and then step back and look at it this way because you deserve this credit: if what they were saying to you or behind your back about you was true, would it really hurt so bad?

After all, if you were the things they said about you, how would you really feel cheated by their "false testimony" on the inside? Even individuals with abusive, sociopathic tendencies can know when others catch on to their illegitimate character personas. While abusive, sociopathic individuals might stress and ruminate about a character attack they experience because they value their reputation in the eyes of others, solely for the doors their false personas can open for them, do you think they feel sincere agony when attacked for their "exposed" phony character like you do when misjudged for your authentic virtuous character? So about that ice cream, I wasn't asking; I was telling. You deserve it.

Imagine the following scenario: assume someone is guilty of being an abusive sociopath who has been selfishly manipulating others through utilizing a false persona to project a false image of his or her character to victims for his or her own benefit. Others, fortunately, catch on and expose this individual's true character. What others are saying that is true about an abusive sociopath's character does not truly cheat that person's character because—as even the abusive individual might fully know—the allegations against his or her character are merited. Please remember, that does not mean that an abusive person will admit to what he or she possesses cognizance of, change, or even that he or she will care.

You see, the same blow causes different pain to different people. Not necessarily because one individual might or might not have a greater capacity to feel empathy for others but because the wrongful attack on an honest person, full of integrity, most severely cheats the character that the honest, ethical person in actuality, truly possesses—like being wrongly accused of a horrible crime then publicly shamed.

Honest, ethical people—that can be why you suffer. And no, I am not going to bring in the overused pop psychology cliché that you should try not to care what others think. Though on the surface it appears so rational, it is about as insensitive and pointless as telling people they should flap their arms and fly above a traffic jam to get to their next destination on time. And besides, in my opinion, having the capacity to care what others think is a virtue.

If you are a nonsociopath, you most likely cannot help but care what others think and *that others think*. Sure, this often puts you at a competitive disadvantage compared to an abusive sociopath on the sociopathically adjusted playing field. But from my perspective, you receive a greater advantage than disadvantage: through being wired to care about others and what they feel and think, you are experiencing life on an existentially deeper level than the abusive sociopath. Remember, you can take action by becoming metacognizant of this phenomenon of so many, for their own convenience, being so ready to judge character superficially and erroneously in order that you may find peace, solace, and closure for the undeserved false testimony *you* yourself have experienced.

Lastly, it probably wouldn't hurt, in your own acknowledgment of others' character attributes, to commit to being much more cautious in accepting the positive character attributes others wish to project concerning themselves for their own benefit. I by no means reason that you should go through life overly skeptical and cynical toward humanity as some sort of misanthrope or grouch. I merely suggest remaining mindful of who is trying to sell you a version of him or herself so as to take advantage of you down the line. And yes, remaining mindful through all the deception is no easy task.

The "Propensity and Inclination to Judge Others for Judging Others" Tactic

A legitimate contention appears evident from the ad hominem identity tactic, chiefly: is judging the character of others ethical? And furthermore, does judging another imply sociopathic behavior? In regard to the first question, obviously, judging others possesses the possibility of carrying negative connotations; but we, for the good of one another and ourselves, have to put some effort into whom we trust, right? I mean, we need prisons, do we not? Should we no longer have courts and trials? Should we no longer label individuals who commit certain crimes *criminals* so as not to be judged as judging others? Should we go out of our way to let individuals do as they please regardless of the danger they put others or themselves in past, present, and future?

The answer, of course, is obviously not. Therefore, in regard to the second question—if well-intentioned judgment is present and made in good faith and rendered in a psychologically healthy, constructive manner—the act of judging others' character or actions does not qualify as a sociopathic tendency. As a matter of fact, an assessment of another's character or actions may be, objectively speaking, factual.

Action Plan

Judgment, within and of itself, is not inherently flawed or immoral. As Martin Luther King Jr. famously stated with his phrasing "content of character," it can be interpreted that we can look, and even feel, for the character within others. Be mindful not to project positive character attributes onto others that are inaccurate; for instance, the particularly charismatic individual might appear the most "likeable" in the room but just might secretly be the most destructively abusive. Simultaneously, remain mindful of those most deserving of acknowledgment for their positive character attributes—especially through noticing how such individuals so often and so humbly put forward the least amount of effort to seek the recognition of others.

However, for reflection, you have undoubtedly experienced an individual justifying abusive behavior with the intentionally deceptive argument: "You are no better than me, just on the grounds that you are judging me yourself." Be ready to identify the individual as lacking remorse for his or her actions, disregarding accountability for his or her behavior, and possessing a willingness to attempt to manipulate others.

Remember, an abuser making that argument desires for you, in a most convoluted way, to reason you are at fault. Resist internalizing that your addressing an issue or communicating a situation with an abuser identifies you and your healthy behavior as condescending. In such a scenario, the abuser desires to lure your conscience into feeling guilt and blaming yourself for even attempting to identify his or her destructive behavior.

"Have You Really Thought About Why I Don't Take Sides?": The "Sociopathic Neutrality" Tactic

I magine a movie-preview announcer with a deep voice reading the following script: "An age-old problem—three people—one conflict—in a world where only one person can be right. One person has to be wrong, and one person—must choose which of the other two people is right." [Cue dramatic thunder clasps.] Everyone you will ever meet possesses convictions—convictions concerning who and what is right or wrong. Sometimes we don't know what to believe, what to think, or whom to trust. It stands to reason then that sometimes we don't know which side to take.

Though many sociologists and political correspondents may disagree, collectively, we often tolerate one another's uncertainty toward choosing goods and services, and often quite sympathetically. Essentially, while some individuals might tell you what you should think if you are "smart," we tolerate the idea that others think differently than ourselves—and sometimes we tolerate quite well. For example, you might reason each individual doesn't like the same foods, same interior-design ideas, and is not necessarily looking for the same qualities in a life partner.

Another way of thinking about this is, does your neighbor knock on the door and tell you what brand of doormat you must buy, or else? And you may think the doormat of your neighbor is the most god-awful, abominable piece of garbage your eyes have ever had the displeasure of laying upon, but you know—it's unreasonable of your neighbor to expect you just to go out and buy a new doormat that meets his or her visual preference, right? Okay, what's the point?

We tolerate that others do not necessarily take the side we do. We even—political pundits skip this sentence in three, two, one—have shown an ability to tolerate that others might be just as right in how they perceive "things" and "choices" as we are. And no, I am not endorsing ethical relativism. Notice the qualifier *might*. Welcome back, pundits.

However, though we tolerate that others choose differently than ourselves, we stop too soon in trying to understand the motives of sociopathic neutrality. By that, I mean a party's neutrality that is not rooted in considerate, sympathetic toleration of—as well as empathetic consideration for—the feelings of others involved in a conflict, but "neutrality" rooted in self-interest or possibly even numbness for others' feelings. Translation: Kayla feels numb toward her closest friends' feelings for different, more complex reasons than why she might tolerate ugly doormats. Wait, but who is Kayla?

Here's a hypothetical scenario to show how a sociopath experiencing "numbness" might think through the decision of which side to choose between two valued interpersonal relationships. Maggie, Annie, and Kayla, for most of their lives, have been the best of friends. The three did everything together. One day, a huge argument ensued after Maggie started dating Annie's ex-boyfriend, Jim.

Though Annie and Jim terminated their relationship a year ago, Annie still possesses some sort of romantic feelings for Jim. Maggie, never originally intending to date Annie's former boyfriend, started developing feelings for him as she and Jim talked more and more after Jim and Annie's breakup. The romantic spark between Maggie and Jim all just happened recently.

Meanwhile, since the breakup, Maggie and Annie have talked as friends almost every day. On occasion, Maggie even consoles Annie, who feels pained by the loss of her ex-boyfriend. Now, Annie feels devastated to find out that Maggie is romantically interested in Jim.

And Maggie, upset that her friendship with Annie is on the rocks, still wants to see where her relationship is going with Jim, her new romantic interest. But to make matters worse, Kayla, the third musketeer, now feels forced to have to choose how to respond to both Maggie's and Annie's versions of the dilemma.

Kayla wants to keep alliances with both friends. Kayla even desires for everything to stay as she remembered it. But she knows that may not be possible. Kayla feels emotionally exhausted just trying to sift through both of her friends' feelings. Well, to put you on the spot, what should Kayla do?

Should she be forced to choose a party to endorse? Should she wait until Maggie and Annie are at each other's throats and then side with whoever appears slightly less classless? By the way, have you noticed that sometimes, when people do eventually choose which party to endorse, the less-egregiously nasty behavior by each disputant serves as a frequent justification for the third party's decision to choose a side?

Okay, you haven't decided whom Kayla should side with yet? How about this, Kayla agrees with Annie that is was misleading of Maggie to console and talk to a heartbroken Annie every day—especially while Maggie did not disclose that she was developing feelings for Annie's ex-boyfriend. Okay, maybe you'll buy that, but there is one other option—an option to rule them all (forgive me, Tolkien fans, I had to go there).

This is tough for Kayla. And you know what, she knows other people know it's tough for her, too. So she internally reasons that her best option appears to be choosing not to choose. Eureka! Others outside of the situation will understand this, right? As a matter of fact, they will likely sympathize with her after the other two girls obviously put her between a rock and a hard place with all the ensuing drama, right? Certainly, even if you don't buy that, rest assured, others will.

So what's wrong with Kayla's choice? Well, nothing—if she genuinely means to stay out of it because she loves both of her best girlfriends and desires more than just about anything not to hurt or disappoint either one of them. But the truth of the matter just may be—what

Maggie and Annie don't know about Kayla—that Kayla doesn't really feel and experience them like they feel and experience her.

And to be fair to Kayla, Kayla may want to care, but she cannot experience caring about others' feelings like her best friends. It's a secret deep inside of Kayla that she finds incredibly difficult to explain, and every time she has ever tried, people find her way too sociable and charismatic to understand what she really means. Kayla, to her credit, comes across to many others as a social butterfly, someone with a natural zest for life, who appears an extraordinarily capable people person. Though Kayla considers Maggie and Annie her closest girlfriends—and even does nice, considerate things for them—she struggles to feel Annie's sense of betrayal due to Maggie's developing romantic interest in Jim, as well as struggles to feel Maggie's desire for Annie to understand and be happy for Maggie's potential future with someone whom Annie once dated.

Kayla knows something else, too. This is not Kayla's first rodeo. Kayla has found herself in these situations her whole life, and if there are three things she has learned, they are that, first, other people generally sympathize with Kayla when she is in difficult positions where she is expected to choose a side; and second, because of that sympathy, she has learned others have never prodded deeper into Kayla's intentions to remain neutral. Others would never suspect, and hardly would believe, that Kayla doesn't want to choose a side because she cannot care. And third, Kayla has learned, at least subconsciously, appearing neutral in certain situations at certain times and in certain ways can help build networks of people that project onto her, ironically enough, the character attribute of being a particularly caring person.

Action Plan

First thing is first. Understand, it is not right to persecute Kayla for her inability to care; for all scientists know, at this point in time, she may no more choose her fate to struggle to care about others or their feelings than a paralyzed person may choose to endure paralysis. Kayla can be any one of us. Just blaming her doesn't necessarily accomplish anything. If you are not seven feet tall, do you want others to blame you for not growing to be at least seven feet tall? Can't you imagine yourself developing resentment toward the people who always point out that you never made it to seven feet? Ask yourself, how do you imagine you might treat others as a result?

You are essentially helpless in achieving another's expectation of you for not being naturally particularly tall, right? So the point here is to be careful not to project expectations that are unfair on a potentially neurologically disabled individual. Well then, what is fair, and where do we go from here?

If Kayla—in her quest to build a self-serving, superficial social empire—manipulates and steps all over the feelings of others to get what she wants, betraying others' trust in her by remaining conveniently neutral in self-serving situations, sure, we can find her at fault and hold her accountable. But for her potential medical inability to care, we can no more assign her blame than we can assign blame to every person who never grew to be seven feet tall. So productively, if we find fault with Kayla, it should not be for her potential disability but for her chosen intentionally destructive actions, or—potentially in this case—intentionally destructive inactions.

I have offered that abusive, sociopathic neutrality can be dressed up as peace and adult maturity. But with respect to the context of a particular interpersonal circumstance you might be contemplating, I urge you to reflect on the following question for yourself: is the neutrality administered by a potential abuser the same as peace and meant to imply peace? I cannot answer for you.

The "Disingenuous Voluntary Recusation" Tactic

Closely associated with the sociopathic neutrality tactic is the disingenuous voluntary recusation tactic (DVRT). Arguably, the DVRT is not a subtype of sociopathic neutrality but a sister concept. Two identifiable distinctions appear to separate the ideologies.

First, the sociopathic neutrality tactic involves abusing others, though possibly inadvertently, by not taking sides due to a general numbness toward others' feelings, perspectives, issues, plights, or concerns; whereas, the disingenuous voluntary recusation tactic is meant to imply not taking sides for self-serving interests *while* clearly possessing the power, authority, or evidence of whatever sort to assist disputants in need. Simply put, disingenuous voluntary recusation involves individuals with the power to influence positively the outcomes of others, dishonorably disqualifying or excusing themselves from participating in conflict resolution for selfish purposes. And a second and rather superfluous distinction between the two concepts presents itself through considering the sociopathic neutrality tactic as a long-term general lifestyle disposition equatable to a numbness toward others' issues or feelings—whereas voluntary recusation is meant to imply advantageously espousing "neutrality" in specific instances or circumstances for an abuser's direct and immediate situational benefit.

Voluntary recusation, as a tactic, might be clearly and intentionally reckless, as in the case where someone with the leverage to help others chooses inaction out of self-interest. For example, some people refuse to take sides in fear of losing favor with some constituency—political, social, or otherwise. But the argument can also be made that voluntary recusation can occur due to an innocent sense of genuine confusion within an individual powerful enough to influence the outcomes of disputants. For example, sometimes individuals believe they cannot help others when, in all reality, they potentially can. In effect, this is to say that some people voluntary recuse themselves from arbitrating others' grievances because they possess a self-fulfilling prophecy that any action that is taken will be ineffective and fail.

Take, for example, the following situation: a frustrated parent may tire from attempting to determine which of his or her two children instigated the most recent quarrel between the siblings. Perhaps the parent may figuratively throw up his or her hands and declare a feeling of powerlessness. Perhaps the parent may reason, "I can't help them. Everything I have ever tried obviously has not worked, so there is no point in attempting to arbitrate their grievances anymore." Yet that parent, more than any other individual, might have the most influence within those particular siblings' minds. In other words, that parent, more than anyone else, may truly remain the most effective and capable resource to bring justice, growth, and resolution to the siblings.

Examples of innocent and honorable voluntary recusation abound. Individuals may recuse themselves due to a genuine conflict of interest, such as the insurance claims adjustor who is assigned to assess the damage of his or her neighbor's automobile, or the judge who owns shares in a corporation and is asked to rule on a company dispute. From these perspectives, to recuse one's self from helping others may be innocent and good-intentioned and not necessarily a sociopathic tendency—but rather, more precisely, a matter of an individual's perplexity in assessing a situation with objectivity in relation to his or her own self-identity. However, the argument can be made that an empowered individual disqualifying him or herself from choosing to bring justice between disputants for a petty or selfish motive—such as fear of losing constituents or even out of a lack of empathy to care about others' feelings, especially when one disputant is clearly proven to be guilty and the other innocent—actively engages in the sociopathic tactic of disingenuous voluntary recusation. And the argument can further be advanced that an abuse of power is an abuse of people.

Action Plan

Remember, one of the most ironic concepts about disingenuous voluntary recusation is that it is deceitfully packaged as honorable voluntary recusation. Listen for the following themes in the phrases you hear: "My hands are tied." "There is nothing I can do." "It won't make any difference if I address that with them anyway." "I'm not touching that issue." "It's in the past. I'm not revisiting that." And, "I don't know what it would accomplish, anyway," etc.

Also, the absence of such words and phrases may speak loudly. For instance, have you ever noticed how a "neutral" party may avoid even verbalizing such claims of feigned hopelessness? An argument can be made that to recuse one's self voluntarily without words can be even more subtle, tactful, and powerful than with words.

Nonetheless, when a manipulative and deceitful individual engages in voluntary recusation, prepare for the onslaught of excuses and justifications. Ask yourself, "Does this person have the power to affect a situation at hand? Does my gut tell me that this individual lacks a desire to use his or her authority, position, or leverage to help others in need? Do I identify any excuses and justifications? Do I hear any attempts by an individual to establish chronologically unrelated cause-effect relationships to justify past instances of his or her inaction as now resulting in positive aspects of an issue's present circumstances?"

Obviously, if you are experiencing these indicators, you are likely in danger on the sociopathically adjusted playing field. Remember, you cannot count on rationalizing that, in return for treating an individual particularly well who engages in dishonorable voluntary recusation, you will be immune from his or her wrath in the future. With good fortune, you may identify an abuser, establish distance, and the individual deceitfully and dishonorably engaging in voluntary recusation may be exposed for abusing his or her position for self-serving interests.

The "Judge, Sentence, and Endanger" Tactic

If you have never driven or been a passenger in a vehicle, well, I have absolutely no idea how you got to this book. However, if you have traveled in a vehicle, chances are, you have probably experienced being tailgated, flipped the bird, and swerved in front of so aggressively that your heart beat like the last time you ran on a treadmill. Let's break this down component by component to see how it hits an abusive, sociopathic home run.

First, your vehicle was found to be in violation of the subjective judgment of another. After all, unbeknownst to you or even an abuser's potential lack of conscience, subconsciously, you were identified as a competitor for roadway and perceived as an animate waste-of-space deficiency impeding another's use of time and territory. Second, after you were established as a competitor for time and space, when the "bird" was flown your direction, you were shown, with all due viciousness, the misery that another wished to make you feel. However, the perpetrator communicating insensitivity to how you feel—as well as a blatant disregard for the fact that *you feel*, for that matter—was not enough. Swerving in front of you, almost clipping and potentially destroying you, was your punishment for wasting the abuser's time and impeding the road ahead.

Never mind the fact you were obeying traffic laws. Never mind you may be so broke and such a good, honest, decent human being struggling to feed a family who cannot afford a speeding ticket in the first place. The impulsivity experienced by the hostile driver through a rush of rage and aggression took for granted whether or not you had the reaction time to hit the brakes when the abuser swerved in front of you at what may have been one-hundred-plus kilometers per hour. Families lose loved ones because of this sort of aggression spurred by malicious intention. The abusive, sociopathic behavior of swerving in front of you symbolizes the "judge, sentence, and endanger" tactic as it intends to make you feel afraid for your life for that split second as a punishment when all you dared to do was drive the speed limit.

Okay, so you might be wondering, am I arguing that everyone is a sociopath who has ever experienced anger or frustration behind the wheel? No, but tit for tat, retaliatory behavioral manifestations of aggression, at the very least, suggest deficiencies in self-control and anger-management issues. Moreover, it seems many people reason within themselves that it is okay to throw temper tantrums and put others' safety in danger—which reeks of unfettered abusive sociopathy. In the action plan, I will address two clues that may help in determining when an individual engages in the ever-so-self-serving and destructive "judge, sentence, and endanger" tactic.

Action Plan

Identifying an instance of an individual engaging in "judge, sentence, and endanger" may appear rather difficult—though, with the aggressive, reckless driver, it remains easy enough. But this begs the question: what about "judge, sentence, and endanger" behaviors that occur more subtly? Perhaps a piece of what was supposed to remain confidential information between "friends" begins to float around and, somewhere along the line, becomes intentionally twisted out of context as the latest gossip among many people. Finding the "leak" may be hard enough, but the guilty party with a vendetta, if even identified, so often plays the ageless card of, "Oh, I didn't think that was supposed to be a secret—sorry."

So could it be that the leaker of a piece of gossip wishes to encourage the demise of an individual victim affected by the gossip—in effect, utilizing the "judge, sentence, and endanger" tactic? Absolutely, it could. Yet, as you can imagine, this situation is much murkier to decipher than an instance of intentionally reckless, aggressive driving.

For instance, the achieved anonymity of the sociopathic abuser spreading rumors and willfully engaging in defamation serves as the figurative getaway vehicle. Or—even when "who" said it is well established—that getaway vehicle may be figuratively represented by an abuser's achieved guiltlessness in others' minds regarding the possible presence of his or her actual malicious intentions. Where the blame should be directed, not to mention whom it should be directed at, can be so well crafted and concealed through subterfuge that leaked information by one party can appear an unintentional accident altogether. However, I have observed two key criteria that I believe to help in determining whether an individual intentionally engages in the "judge, sentence, and endanger" tactic. Asking these two questions should assist you in determining incidence from coincidence.

First, does the given situation at hand cause you to conclude with probable cause that a transgressor perceives himself or herself as "rules-negotiable" and more important than others? For example, the action of the aggressive driver makes the statement, "My time is more important than your safety, and for trying to control my time, I will make you pay by violating your safety. Furthermore, I will sadistically derive pleasure from making you feel fear." In effect, the aggressive driver's action implies that his or her time, agenda, and well-being are somehow more important and valuable than his or her victim's. Ergo, probable cause definitely is established.

With the gossip situation, where there is no vehicle blatantly swerving in front of a victim for which to assign responsibility to a specific driver clearly and quickly, it may be more difficult to identify if "judge, sentence, and endanger" transgressors believe others are less important than themselves. However, if a likely leaker of confidential information manifests insensitivity to the plight of a victim personally affected by the release of gossip after the fact, it may make a case for probable intent by the perpetrator to wound or destroy victims negatively affected by a particular disclosure. Such insensitivity by a potential abuser might manifest through a comment such as, "So they feel embarrassed—so what? What's the big deal?"

The second question to help you determine incidence from coincidence in a given scenario is—pardon the play on words—is there a getaway vehicle? What does that mean exactly? Notice that in the example of the aggressive driver who "swerved" in front of the victim dangerously, the transgressor was visible. How visible? The "judge, sentence, and endanger" perpetrator was so visible that he or she was right in front of the eyes of the individual victim who had to slam on the brakes.

Here is a key distinction: though the perpetrator was momentarily visible to the victim, a getaway vehicle was in use to speed off into the horizon. The perpetrator remained not only difficult to identify by the victim but—for all intents and purposes—untouchable. Why is this important? Think of it this way: if someone engages in "judge, sentence, and endanger," a getaway vehicle helps to escape responsibility for one's actions, literally and symbolically. However irrational those actions may appear, life's getaway vehicles remain extremely rational and calculated—be such getaway vehicles literal (like fast cars) or figurative (like abuses of authority, abdication of responsibilities, or even playing ignorant after intentionally manipulating another's trust—ahem, intending to gossip about a competitor or confidant to gain some advantage or bring pain to another).

Getaway vehicles remain products of planned rational thinking as they not only allow perpetrators a means to escape punishment for transgressions against others but afford such transgressors future opportunities for the perpetuation of behavioral abnormalities yet to come. Why do some people attack others when and only if there is a getaway vehicle? Because they figure they can get away with doing as much, and unfortunately, a lot of the time, they are right—which is a great reason, within and of itself, to address this phenomenon.

Redefining MVP—The "Most Valuable People" Tactic

Perhaps you have heard someone say something to the effect of, "Well, important people think..." or, "We have some important people coming in today. Let's all show them how great of a job we do." And perhaps that doesn't sit right with you, especially if you do not think anyone is any more important than anyone else. Unfortunately, some people view people like objects, literally things, instead of people. Of course, expecting people to admit this with words is no easy task. However, if you believe actions speak louder than words, perhaps you have noticed some people's actions seem to reflect an attitude that some individuals may be more important than others.

Moving forward, there are logical contentions that need to be addressed concerning the concept of "important people" when multiple individuals are involved in a team project. *Teamwork*, a phrase that conjures the collective ambiguity of positive thoughts circulating within various minds regarding constructive group effort—ambiguously enough—may also incur the minds' negativity. How so?

Well, for starters, are all teammates within teams satisfied? Does the worker declared "project leader" always deserve the credit? Does the athlete really believe in the coach's vision, even if it means the athlete has a minute, insignificant role relative to the next player on his or her team? Does teamwork always resolve conflict, or can it, within and of itself, contribute to, and even create, conflict?

Well, the real point to be made here is not at all to knock effective teamwork but that who or what is considered "important" and *why* is widely contested, even within the confines of the minds of individuals engaged in teamwork. While it might stand to reason that if no one is inherently any more important than anyone else, then no teammate should be any more important than the next, right? Unfortunately, the reasoning is wrong.

To borrow the athlete's predicament, remember that often the athlete envisions the success of the team through an opportunity for more individual contribution—and sometimes the inclusion of some players actually can be proven to increase the odds of victory versus another group of players. For a detailed explanation of this phenomenon, visit Las Vegas. Moreover, of all the human beings on the planet, certain individuals repeatedly win gold medals and world championships against the odds of ever repeating as victors.

Think about it this way: billions of people live on the planet. The odds might be one in billions for any one individual to win any specific Olympic gold medal, but repeating as the winner in the next Olympics—those odds should be exponentially insurmountable. In effect, repeating as a champion in a global competition should be virtually—well, mathematically impossible. Yet multiple human beings have done just that. And with regard to team sports, certain individuals actively competing on a team, just by contributing to a team, statistically speaking, increase the overall probability of a given team's chances to win a championship.

Action Plan

On the one hand, generally speaking, nobody may be any more valuable or important than anyone else as a "human being," but on the other hand, specifically speaking, certain individuals are determined by others to appear more valuable and important in achieving specific task-related outcomes. However, remain mindful of the following abusively manipulative sociopathic behavior: self-objectives may be dressed up as group objectives.

For example, pay attention for when the team "concept" is set up to serve the needs of the individual. Imagine the athlete, as they say, who takes too many contested shots in basketball, or the soccer player who always attempts a shot on goal instead of passing to an open teammate. Perhaps, after the game, both profess a commitment to the importance of teamwork with a sense of regret that their teams lost. Though, perhaps, both view their losses not as a result of their own squandered opportunities to score but as a result of their team-mates' failure to pass them the ball for even more individual oppor-tunity. Similarly, in the workplace, some sharks are ready and willing to run up and accept the "wins" of their teams, but run even faster to distance themselves from their teams' "losses."

Getting the right teammates and putting them in the right positions is fine, but the "most valuable people" mind-set transitions into a tactic of abuse when it becomes all about exploiting others for one's own self-interest—or, to borrow and openly interpret phrasing offered by the American Psychiatric Association's alternative model for diagnosing antisocial personality disorder, "goal-setting based on personal gratification" (2012, 2013a). In essence, the "most valuable people" *concept* reduces to the "most valuable person" *mind-set* under the guise of team-centered objectives for a given individual to engage in exploiting others. In effect, figuratively speaking, while there is no *I* in *team*, the argument can be made that, for some individuals, there is definitely an *M* and an *E*.

So what discernable sense do we make of all this? Well, I, for one, think it would be a stretch to assume people are sociopathic because they are cognizant that the inclusion of certain individuals and their respective potential individual contributions may increase the odds of achieving a group objective. Would you want just any random citizen to play if you were trying to win a World Cup soc-cer championship? But in day-to-day living, we are surrounded by phrases like, "She is a nobody," or "He doesn't matter," or "Who are you again?" Such phrases exhibit elitism as well as a disregard for some individuals as being below others. Is there pettiness in such self-aggrandizing phrases? Certainly, there is.

Also troubling in such verbalizations is not only the objectification of others deemed less inherently valuable but also the rationalization that one's "lack of value" justifies how an individual deserves to be treated. What we can do is scan for and identify words and actions that appear to suggest an individual operates on the egocentric assumption that some people are more valuable or important than others as human beings. Through our own words and actions, we can set an example that we wish to see in the world. In effect, we can vigilantly defend the premise that others are not objects to be manipulated or exploited but people to be validated and appreciated.

The "'Reset Button' False Commitment to Commitment" Tactic

What does commitment mean to you? If you shake a hand, if you sign a contract, if you pledge to be there for another, how long are you obligated? Are you obligated unconditionally? If someone else cheats you or ceases to commit to you, are you relinquished of your responsibility to commit to that individual? These are questions we all have differing opinions about. So many circumstances occur that can change how we view not only others but how we view our obligations to others.

Okay, so that all sounds like common sense. But what if someone came up to you right now and said, "I will pay you one million dollars a year, every year, for the rest of your life, but there is a catch. You have to agree that you will not talk for a consecutive thirty-day period every year. If you so much as speak a word, you have to pay everything back that you ever made from the agreement. If you accept the offer, understand that you also agree that there will be video cameras and sound recorders everywhere to survey you and make sure you keep your word that you will not speak. Lastly, I will determine which thirty-day period of the year you are not to speak and notify you in advance."

Would you take the offer? How about this? Let's make the offer more interesting. What if you only had to agree not to talk for one week of seven consecutive days of the year? Okay, let's make it even more attractive. What if the catch was you had to agree not to talk for one day, the whole day, of the dealmaker's choosing every year?

Chances are, you probably think that is not a bad deal. But did you catch the part about how if you cheat, you have to pay everything you ever made back? And let's assume, if you mess up, "they" will know. Do you still want the offer? Are you sure?

Many people would agree to this arrangement, possibly most people, for one day every year for one million dollars. While some people, however, would not take the agreement because they would not feel comfortable and certain that they could keep quiet every day required in the future. For instance, what if you become senile? Assume if you broke the rule in the future, you would still be required to relinquish the treasure gained from the past. Can present you speak for the commitment of future you?

This scenario exemplifies many people's ill-advised commitment to commitment; it describes how some abusive sociopaths make decisions concerning jobs and relationships. Perhaps you have had a former close friend who intentionally abandoned and severely disappointed you in the past say, "Hi, let's start over. My name is———." Did the once seemingly committed individual undergo an internal metamorphosis and become a new person? It is not likely.

What likely happened here is that the sociopath abuser utilized a tactic I call reset. Obviously, both people remember who the other is, and remember their shared past personal history. Let's assume the individual initiating "reset" through the preceding reintroduction lacks any traumatic injury or amnesia. The network of people once socially interacted with—as well as the commitments entered into in the past that were agreed upon by an older version of the self—are displaced and abandoned by the present self. And while an abusive sociopath might try to convince others otherwise, he or she really is not losing sleep over whether the severances that have been initiated were mutual.

Reset does not just reside in the personal relationship playing field; it inundates the professional arena as well. And through the "false commitment to commitment" tactic, reset even allows for intrapersonal reneging of responsibilities to one's self. In effect, some abusers possess a trait of irresponsibility not just to others but knowingly lie and deceive themselves, even at their own expenses. Hence, some individuals go through life intentionally making false commitments to future commitments.

If feigning commitment is not easy for you, imagine how easy it would be for a "reset" agent in a job interview to claim to be, with a strong sense of commitment, who he or she thinks interviewers hint at that they are looking to hire. Imagine playing that role so believably that you basically glow in a figurative aura in the minds of interviewers as a perfect fit for the potential job offer at hand. What reset allows for is full-scale, no-holds-barred commitment to the future in the present moment—of course, with no intention to follow through on future commitments. Unfortunately, a lot of hiring managers are completely unaware of "reset" and sincerely judge applicants' momentary energy, enthusiasm, apparent lack of deception, and presence as indicators of positive attitude and long-term employee commitment—translation: advantage, abusive sociopath.

Action Plan

First, recognize that not everyone desires to honor commitments they undertake, even commitments to themselves. And remember that though your emotional connection to another may be personal to you, it is not necessarily personal to an abusive sociopath. What you may feel as a mutual connection may only be one-sided. And though you may feel personally abandoned to be thrown out of someone's life at some point, never buy into the baseless notion that such an action means you are worth throwing away.

And if you catch yourself thinking, *Why can people not stand staying with me?* remember, everyone has his or her own personality quirks, and it may have nothing to do with your personality. So do not beat yourself up, questioning, "What's wrong with me?" when you feel abandoned. After all, there is a chance—in situations where a significant interpersonal connection in a relationship has been established, and one party later treats the other like an undesired stranger or acquaintance—that the motive for abandoning a victim may be as simple as one party feeling threatened by having some sort of obligation to maintain a commitment to another.

If that seems foreign, just imagine what it might mean to have a quasi-experience with authentic interpersonal commitment toward others for someone who cannot handle commitment and perhaps even feels incredibly uncomfortable around it. Hence, in the case of interpersonal abandonment by one party, it may not be what one party was used to and comfortable with, and that person needed to distance him or herself from it. And if you are not at fault when another rejects interpersonal closeness with you, do you know what that means? It means you cannot rule out that you are desirable and lovable, which should be encouraging thoughts. If only more heartbroken individuals resisted beating themselves up over the fact that many abandoners may lack a desire to continue relationships not because they inherently reject the people they abandon but because they may inherently reject interpersonal intimacy with people in general.

To the beautiful, heartbroken, downtrodden, wounded human being dealing with tremendous pain, grieving for who or what you may have lost, think of it this way: if someone you courted abandons you because that individual is uncomfortable due to the effects of the powerful, forging interpersonal intimacy of your relationship—and that individual chooses a new partner—this does not mean the abandoner will magically desire emotional intimacy or meaningful interpersonal connection with the new partner either. A new life partner may have been chosen by an abusive abandoner for the express purpose of attempting to have a relationship that lacks an authentic emotional connection.

In essence, there may be nothing to feel jealously about because the future relationship with the new partner lacks the very unreciprocated intimacy you may have desired with the abandoner—and perhaps even feel was lacking at the untimely termination of your relationship with the abandoner, which should also be an encouraging thought, reflecting your lack of fault in being abandoned. In certain situations, I'm willing to bet that an abusive, sociopathic partner, feeling threatened, will fight that emotional intimacy connection every step of the way because it is just not comfortable when he or she may have only ever known present commitment in life with a future reset button.

Not Quite Name-Dropping: Welcome to the "Norm-Dropping" Tactic

Just like that, like lightning and thunder. Come again? Lightning and thunder allegorically symbolize what happens during norm-dropping quite well. Norm-dropping, as you may have noticed, sounds similar to "name-dropping." Pardon the refresher. Here is an example of name-dropping: "Last week at the mall, I saw [insert celebrity]." Okay, norm-dropping is a little different. Did you notice a norm that was just subtly dropped, albeit innocently enough? In a nutshell, I define norm-dropping as an individual communicating to another what shall be henceforth acceptable or unacceptable to prioritize or think.

Lightning represents when others, for a split second, elucidate your mind with their surprising perspectives. And afterword, thunder, in close association with lightning, represents the boom others figuratively feel within themselves when lightning strikes. Okay, okay, I'll be more direct.

Here is the issue: sometimes people with power over others very quickly, very subtly, very manipulatively—and often with very few words—communicate to others with less power what will now be acceptable to believe. Perhaps you listen to a press conference. You hear a famous person tell his or her side of a story. It sounds contrite. It sounds like he or she will soon be exonerated by public opinion, and all of a sudden, the individual says something completely untenable. And accompanying what came across as so undigestible is an implication that "if you can't see it my way, you're a———." Well, feel free to insert your own choice word.

So that's lightning and thunder. During the press conference, everything was okay, and all of a sudden, allegedly crazy showed you some authentically crazy. Here is another one: Jane's boss tells everyone in a group meeting a little white lie to modify the version of what actually happened with what seems a little less likely to focus liability on her boss's mistakes. Others pick up on the new norm that has been established.

And to provide yet another illustration of norm-dropping: someone with power accuses someone innocent of being guilty. And now imagine—that accused but innocent person is you. In other words, the new norm "dropped" is that you are deemed to be in the wrong and will be made to pay, regardless if that affects your reputation, livelihood, mortgage payments, or really anything you hold dear. So lightning here would be your mind's realization that you have been targeted by another's malicious perspective that you did not anticipate. And thunder would be the feeling in your gut when you feel tremendous pain and fear and ponder, *Oh, brother, what did I ever do to deserve this?*

Well, what you likely did, without your knowing it, or at least knowing it in time, was register within the mind of an abusive sociopath that you were a possible competitor who stood in the way of the abuser's agenda as some sort of threat, competing to acquire a coveted resource. From that vantage point, one can perceive anew where some personal attacks are truly rooted—and that is a *truly* empowering thought. For, you see, there is liberation and healing in understanding that the questions "What is wrong with me?" and "Why have others personally attacked and scarred me?" authentically equate to the answer "Nothing is necessarily wrong with me. It quite possibly was a matter of how I, even incorrectly, was perceived to be obstructing what was desired by someone else."

Action Plan

Let's take that example of being falsely accused by a more powerful person. Unfortunately, when you are less powerful and more ethical than someone above you, you just might find yourself in serious trouble. This is absolutely horrible to go through. Not only do you know you are falsely accused—you know your perpetrator knows you are falsely accused as well. The problem here is that only one of you cares. And that presents a big problem.

But at least both of you agree that the perpetrator's actions affect you, right? Wrong—remember the flawed presumption that some truly believe one person never affects the next, that everyone individually controls his or her own feelings? For a refresher on that concept, see tactic 1. Likely, only one of you will believe one person's actions affect another. And what about *your* own emotional well-being and peace of mind? Sadly, so often in these situations, probably only one of you cares about those as well. Here is what you do.

Consider remembering and repeating the following passage, and please read it aloud:

> I am undeserving of another's accusation against me. All I likely did, without me knowing it, was register within the mind of an abusive person that I am a competitor who stands in the way of another's agenda as some sort of threat. This does not mean that I did anything wrong, and it does not mean that I am a bad person. While the person who did this to me doesn't appear to care or, for that matter, understand how I now suffer due to his or her actions and words, I will commit to realizing every future second is worth more than that person's objectification of me. In life, this was bound to happen. If it didn't happen here and now, another abuser would have done something similar to me down the road. I will move past this and live a positive, healthy life to

the fullest every single waking hour of every single day. I believe in me, and I know I can help do great things.

And now consider reading it aloud again or even put a bookmark on this page. Sometimes all you did was scare others into thinking a thought they are too afraid to express: you just might be the real deal. You just might have the sort of altruistic intentions they doubt can exist, and they just might feel insecure and jealous because they may not be able to feel how you feel or care how you care, no matter how hard they have ever tried. And the fact that you might feel sorry for them for as much might only make them more resentful because they may not be able to experience what it feels like to feel sorry for someone else with the depth or frequency that you can.

On another note, there is hope through documentation. When being targeted, documenting everything just might make the difference to give yourself a fighting chance to convey to others the imposition of another's unfair norm imposed upon you. Others might possess the power to bring to light, and even subdue, any intentionally reckless norms, and of course, the term *reckless* conveys those "norms" intended to cheat, hurt, or—in general—abuse others.

Also an encouraging thought: there remains the chance that others with enough power to do something in your defense have a suspicion of the type of character with whom you are dealing. Although, sadly, there is a chance that the others with enough power to help you—upon receiving solid documentation from you—do not and will not care about your struggle. Nonetheless, be quick in mind like lightning and powerful in character like thunder and do the great things you and I know both you *can* and *need* to do.

And on that note, that is part of the reason this book needed to be written—because where are we going? Do we intend to just sit back and sweep abusing others under the rug while future generations wordlessly learn to equate success with self-serving, destructive behavioral patterns that promote lying, cheating, stealing, manipulating, deceiving, and ruining the lives of others who are innocent, or are we going to make the world a better place to live? The APA's

Diagnostic and Statistical Manual of Mental Disorders, fifth edition, arguably hints at this phenomenon of groups endorsing questionable treatment of others through the term "culturally normative ethical behavior" (2013a, pp. 662, 764). And make no mistake, the powerful, abusive adult who drops the dishonest norm on a subordinate can be as much of a bully as the child who threatens to beat up others on the playground—period.

The "Formality Paradox" Tactic

Ask a parent who decides to pick up an order from a restaurant if he or she would want a son or daughter who works at a food establishment addressing him or her by the first name to communicate that an order is ready. Though not for all, it's unsettling for many. Also, many people, especially in American culture, when frequenting restaurants, do not like to be asked to provide a first name for a table request when they have identified that someone much younger will likely be calling out their first names.

In many cultures, it is generally better to come across as a little too formal than a little too informal. But an assumption must be addressed. Specifically, because someone refers to someone else formally—for instance, "sir" or "ma'am," "mister" or "missus," or "doctor," etc.—that does not necessarily mean an authentic intention to respect or consider another is present.

That said, it should be noted that many employees are instructed to address others formally, and nothing is necessarily wrong with that. Nonetheless, when others call you *sir* or *ma'am*, be on guard. For instance, some manipulative individuals might simply desire to live in a world where other people are always treated as superficially significant—you know, in an idealized, on-the-surface, sort of way—while such manipulators simultaneously take advantage of victims.

Through subterfuge, manipulative people can utilize formality for at least four purposes. First, through the utilization of formality, manipulators desire to appear that they are engaged in civilized, higher-road dialogue. Second, manipulators utilize formality to trick others into believing that, through being called *sir* or *ma'am*, they are valued. Third, formality may simply be utilized in an effort to test and "feel" out the relationship with another for exploitable weaknesses through another's response to receiving formality.

And fourth—a big fourth at that—formality is utilized to create leverage over others. What does that mean? Do people say *sir* or *ma'am* to bosses or others in hopes of getting ahead? Sure, but that's not necessarily what utilizing formality to create leverage over another encompasses. For clarification, it means that some people will do and say anything they want to you, however they want to do or say it, but through addressing you as *ma'am* or *sir,* or offering a phony "please," or "Thank you"—or even just making a point to begin a steamrolling session with a substanceless "How are you?"— they will argue to others, even internally rationalize, you were treated with all due dignity and respect.

Such people might quickly bring to mind to others how you did not reciprocate their formality and therefore rationalize you as having inferior behavior, comparatively speaking. Leveraging formality is part of the sociopathically adjusted playing field. We endure socially unchallenged superficial formality divorced from authentic sincerity every moment of every waking hour.

Action Plan

You might be wondering, then, so what happens when a nonsociopath utilizes formality to address an abusive sociopath? The attempt at showing an abusive sociopath courtesy by referring to his or her position or title during conflict will likely go noticed but remain uncared about. Expecting an abuser who has lost it to recount that another called him or her *sir* or *ma'am* is really expecting too much. Sometimes abusive, sociopathic individuals, when receiving formality in conflict, possess no intention of returning formality or working toward resolution and will show you their true colors through refusing to care that *you honestly may care*, as evident through your action of respectfully addressing them.

In effect, your good-faith effort of respectfully addressing another to show you wish not to attack another but to work through something disputed may go unappreciated. Additionally, the argument can be made some individuals can be so abusive when they lose their tempers that every time they are addressed as *sir* or *ma'am* when they have lost control, it strengthens their resolve to rationalize within themselves that a disputant deserves their wrath. Where the nonsociopath might reason through showing the deference of a "yes, ma'am" or "yes, sir" in the middle of another's temper tantrum that such a courtesy of formality will calm the tension, the abusive sociopath may internalize a received formality as a momentum changer. Something akin to reinforcement that another concedes to wrongness and, if the attacker is impulsive enough, deserves all the more to be subdued and embarrassed, possibly in front of others.

The formality paradox is not as indirect and subtle as some of the other tactics abusive sociopaths utilize, but it affects everything. The people who come to work not when work starts but who come in early or stay late often set the precedent for working hard, right? Likewise, so too can the insincere formality used in interpersonal communication set the low precedent for how others are to be treated within a group, even when the only thing apparently sincere about such formality is a group's current lack of prioritization for addressing it for what *it* truly is.

If you actually play the game, you still lose. Why? Because—you can be labeled as too formal, too respectful, too deferential, etc. And who judges that? That's right. Think of how preposterous that is: someone else who was going to manipulate a situation by claiming you were too informal now reasons you may be too formal, yet refuses to acknowledge how your formality may constitute a good-faith effort to work through conflict like a grown-up. So the point here is that this is a game you win by understanding, not by playing.

When you observe the paradox, when you perceive how the respectful greetings and pleasantries don't parallel the cutthroat actions and callous disregard for others, guess what? You still make out for the better because you can start to cut your losses now and even leverage today for a healthier tomorrow.

The "'Ego Advantage'
Practitioner" Tactic

Imagine people you perceive as the most talented public figures in your mind. Perhaps you have conjured up a list of actors, musicians, athletes, broadcasters, and possibly even some politicians. What do they have in common? Why are they as successful as they are? Is it a matter of lucky breaks, or talent, or perhaps both? Could you do what they do as well as they could? And I don't mean could you, with a beating heart, live a couple of days in another's shoes collecting beaucoup bucks, but could you be received as well as them?

With regard to actors, I'm sure I could remember a couple of lines, but coming across as believable on the big screen or on Broadway, I'm not sure I've got that "it" factor. With regard to athletes, I don't expect to get into a pool and swim down an Olympian in a race any time soon, and I'm moderately athletic. With regard to broadcasters, I have no inclination to believe my voice will project the favorable, authoritative, likeable sound waves and smooth delivery execs looks for to build networks of millions of listeners—and politicians? Well, let's not go there.

But what I'm getting at is not just that successful people demonstrating incredible talent can do ordinary things in extraordinary ways. Rather, some people—through excessive self-admiration, or delusions of grandiosity—mistakenly believe they can do just about anything better than anyone else. I'll take it a step further: some people believe not only can they do just about anything better than anyone else—they believe, through such delusion, they are of superior qualification compared to others to be most deserving in just about any pursuit at anything. For the sake of clarity, assume that the judges of talent remain the public at large, not one individual, say, in the local music store who might assume as he bangs on a drum set that he will be vindicated in the minds of others who hear him as the most talented percussionist in the world.

If you are like me, after reading the last sentence, a sense of negativity appears evident. You might be wondering, *Is this author one of those people who thinks kids should not follow their dreams of stardom because most will eventually and inevitably fail in achieving them?* Au contraire, I am actually all for following dreams. When you don't arrive where you set out to be, you still can find you arrived where you'd rather be.

You might suffer from chronic negative thinking, always belittling your self-worth and condemning yourself to automatic failure in the minds of others. And of course, you have, by now, heard this type of thinking is unhealthy and not *necessarily* necessary. But some sociopathic individuals with a tremendous sense of ego have a huge advantage: they don't have to live like this.

They can basically walk up to anyone, anywhere, without the slightest semblance of fear of failure or rejection. They can shine with persistence, persuading and closing a sale, even when buyers are not even remotely aware they are shopping. When desiring someone or something, they don't necessarily have to fear the competitive structure as it stands because they may be oblivious to who might be considered or prove more desirable, beautiful, handsome, personable, charming, likable, attractive, considerate, or even talented.

But more powerful than potentially being oblivious to the competitive structure, they don't necessarily have to care what the structure is or how other people will judge an unworthy breach of it. Think of it this way: when you observe individuals who think they are an undiscovered superstar due to their dancing or singing skill, and you do not share in their opinions, they strike you as delusional, right? However, behind that delusion may be false pride—but an individual may interpret that false pride as authentic confidence and belief in one's self.

Let's take the singing and dancing out of the equation. Let's say someone feels that one's talent is that he or she is great at meeting people, conversing with them, and believes—I mean really, truly believes—others perceive him or her as an extremely likeable person when that person is a really abusive, toxic, dangerous individual. This belief in one's self reinforces that person's potential to strike up a conversation with anyone and everybody, from the socialite to the quiet, introverted soul, and even the grouch. And what often happens after the boldness and courage of striking up such conversations?

In addition to flat-out rejection, often, people approached feel flattered and obliged to accept a new acquaintance. And when people accept a new acquaintance over and over *and over*, a person who may not be all that authentically likeable may have amassed a network of thousands of people. Again, the thousands of friends or even social media acquaintances do not mean that person's real character is truly likeable, any more than a self-confident but talentless singer or dancer truly has the talent to be a multiplatinum superstar. But the point is, the possibility exists that when some abusive people believe in themselves through delusion, they can achieve seemingly unbelievable results—hence, the title of this tactic: the "ego advantage" practitioner.

Action Plan

So you might wonder where the obligatory sentences concerning believing in yourself in an unrealistic manner to increase your "ego advantage" are located. They are not here. I reason that to assume a solution for gaining self-confidence exists by believing in your own positive character attributes with an overexaggerated fervor does a disservice as it translates to wishful thinking.

Sure, some people might be able to do this, in effect, believe themselves to possess abilities they do not, but who am I to tell you what you can believe? That stated, if you tell yourself, "Self, you can fly now," please try this thought experiment close to the ground. Kidding aside, believing you can fly may be as hard for you as believing you are extremely qualified to do anything else, even something in which you might have tremendous proficiency—so do not discredit and undervalue your abilities.

Sometimes we do not know how far short we fall in giving ourselves enough credit. Sometimes you may not want to believe it, but you just might have what it takes to outcompete others at something; while, at other times, you might believe you have what it takes to outcompete others, give it your all, and then come to realize you are outcompeted.

With regard to whenever you feel outcompeted, remember this: your worth is not defined by your limitations. And it is not a shot at your self-esteem to acknowledge your limitations. As a matter of fact, the argument can be made that being honest with one's self is an attribute of positive self-esteem and, in turn, a *healthy* ego.

The "Mini-Death" Tactic

I can imagine a reader thinking, *Okay, look, you can't just make up words—"mini-death-ing?" Are you serious? What in the world does that mean?* Yes, I am not just serious; I am dead serious. Okay, please forgive the cheesy play on words. And "mini-death" means basically this: people intentionally, for a variety of reasons—well, that's fudging it—really for a variety of excuses, treat other people they were once close to, or at least frequently interacted with, like they are already dead. Similar to the unofficial term *mini-death* or *mini-deathing* presented within this writing is the officially recognized psychological term *social death*—a phenomenon that can occur when groups ostracize or antagonize a particular member, thereby excluding a specific individual from receiving future equitable treatment (American Psychological Association, 2015). Such termination of group membership privileges can negatively affect a targeted victim's ability to satisfy his or her necessary psychological needs, regardless of whether or not expired interpersonal relationships were ideal or even healthy. In effect, through "social death," groups intentionally terminate social—and often even physical—interaction with targeted victims. Subsequently, victims stand to suffer distress as they lose access to previously relied-upon interpersonal resources utilized to meet and fulfill personal desires. In any event, where "social death" might deal more with groups abusively excluding an individual, "mini-death" is meant, herein, to communicate not a group's effort but an *individu-al's* effort to shun or ostracize a targeted victim.

Obviously, no one assumes someone else alive is literally dead. But sometimes people, for abusive intents and purposes, treat others from their past like they are all but dead. Translation: abusers warm victims up, get what they want, move to the extraction point, and complete the mission. Sadly, when someone is removed from the life of another, that often really is it—that might be the last those two people will ever see or hear of each other. Of course, people have to move or leave for unintended reasons and unfortunately lose contact with others, but this is not what is intended by the "mini-death" concept.

To mini-death another is a deliberate, intentional, selfish, and abusive action. However, here's an important caveat: to cut ties with another is not always ethically wrong. For example, if one is abused, is it necessarily fair for someone abused to maintain a relationship with his or her abuser? The answer is obviously *no*.

And also, mini-death is not exclusive to individuals with socio-pathic personality disorder; nonsociopaths can learn to cut others off too. I will go so far as to say this: people go to therapy and, in some cases, are told messages like, "Believe in yourself—if you just stay open and positive in your attitudes toward others, others will not want to leave you." Maybe that is true for some situations. But as a blanket statement for all situations, I have four words—*how dangerous and reckless*. First of all, I'm willing to bet the therapists who rationalize others' futures solely with positive outcomes are not thinking about, or perhaps even grasping, the fact that the wounded individuals they are compensated to help might be living a life full of being considered all but biologically dead by others.

Some people have it so badly. If you are having a particularly bad day when people have been mistreating and swindling you over right and left, remember that and remember them. Some poor indi-viduals are suffering, more alone than almost anyone, no matter how surrounded by others they might be—due to chance that many of the abusers who have been a part of their personal history, in a most traumatizing manner, used them and then figuratively threw them away.

If other people who you were once close to treat you like you don't exist—like you are not there, like they never interacted with you in the past or cared about you—how would you feel? If you feel interpersonal connection deeply, you probably would feel extremely devastated and perhaps become clinically depressed. You probably would wake up thinking about how to make sense of another's ostracism and admonishment of your existence. You probably would assume that the person who killed you off through "mini-death" feels your fondness for them, and you probably would ponder what you can do to fix things so that the relationship abandoner might feel the meaningful connection you had always felt—perhaps even continue to feel toward him or her into the present moment.

To mini-death another doesn't necessarily require once claiming to love or like another. It simply can be a matter of acknowledging someone, even through a superficial relationship, and then throwing that interpersonal communication pattern away—simply discarding another, completely removing another person from one's life. It doesn't hurt everybody.

If you don't feel deep emotional connections to people, spending mental energy to ruminate upon being "mini-deathed," or "mini-death-ing" another might be about as important to you as the need to ruminate upon a random raindrop and visualize the cloud it fell from. Some abusive, sociopathic personalities live and die by the mini-death *figuratively*. Surely, you've heard someone dangerously prescribe, "Look, you don't have to care what other people think or feel" as an elixir to cure a troubled mind. With mini-death, you can even simplify that concept to, "Look, you don't have to care that there are other people that think and feel," which can be simplified even further to, "Look, you don't have to care that there are other people."

Mini-death is selfish. It's "communicate with whom I want something from when it's in my interest, and on my terms, get what I want, then throw them away." It's "People are things to be communicated with by me when convenient," not "People are *people* to be communicated with in sickness and in health, even when one person no longer perceives an end to be gained for him or herself through prolonging the means of communication with another in an otherwise healthy friendship." In brief, look out for people who do not want to get to *know* you but want to get to *use* you.

Am I saying that I feel we are obligated to develop interpersonal relationships with every person we ever meet or pass on the subway? No, but I am saying, figuratively, we need to wake up. People are in a tremendous amount of pain because of this phenomenon, serious psychological distress from the all-too-often tolerated ostracism, and we need to get to work.

Action Plan

If you ever felt emotionally ravaged, truly devastated, by someone who claimed to love or like you in some way, someone who seemed to appreciate and value you, or even merely acknowledge you, who, suddenly with what seems like the effort of flipping a light switch, no longer acknowledges you're alive, know this—you are not alone. You are a victim of a traumatic pattern of abuse we are not quite currently ready to address in our contemporary moment. From me to you, know that you matter and that I think your ability to think matters, that I care that you think and feel, and one more person on earth roughly knows what you were or are going through during your past or present moments.

I'm willing to bet that it's not just me but millions, if not billions, of people feel similarly due the anguish you are enduring. They know, like you, what it's like to be thrown away by someone they were good to, and they know the feeling of others not really understanding the significance of the grieving you endure to be treated as somehow erased. Please understand, you matter. You possess priceless worth, and you *must*—yes, my subjective opinion, *must*—march on and give the world day by day all of your beauty, you wonderful, life-changing, meaningful human being.

The "Word-Wiggling" Tactic

Perhaps another person, say for example, in the workplace has said something abusive, or at least hurtful, to you. You remember the other person's words like your date of birth. They probably, deep down, remember as well. Of course, others often won't admit when they are guilty of saying something to another that can be construed as negative. So at this point, person A who mistreated person B may simply let time pass and hope that, after a while, after more interaction, the offense will be treated as something at least diminished or at best completely forgotten.

This sort of thinking happens to virtually all of us. After all, who does not sometimes say things, even positive things, not intending to hurt others' feelings, that do, somehow or another, hurt others? For instance, even a positive comment can hurt another. Have you ever given too much credit to one person and not enough to someone else, someone whom, unbeknownst to you, may have worked the hardest of all?

An honest answer to that question may be *yes*. But an equally acceptable answer to that question is, "I don't know." And since we don't always know who is most deserving for a job well done or who has the best intentions, we might incidentally mistreat someone who helped make something possible by giving credit disproportionately.

Now that we have touched upon the positive remark that featured no intention to mistreat another, let's return to the scenario featuring the intentionally negative remark that person A intended toward person B. Let's assume person A, Mr. Jones, said something negative to person B, John, when Mr. Jones lost his temper while feeling irritated by John.

Consider the following hypothetical scenario: John, age twenty-three, says, "Mr. Jones, would you like the quarterly reports in PDF or through the newer version of the database software?" Mr. Jones replies, "John, are you seriously asking me this question? What a stupid thing to say. You have been here, what, six months? And I have to wet-nurse you for even the smallest detail you should have by now noticed. What's next? Do I need to hire a five-year-old to teach you how to do your menial job? This is absolutely ridiculous. Get this out of my face."

John, a nonsociopath, never intended to incur Mr. Jones's wrath, let alone challenge Mr. Jones. Yet, at the end of the conversation, John feels pain that is very difficult for him to convey to anyone else. John has learned in his life that making disclosures about his pain to others will often be construed as examples of "thin skin" and a lack of toughness. And John knows not everyone will care what he feels or endures, so he tries to keep quiet and pay bills—though, inside, every day, when he returns to work, he feels the tension broadcasted by Mr. Jones toward him, which reinforces John's feeling unwanted, incompetent, and irrelevant.

Imagine, weeks later, Mr. Jones has come after John multiple times. It has gotten so bad that John not only would change jobs if he could find another, but even Mr. Jones (an abusive sociopath who can't care about the importance of John feeling welcome and valued) realizes he probably should make a concessionary speech to John, fearing that his subordinate might complain to human resources—a move that, if conducted with tactful precision by John, might hamper Mr. Jones's chances of promotion, as well as threaten the perception of Mr. Jones's reputation among other key decision-making administrators within the company.

So Mr. Jones finds John sitting at his desk, diligently typing a document, and Mr. Jones enthusiastically offers, "Hey, John! How are you today? Did you see the game last night?" John—experiencing surprise, suspicion, uncertainty, and fear all at once—looks up to Mr. Jones and says, "Hi, Mr. Jones. I was working on a report last night and had to switch file formats for it to load properly so it could be ready ahead of schedule. I didn't have a chance to watch any television." To which, Mr. Jones replies, "You know, John, that's one of the things I like about you. You are so detail oriented, always on the ball when it comes to organizing and choosing the correct file format."

John, at this point, with mind racing, wonders why and how Mr. Jones can say this to him. John reasons internally, *He thinks I'm stupid and incompetent, like a child, for the questions I have run by him, and here he is complimenting me on a "strength" that he has more than just once criticized as a "weakness." What gives? This has to be disingenuous.* John's thoughts rush within him as he partially wishes to address the inconsistency of Mr. Jones. He feels the fear of losing an ounce more of job security, physically manifested by an increased heartbeat and sensation of swelling in his gut, and simply replies, "Thank you."

What happened here is Mr. Jones realized that he had been picking on John long and hard enough, and he knew it was time to "word-wiggle" for his own sake. Mr. Jones also could have "word-wiggled" after an initial round of disingenuous positive reinforcement by saying, "John, I know you think that I called you incompetent and stupid, but for the record, I never said that. I just thought the mistake you made was stupid, not you."

Or Mr. Jones could have started by saying, "John, it's okay. I won't be mad at you for sharing with me. Did you think I called you incompetent?" Perhaps to which John might nod in the affirmative, though out of intimidation, not likely. Mr. Jones might, in turn, shake his head in the affirmative, slightly smile, and say something to the effect of, "Well, I never said that. You misinterpreted what I said."

And here's a telltale abusive sociopathic word-wiggling favorite: "Some people are too sensitive to that kind of humor and seem to have difficulty knowing when someone is joking. You are one of those people, so since you have trouble knowing when I'm serious or joking, I'll try not to use humor around you since you can't understand it." How condescending, right?

In these instances, Mr. Jones is indirectly communicating to John that, as one of John's bosses, Mr. Jones is willing to change his story so that he won't have to accept responsibility for any grievance John brings against him. And if John tries to accuse Mr. Jones of excessive hostile negativity, Mr. Jones will go on record today as saying something positive to John. It's all very calculated on Mr. Jones's end as he walks John down the red carpet. For instance, the conversation will be dressed up by Mr. Jones for human resources as a superior taking the initiative to communicate with a subordinate while also utilizing positive reinforcement to discuss work-related activity.

Meanwhile, John not only wants to feel validated and welcome in the workplace, he wants to put the past in the past and believe that the abuse is all over now that Mr. Jones appeared to turn over a new leaf, and seems to understand what he did wrong. John hopes and believes that everything is going to be better from here on out. And to Mr. Jones's credit, very cleverly, through his own life, he has learned wiggling out of problems he has contributed to may be a matter of persuading others to hope, even believe, he has changed or feels remorse for his mistreatment of them.

Action Plan

In life, everyone who speaks words is given the chance to word-wiggle. And in fairness, word-wiggling is not necessarily unhealthy and intended to hurt another. For example, ask a parent who takes a small child into a grocery store how hard it can be to deal with the persistent requests from a young one who desires to acquire what seems like every toy and piece of candy on every aisle and endcap. Obviously, for the child's good, many parents, even if they can afford to, will not want their young one accustomed to receiving everything, perhaps a gift a parent can bestow upon a child with far more substance than any toy collection. Nonetheless, finding the right words to word-wiggle to calm down a child while shopping in public after, "But why won't you buy it for me?" [breathe in, pant, breathe out, pant, moan, cry, scream] can be daunting.

But word-wiggling that is not well-intentioned can be a means to abdicate responsibility for past verbal disclosures that are interpretable as impulsive, hostile, rash, harsh, unsupportive, ugly, unsettling, and in general abusive, etc. Strategic word-wiggling allows an abuser a passive-aggressive means to retain control. The argument can be made that, through aggression, word-wiggling allows an individual with some sort of leverage or power to strong-arm a victim through renouncing what was actually said as something never to have occurred—for instance, Mr. Jones's phony denial of ever berating John. And through passivity, word-wiggling allows a more powerful individual the opportunity to deceive a victim through pretending to display remorse, as well as to present one's self as having turned over a new leaf to the victim.

In line with the classic adage, "It is not only what you say but how you say it," when trying to convey certain verbal messages, not only do individuals utilize tonal inflection, they also make an effort to choose the right words. The word-wiggling tactic allows an abuser to communicate a manipulative, disingenuous message in order to fool a victim. Documenting what was said as soon as you can after it was said is a good way to build evidence against an abuser. If you have documented nearly verbatim the words an abuser uses, he or she might contradict your documentation by making up "the real version" of what was said while speaking to another party, such as human resources.

Unfortunately, sometimes victims are not just dealing with an initial abuser like Mr. Jones but also with an inert organizational culture willing to make up "the facts" as they go along, with an agenda of not letting a guilty Mr. Jones "look guilty," so as not to tarnish the company's brand equity. Even if you are extremely well documented, there may be little you can do because how they treat you might not technically be "illegal." And even when your mistreatment is illegal, legal expenses are, well—expensive; not to mention some law professionals might be unwilling to take your case, in fear you might be lying, that you don't have enough evidence to win, or even because some litigators might sociopathically perceive your case as something irrelevant toward their self-centered career goals.

Documenting and seeking recourse aside, I think there are two things you can do regarding abusive word-wiggling. First, get as far away from the abuse as possible. You don't deserve it. It's not your fault. Ugly-hearted people will lie about you in a heartbeat and tarnish your name before anyone has time to see who they really are and who is really responsible. Please do not settle for the status quo. As a human being, you do not deserve to be someone's emotional punching bag.

Second, don't be part of the problem; be part of the solution. After all, what would you be teaching everyone else if you have leverage and word-wiggle to abdicate responsibility when it appears convenient for you? You need positive energy. You have so much within you to contribute and do not deserve to be around an abuser or abusers who only know how to objectify your value for what they perceive you bring to the table and, along the line, fail to see the value of what you have within you. Please never forget that value.

The "Button-Push Forecaster" Tactic

Like a bloodhound running down the scent of a perpetrator hiding in the woods, a skilled sociopath can sense his or her environment. A master sociopath can even walk into a room and, in a matter of minutes, know who calls the shots, who wants the power, who appears easiest to manipulate, who is most likely to be intimidated, who is too straitlaced to corroborate in gray-area endeavors, and—who else in the room intentionally operates on the dog-eat-dog sociopathically adjusted playing field. It is a truly remarkable ability and skill set, though with major drawbacks and limitations. The individual with sociopathic abilities constantly, and perhaps even subconsciously, scans for others' weaknesses and exploitable vulnerabilities, particularly through others' personal disclosures—much like the forward-thinking meteorologist forecasting in advance for inclement weather.

The idea that whatever you say can and will be used against you by another is pretty self-explanatory. But what if you disclose confidential information and it is used against you, even altered intentionally, by someone else in the future? For example, perhaps an individual remembers something you chose to disclose that you communicated as personal and privileged; then that person intentionally disregards a connection to your mentioning what you disclosed as private, as well as the pain within you that corresponds with whatever you communicated—a connection obvious to you. And lastly, somewhere down the line, that person utilizes, perhaps even manipulates, what was disclosed as a strategy to wound or destroy you when doing so may serve to benefit him or her in some way.

In effect, some individuals possessing malicious intentions or simply even self-centered agendas, knowingly or otherwise, scan for others' "buttons." And the act of doing so—in effect, pushing others' buttons to forecast for their reactions—may have several potential motivations. For example, abusers can push others' buttons to identify what makes a victim suffer or even simply to assess how best to "use" a victim toward a desired end through testing their reactions to unwarranted advances.

Have you ever noticed somebody testing you? Maybe they violated your trust just a little, and it left you wondering, *Did he or she do or say that on purpose?* Perhaps a situation got worse over time, transitioning from a leaky faucet drip by drip to a full-on bursting pipe. Sometimes individuals with sociopathic tendencies are intentionally sizing you up by pushing your buttons, concealing their less-than-innocent intentions.

Perhaps you might be thinking, *Why would someone choose to act like that, and what would be in it for them?* Most obviously, testing others' boundaries can be a mechanism to "feel" out a situation for what manipulative behavior will be tolerated moving forward. Without directly asking a victim, "how would you respond and react if I...," the abuser can nonverbally inch his or her way toward a desired objective. Through subterfuge and subtle digression, a victim remains much less likely to catch on to an abuser's true intentions.

For example, imagine an individual named Jan who befriends a part-time salesperson for a cosmetics company, Tracy, at a mutual friend's dinner party. Both really seem to hit it off and discuss a wide range of interests. Days later, Tracy sends Jan a social media friend request, which Jan accepts. Assume that, with this connection, Tracy now has access to view and communicate with Jan's entire online social network, person by person.

The two new friends begin making more and more time to socialize together. Weeks pass by, and Jan receives uncanny messages from nearly ten of her friends on social media. All the messages insinuate that a stranger named Tracy, claiming to know Jan, direct-messaged them to offer discounts on cosmetics—and the messages just keep coming. Jan contemplates this and determines, not so much by coincidence, all these unsolicited offers came to people judged to be within a certain age range corresponding to the products that Tracy has access to sell.

Perhaps Jan discusses this with Tracy, who then profusely apologizes, claiming she did not think Jan would think it was a big deal—after all, Tracy framed the argument that she wanted to help out Jan's friends with great bargains. Moreover, Tracy not only so convincingly urged Jan to see it as a nonissue but also pressured Jan to feel like she is being "uptight" and "square" to make a situation out of it and needs to "relax." Suppose that Tracy—in her thirties, like Jan—intentionally attempts to access a part of Jan's personality that enjoys feeling like a teenager again when she interacts with Tracy, though Jan may lack conscious awareness of this. Further, suppose that the initial connection they had was not mutually authentic, and that Tracy was willing to invest time to socialize with people like Jan in order to gain some benefit—like access to new clients.

In other words, Jan enjoys the way Tracy makes her feel, though the "Tracy" she perceives is not real. Imagine that, as time passes by, Tracy e-mails nearly fifty people over and over again, people to whom she gained access through Jan's personal social media network, leading to even more complaints heading Jan's way. Deep down, Jan may feel abused but finds herself rationalizing that Tracy is right—she needs to "relax." However, Tracy is remorseless about any inconvenience or strain this causes on Jan's other interpersonal relationships and displays shallow affect.

Action Plan

When you observe abusers exploiting others' boundaries, or even privileged information shared in previous personal disclosures, be on your guard. You may be very close to a toxic personality. And if you reflect and find people have terminated interpersonal goodwill toward you in a similar manner, time and time again, realize that you may be getting forecasted for what gets the most rise out of you, or what causes you the most pain—or even what's the most effective way to manipulate you—every time you share something personal with someone underserving of your disclosure. Such individuals, at some point, may be willing to use what caused you pain against you *to use or abuse you*. To prevent this from happening, reflect on the following "empathizations."

A common empathization is the erroneous belief that through intentionally disclosing one's deepest feelings and secrets to those who are desired to be closest to an individual discloser, interpersonal bonds and emotional intimacy are, by default, mutually strengthened for both parties. In effect, the empath often believes that through voluntarily divulging information that exposes one's self as vulnerable, the interpersonal bond with a receiver of a message will necessarily grow stronger. It is like a conscious desire to hug another tighter, or even to water and nourish a beloved plant. Empaths often desire such closeness and connection with their confidants and enjoy strengthening interpersonal intimacy.

However, the empath often engages in another "empathization" in the process: the belief that all people are inherently well-intentioned and desire interconnectedness with others. Thus, the empath further stands to reason, erroneously, that the action of sharing his or her time, personal feelings, or secrets with a receiver—while possessing a good-faith intention to treat a receiver honorably forever, in perpetuity—automatically equates to an abusive receiver of a personal disclosure equally valuing and honoring the disclosing victim and the interpersonal relationship between them.

The "Sigh-and-Exhale" Tactic

Perhaps you have experienced another expressing irritation with you directly after your verbal or nonverbal behavior through one of those grandiose sigh-and-exhale "pieces"—maybe even featuring one of those pronounced eye rolls or recoiled facial expressions. Now, I'm not talking about when others "sigh-and-exhale" when you make a mistake that is truly your fault, which costs the team because you got to work late and others will have had to pay for your mistake. I'm talking about when you, in good conscience, mean no offense, and another can't seem to stand that you are a creature that speaks. You know, where someone else, without using the words, basically communicates, "Woe is me. This other person annoys the heck out of me. He or she is such a waste of life." Hypothesis: the sigh, with pronounced exhale, symbolically represents the abusive sociopath's plausible irritability and contempt for your perceived intrusion into their realm.

Of course, like not yawning when others speak to us (by the way, a concept that is an investment in your future worthy of paying for this book in as little as one sentence), we can also keep ourselves from sighing and exhaling while others speak. Sometimes, sadly, it appears the closest to consideration you are shown by others is their commitment to wait to "sigh-and-exhale" until immediately after you have finished speaking—how generous, right? And of course, the sigh-and-exhale behavior is also reverted to by nonsociopaths who have lost their sense of patience or tempers.

It is a passive-aggressive behavioral expression of partially communicated interpersonal hostility. And like some other abusive, sociopathic expressions, it can be considered tolerable behavior. When was the last time you saw an incident report form that had a "Someone else repeatedly sighs and exhales during or after when I communicate and also does this to undermine and embarrass me in front of others" checkbox?

The repeated sigh-and-exhale behavior by an abusive individual with sociopathic tendencies invalidates another's voice and, in so doing, undermines another's dignity. The sigh-and-exhale can say, without words, more than, "You irritate me." It can say, "I don't care what you think. I think you are inferior. Why are you even in my presence? You don't even matter. I'm right. You are wrong, and you obviously don't understand how stupid, annoying, and irritating you come across, and therefore, you deserve to feel embarrassed when I undermine you in front of others."

Action Plan

Earlier in this tactic, it was implied that a recoiled facial expression might, in some cases, be a subconscious physical manifestation of an abusive sociopath's antagonism for a particular victim—sort of like when the human brain first registers it perceives a venomous snake nearby. However, more than just a neck jerking backward in revulsion, or recoil exhibited more subtly through a lightning-quick abandonment of a previously held smile upon initial sight of a despised victim—the argument can be made that sociopathy presents in another common-enough facial gesture as well.

Imagine humans playing a ridiculous game where they each took turns putting on a lightweight, square-foot-sized box-shaped helmet that fit snugly around the neck. The walls of this apparatus consist of breathable mesh screens. However, inside of this enclosure are live biting mosquitos! Revolting to say the least, but the point is—pay attention for a facial expression that looks like a listener is trapped from the neck up in a box swarming with mosquitos.

Quite an unusual image, to be sure, but imagine how a sociopathic individual may clamp down facial muscles as if to suggest an experience of discomfort, disgust, annoyance, impatience, or even rage, with "wasting time" going through the motions of pretending to listen to and value a sender. Have you ever tried to briefly and concisely communicate a message and received such a facial expression that indirectly communicated, "Wrap it up already. You're figuratively killing me"? If so, perhaps such a message you recall communicating was not even necessarily relevant to conflict resolution but simply a "How are you?" met by a feigned verbal reciprocation *teeming* with another's visually observable mosquito-enclosure facial disdain. Obviously, knowing what is likely transpiring in another's mind in such a situation empowers you to acknowledge an individual's potential incapacity as you plan and navigate going forward.

Now, directly regarding the sigh-and-exhale, this is one where it is arguably best to lead by example. It can be tough not to sigh-and-exhale when you hear something disagreeable. Obviously, not everyone agrees with what another says. And sometimes abusers try to fish for, and then push, what they perceive to be your buttons, desiring to elicit a negative response from you to facilitate your demise. Some may want to get that rise out of you—for instance, you may have, for all you know, outcompeted another by beating another's reasoning through your empathetic perspective, so all the individual has left is roiling you up to conduct the ad hominem counteroffensive.

And when you sigh-and-exhale for others, you may be playing right into a manipulator's hands and giving over your control of your behavior to them as they now can build that momentum to paint you any number of negative connotation choice words because of your perceived negative attitude—which, by the way, may be true. Understandably, it just may be the case that you might exhibit a visibly upset demeanor and cease listening to abuse once you have identified, in a given moment, that someone is intentionally trying to push your buttons.

For instance, if someone says something particularly egregious or engages in "sigh-and-exhale" at an opportune moment in an effort to undermine your good intentions and character, or just to communicate insensitivity toward your feelings, you may have an understandably negative attitude and perhaps even desire to engage in argument with a manipulator once it registers within you that an individual is "off base"—an American baseball colloquialism that loosely means an assumption is inaccurate or unfounded. Also, if you go tit for tat and engage in "sigh-and-exhale" with another who sighed first, you might foster resentment more than mutual understanding and trust. And that represents a behavior just as unproductive as literally pointing your finger at another on the grounds that he or she pointed first. So is it realistic to presume no one will sigh or exhale ever again when irritated? Probably not—but you can make a mental note to bring this concept to the forefront of your conscious awareness to remain mindful of what the sigh-and-exhale "bit" implicitly communicates to others.

The "Assume, Act, Abdicate, and Repeat" Tactic

"Assume, act, abdicate, and repeat," depending on how you look at it, is a three- or four-step cyclical process. It represents, first, the dawning of a generally inaccurate, even unfounded, assumption, followed second by an action—often but not always impulsive—that is influenced by an abuser's initial inaccurate assumption. Following that initial assumption and reckless action is the third step: the abdication of responsibility and ownership for actions and assumptions that are incongruent with the appearance of positive character attributes desired by the abuser.

An example of a positive character attribute that an "assume, act, abdicate, and repeat" practitioner might desire, simply enough, might be achieving others' perception of an abuser as not being particularly impulsive and presumptuous. But straight to the abuser's major benefit to utilize this tactic—how many times have you experienced another presume something incorrectly, take some action, make a destructive mistake, and not accept responsibility for their presumption, action, and subsequent abdication of accountability?

Last but not least is the fourth step, classifiably debatable due to its repetitiousness: repeating steps one through three. While that may seem semantically repetitive, perhaps the best defense for the existence of the fourth step is that it is *assume, act, abdicate, and repeat,* not *assume, act, abdicate, learn, grow, and change*. Here is another example of this tactic in action.

Someone assumes you lost an important piece of paperwork or memo. That person accuses you of carelessness and not being organized enough. Sometime later, the memo turns up within the possession of the very person who accused you of losing it. You know that the person found it and let's say the individual knows you know, too.

So to step three—the abdication of responsibility—the individual who assumed you were at fault and then accused you of losing the paperwork now abdicates. In effect, the individual renounces any semblance of responsibility for accusing you. Instead of an, "I'm sorry to have accused you of losing something that turned up to be in my possession all along," you might get a, "Well, you still should have…," or perhaps you might even receive no response at all—which, if you are a victim, might feel like an overwhelming rush of frustration as you feel another's pettiness, who is perhaps neurologically inhibited from owning the situation and apologizing in consideration of your feelings.

And to provide another type of example, sometimes people "assume, act, and abdicate" without initially desiring to injure another but, rather, to help one another. That is to say, the abuse comes later. Consider the following scenario. Jason and Susan work in a customer service call center and constantly deal with customer complaints and issues through telephone calls. Jason, who has the same job and rank as Susan, has trouble understanding why Susan spends so much time listening to disgruntled customers who appear to desire "aimlessly" venting more than achieving resolution with the customer service representatives. However, Jason does not know he has trouble understanding Susan's motives and simply assumes Susan frequently listens to people vent because Susan is a people pleaser who is constantly taken advantage of by customers through not communicating to disgruntled customers that they need to "wrap it up"—a weakness, according to Jason, that makes Susan a human customer-complaint punching bag.

After internally crafting this assumption concerning why Susan is weak, Jason chooses an action to rectify Susan's alleged malfunction. Jason says, "You are being too nice to them, Susan. If you want to be successful, you know that we have to meet a quota for how many customers we assist each shift that we work." Jason proceeds, "You know, you and I can't afford to be in the red on those evaluation metrics. Susan, you need to be more assertive with disgruntled customers and take control."

Susan responds, "I disagree with you. I really think the best thing to do is let the customer be in control and take the time they need to say what they want to say because that's how I think I would want to be treated. And after talking with us, you know the customers have the anonymous survey option to rank the service we provided for them on the phone."

Resentful to be challenged, Jason angrily replies, "You don't get it, do you? Management doesn't care as much about customer service as they do about how many customer turnarounds we perform. Don't you know they let go of two employees for that reason already?" Jason continues, "I'm just trying to help, but fine, whatever. You're not smart. It's your termination, not mine."

To recap, here in this instance, it can be interpreted that Jason does not understand that Susan possesses a different philosophy regarding customer service, though Jason erroneously assumes the issue is not a difference in philosophy regarding customer service but his egotistical perception of Susan's intellectual inferiority. The assumption by Jason leads to the action of criticizing Susan. However, assume Jason's initial intention was not to abuse Susan by berating her; rather, he initially wanted to help Susan, though conditionally on his terms.

Jason's initial assumption about why Susan does things the way she does them is incorrect. His assumption fueled the escalation from step one, assuming, to step two, his "actions" of criticizing, arguing with, and berating her. In step three, abdication, Jason distances himself from responsibility for his actions, as well as exhibits his newfound disdain for emotionally supporting his coworker through the phrase "whatever" to dismiss Susan's perspective.

At this point, since Susan did not agree with Jason, he dismissed any intention of "helping" her see his logic and established an antagonism toward her. Perhaps Jason felt a need for someone to provide him adulation for his wisdom, and when it was rejected, he attacked. Any altruistic intention at that point, if there ever truly was one, may then have become converted to hostile intention within him.

Action Plan

So this is where the obligatory "Assumptions are bad, so make rational, informed decisions, avoiding assumptions at all costs" section is located, right? Wrong—assumptions occur in our minds all the time. They are not all bad. Perhaps you assume that an alley looks dark and dangerous and take the action of walking a different path. Perhaps that decision saved you from being mugged.

So, if even possible, how might you avoid being figuratively mugged from "assume, act, abdicate, and repeat" practitioners? First, recognize the phenomenon around you. In effect, remain cognizant of some individuals' propensity to make ill-advised, ill-informed assumptions, manifested especially through abusive actions, such as impulsive, accusatory, verbal disclosures constructed to blame others. Remember, awareness helps you navigate the sociopathically adjusted playing field.

Second, when you do suspect the phenomenon, do yourself a favor. Fight any urge to project onto a practitioner any justification that you will be treated differently. If it's nothing for someone to accuse, act, abdicate, and repeat, what should that tell you about your future interaction with that individual?

Consider breaking any habit of thinking assume-act-abdicate practitioners will see your good intentions toward them and treat you differently than others. If you go into a polar bear's den in the wild, tell the bear nice things—*and even bring fish as a peace offering,* guess what? You are still in the bear's domain, and you just may be the entrée after the fish appetizer. Remain steadfastly on the lookout for "assume, act, abdicate, repeat" and resist blindly projecting onto an assume-act-abdicate practitioner the belief that he or she will recognize that you have decided to make every effort to go above and beyond for him or her.

Also consider resisting any urge to project onto assume-act-abdicate practitioners an ability to experience an ideal conscientiousness that inhibits steamrolling whatever, or whoever, gets in their way when they make mistakes and evade owning them. One of the greatest mistakes empaths make is the "empathization" of projecting unto others a notion that abusive individuals wouldn't have fall people or lie because everyone would just feel too much remorse to act like that in the moment—let alone live like that for a lifetime. If you assume this is worth others thinking about, take action and explain this concept to others. Let them weigh and ponder upon "assume, act, abdicate." And then repeat.

From the Top-Down to the Bottom-Up: The "Expectation" Tactic

In the "deconstructive, constructive criticism" tactic, it was offered that some abusers exploit the constructive criticism process by incorporating their malicious intentions. As if to say, "I am going to put you down and tear you apart unfairly and destructively. But I will conveniently spin what I am doing to others in order to reclassify my abusive behavior as positivity directed toward you, constructively."

While that may sound rather unpleasant to contemplate, something very similar to this tactic occurs in top-down relationships that warrants attention. It is similar to the "deconstructive, constructive criticism" tactic in that it features fraudulent, inauthentic "constructive" communication. In these instances, however, such communication emanates from the bottom-up.

In other words, some abusers expect victims only to refer to them glowingly, even when such acclamation fails to appear warranted. Interestingly, on a closely related note to such a situation regarding a more powerful individual exploiting a less-powerful victim—in drafting and revising what would ultimately become the *DSM-V*—the American Psychiatric Association contributed a new criterion for antisocial personality disorder diagnosticians to consider on a case-by-case basis: an incapacity for mutually intimate relationships, and such incapacity might manifest through coercion, dominance, intimidation, or exploitation, of others (2012, 2013a). Paralleling this theme of interpersonal exploitation within this writing through the "expectation" tactic, an individual with leverage establishes the conditions to create a workplace environment where subordinates are informally directed, under their own volition, to esteem and praise a leveraged manipulator—*or else.*

In preceding chapters, it was addressed that some individuals can come across as charismatic, charming, open, warm, caring, considerate, and likeable people without ever truly being any of those things. And not only can they come across to others as featuring these attributes *without truly possessing them*, they can come across with such traits without even truly internalizing how their potential substanceless expression of them might be disingenuous. But such abusers alone do not have to project and market their own positive character attributes. They can also coerce and expect others dependent upon them to build their brands for them—hence, the phrasing *the "expectation" tactic.*

The idea that some manipulative individuals attempt to flatter and ingratiate their way into others' good graces is nothing new. Imagine, for instance, a ruthless, mean-spirited individual who transforms into one of the "nicest" people in the room when interacting with someone possessing something coveted. But a chief distinction between sycophancy and the "expectation" tactic is that, in the latter, all subordinate employees can be expected to speak glowingly of their potentially abusive workplace superiors—not just the sycophants who deceitfully intend to do so anyway for their own advantage.

Perhaps someone similar comes to mind from your memory. Have you or others ever felt expected to describe such an individual glowingly, or not all? And perhaps, "not at all" was *not* an option. Where did that expectation come from? Perhaps it was not explicitly stated, but you found yourself feeling it. And if that feeling did not come from you and it did not reflect your intentions—quite possibly, that expectation came from a manipulative abuser exploiting his or her leverage over you in the workplace.

Similarly, perhaps you have had the displeasure of coming across someone who said, "You're lucky I have been so nice to you," when, really, that person might be one of the most ruthless, callous individuals with whom you have professionally interacted. You might have felt the tension surrounding even considering whether or not to address the hypocrisy. Perhaps such tension might be manifested through a feeling of intimidation swelling within you.

Comparatively to the concept of others erroneously regarding a given individual as having a "nice" character—could it be possible that others may be intentionally manipulated into erroneously regarding an ascending or distinguished individual as possessing outstanding personal character attributes? Do people, in general, easily equate professional accomplishment or esteem, by default, with personal integrity? And do people give a benefit of the doubt to a potential abuser in presuming his or her flawless character compared to less professionally regarded individuals?

Of course, not every highly accomplished professional enjoys public perception as an individual possessing particularly positive character—but does an individual's professional brand provide him or her a favorable competitive advantage? In other words, is it possible that being considered promising or distinguished in a field—or even particularly relevant in a local office complex pecking order—correlates with others being expected to perceive and believe a given individual possesses particularly positive character attributes? I do not know. But if so, there remains the possibility that an individual employee with leverage over others is creating his or her ideal workplace environment through the "expectation" tactic.

If a "distinguished" person comes to speak at an event, he or she is often referred to as nice and kind. But do the individuals communicating as much truly know that about him or her? Have you ever experienced pressure from others to think highly about someone held in high professional regard in the workplace?

This should raise a red flag. It is as if a person's professional reputation automatically equates to some sort of assumed personal character far above reproach. Perhaps you are not interested in prying into another's personal life but have contemplated this phenomenon of adulation for those employees deemed particularly relevant or reputable. And perhaps you have been made to feel uneasy in a given work environment for daring to address as much.

But this example does not just extend to domineering bosses or visiting speakers delivering keynote addresses at business conferences. It might also extend to some "change agents" from outside of organizations hired to come in and help "steer the ship." Regardless of one's under-the-table affairs or backhanded deals, the change agent preaching a sincere and complete unwavering commitment to organizational excellence, in some cases, might better be described as a salary mercenary preaching a sincere and complete unwavering commitment to organizational excellence *to* the highest organizational bidder *for* his or her services. But even for a disingenuous change agent, the pressure to clap remains palpable. Why is that?

Action Plan

To play the game, you should know the rules. Be warned, the game is not fair, and the rules do not officially exist. The game is played like this: this type of abuser wants good things said about himself or herself *always*. The higher such an individual gets in a system, the better the things said about him or her are expected to be. Say something "good" about the abuser, and you are often not going above and beyond; you are merely doing what the abusive organizational leader informally expects of you. Every once in a while, say something "great," and you are brought up to your benefit. Say something "bad" about the abuser, and you are thrown overboard. If you can get to the top, maybe you can end the game. Godspeed.

The "What Attitude? I Don't Have an Attitude!" Tactic

"What attitude? I don't have an attitude!" Have you heard that one before? When someone with potential antisocial personality disorder abusively and vehemently communicates the preceding phrase to you in a repulsive, vile tone, do not worry—you are not necessarily crazy. Expecting someone animatedly livid in a tirade featuring this one-liner to appreciate your point of view—someone frustrated by your apparent inability to mend your wrongness in concession of his or her rightness—is like expecting your oven to buy you groceries. What's likely happening here in this sort of situation is a disconnect within the abuser's mind from rational and empathetic thinking.

This "What attitude? I don't have an attitude!" tactic manifests a tendency to renege responsibility for one's behavior while manipulatively twisting and shifting blame onto others. Obviously, no mutually agreeable end or resolution is sought after or strived for by the individual with a destructive, nasty attitude refusing to be considerate and empathetic toward the victim he or she desires to control.

Action Plan

Get ready. The following question is so important and, at first glance, deceptively obvious that concocting a quick answer may just strike you as incredibly effortless. Here we go: should you always stand your ground during the moment and attempt to teach someone staunchly committed to refusing to take ownership for his or her attitude toward you a thing or two? If you answered yes, please consider the following: when someone refuses to acknowledge giving you an attitude, that person probably isn't interested in acknowledging whatever other words or actions he or she may be utilizing to wound or dominate you with, right?

When someone dismisses you through refusing to acknowledge words and actions utilized against your person, you essentially are treated like an inferior being. On the one hand, you might consider saying to an aggressor—as one genuinely good-hearted and wise person would say to people who think it is okay to talk to others like they are not people—"I wouldn't even talk to my dogs like that."

But on the other hand, keep in mind, if you stand up and say such a thing, what you intend to accomplish—in effect, teaching another a lesson—may not register within an unaccountable individual's mind. Indeed, your standing for a principle might be interpreted as hostility and aggression in the mind of an abusive individual with antisocial personality disorder. As a matter of fact, you might encourage an abuser to mark you to incur his or her future wrath or, worse, instigate an aggressor's potential impulsiveness toward promoting hostile action in the present moment.

Unfortunately, besides any semblance of satisfaction you might glean from altruistically attempting to "help" an individual who has an unaccountable or destructive attitude through standing your ground verbally in the moment, you can gain very little. So often, empaths do not disengage from attempting to teach "right" and "wrong" when another is unreasonable and perhaps out of control—and again, instigation of these types of situations can be dangerous. Please exercise caution. The conscienceless individual might not process altruistic intention.

If you find yourself in agreement with the notion that altruism and love, somehow or another, are inextricably linked concepts, consider this: world-renowned sociopathy expert Martha Stout asserted that experiencing conscience is a prerequisite to experiencing love

(2005, p. 126). And from that angle, it becomes easier to build upon such a premise and theorize that, without conscience—and, therefore, love—a sociopath might possibly lack a singular life experience of ever having felt an authentic connection to altruism. And if that is the case, just imagine how misguided an attempt to convey your intended altruism may be with an individual lacking the capacity not only to appreciate it but to process it—all the more reason not to engage a personally unaccountable, potentially hotheaded and close-minded individual.

The empath often erroneously believes that through standing ground on principle in an altercation, the abusive sociopath might be able to have a concept "click" internally and be "fixed." In such a moment of well-intentioned but wishful thinking, the empath can reason that a concept "clicking" within an unaccountable individual's mind will lead to the learning of a life lesson and subsequent behavioral modification. Moreover, the empath might believe that through standing ground, the abuser will not pick on a particular empath again.

And why does the empath so often believe in these empathizations? Because these would be rational, empathetic assumptions on part of an empath—assumptions akin to standing up to a bully, or in this case, an adamant, righteous, unaccountable individual looking out for "number one" (but bully might work, too). Sometimes, in some dangerous situations, the best and safest way to stand your ground is to avoid abusers and attempt to go through appropriate channels. Discretion remains the better part of valor.

The "Smart Enough to Know I'm Smarter Than You" Tactic

Pop quiz: who is the smartest person you know? If you are absolutely certain it is yourself, feel free to skip this section. Welcome back, everyone. Have you ever noticed that some people feel quite at home telling others how they are not smart enough? Perhaps you have received a "Don't try to impress me. You can't," from someone.

For every person who has ever had the misfortune of being condescendingly cast aside as someone intellectually inferior, understand this: you are not alone, and please consider refraining from putting any stock into other people's snap judgments of your intellectual limitations. Reflect on this: some people feel so comfortable as intellectual authorities, eagerly willing to label and judge you based upon their perceptions of your intellectual inferiority, but their judgment of you is without merit and originates from a disingenuous place—a place where a grandiose sense of entitlement resides, likely fueled by an unhealthy, delusional egocentrism.

Another way of looking at this is to consider that if the people who label you as intellectually inferior compared to themselves or others were so smart, why is it that every single one of them still faces mortality? Why is it that they are not smart enough to end world hunger or homelessness? "Oh, but they are. They just have to deal with less-smart people, inhibiting their grand solutions," some might say? Well then, why is it they are not smart enough to overcome that obstacle as well? I earnestly do not intend cynicism for humanity's potential to solve problems—as I am quite the front-row fan, cheering on my fellow *Homo sapiens*—but I do intend to point out the lunacy of self-serving intellectual segregation.

Similar to the "ego advantage" tactic, the "smart enough to know I'm smarter than you" tactic practitioner can enjoy the privileges of entitlement afforded to him or her by egocentric delusions of grandeur. Troublingly, this poses a dilemma as the self-proclaimed intellectual elitist may operate destructively in interpersonal situations on the grounds that his or her superior wisdom justifies actions that may abuse others. From that vantage point, it becomes a lot easier to perceive how an abuser might self-justify manipulating others because doing so can be conveniently "deemed" by an abuser to be in a victim's "best" interest. Does the intentionally dishonest, "I'm doing this for *you*" sound familiar?

Some famous historical philosophers used to speak of "accidentals." In other words, the difference between two organisms, a characteristic attribute (for example, a height difference), might be considered an accidental—as if to suggest that so many of the differences between two members of the same species are random and irrelevant. Does it really matter if you are taller than a stranger? Does it really matter that we all are not exactly the same height? Does our unique height negatively affect our worth or value as human beings?

So another way of looking at it is this: we, according to many physicists, are composed of subatomic particles, made possible after at least second-generation supernovae explosions—how we even derive the atoms necessary for carbon-based life-forms in our blood. If we are all but slightly different combinations of stardust, theoretically, some of us might be slightly more or less intellectually capable subatomic agglomerations than others; but in the grand scheme of things, such distinguishing "accidentals" remain irrelevant.

I discuss accidentals because taking a step back and trying to see a bigger picture holistically, one can see the lunacy of intellectual prejudice. Expanding upon the example first referenced in chapter 2—regarding implications concerning the irrelevancy of fluctuation in human variation—some people can do more in less time than others on some paper-and-pencil tests. But so what?

Have they cured every cancer? Have they stopped the process of aging? Have they safe-proofed the world from pandemic diseases? Have they been any more successful in finding happiness? Have they concocted a fail-proof escape plan for humanity for when the sun becomes a red giant and consumes the orbital trajectory of the earth? So relax. Others' intellectual capabilities indeed feature limitation as well and are not a negative reflection of your authentic self-worth. You are incredible and incredibly capable just the way you are.

The truth is, we as a species likely have as many or more questions than we do answers, and that is okay. To be better than another at some "official" intelligence quotient test and disregard another as an inferior creature is not. No matter how much "smarter" anyone is compared to anyone else—arrogant people, prepare to feel potentially nauseated—we all can learn from others.

For us to wound or destroy one another through condescendingly dismissing others based upon our perceptions of their intellectual capabilities is also to wound and destroy one another through disavowing each individual in the pursuit of his or her legitimate potential. It is like telling an adult, "You're likely never going to be a professional athlete, so you do not need to bother maintaining or improving your body by doing exercise." Obviously, scientists know that exercise has tremendous benefits for nonprofessional athletes as well. Exercise even helps people live longer, healthier lives. And who are we, imperfect as we are, to engage in the discouragement of another's potential—be it potential for growth in body or mind?

Do we have the potential to solve complex problems that so far remain bereft of solutions? I, for one, hope so—and believe so. There is your capability, here and now, in the present. But that capability is but a temporary limitation to another characteristic of yourself that you constantly develop as you actively grow—your potential. To symbolize capability, imagine raising a hand chest high, palm facing downward and level, under an open sky. At the mention of *potential*, imagine an outstretched hand elevating high above the head, with palm still facing downward and level—as if to represent the figurative limitlessness of potential—as the extended hand symbolically representing potential fails to reach the impeding limits of an established ceiling.

Perhaps, you might wonder if I am implying that I do not believe in the accuracy of intelligence quotient testing. To some degree, yes—even though such tests are normed, they have a long way to go and may currently lack the technology to do what they claim. So then am I also implying that when an educator evaluates students' work, the educator should cease to offer formal assessment? In other words, should educators not engage in the practice of grading? No—grading is not inherently unethical, but I reason and believe that the ability, even privilege, to grade another's work does not entitle or specifically qualify one individual to judge another's intelligence. Rather, grading perhaps best remains treated as an altruistic action not to be abused by an evaluator's potentially antagonistic subjectivity.

Further, the assertion can be advanced that fostering and encouraging others' intellectual proclivity is not some politically correct mind-set to be digested and regurgitated by today's educator or philosopher but an attitude worth internalizing and living, day in and day out. The dismissal and rejection of another through intellectual prejudice—over an arguably distinguishable difference the span of a minute, quantum, microscopic distance—is sheer madness.

Action Plan

What can you say? What can you do? If you consider believing and potentially internalizing the following words—not just recalling them when it seems like the appropriate moment—you might experience surprise and begin to perceive the world slightly differently. Are you ready? "I'm smart enough never to assume that I'm the smartest person in the room."

Humility is healthy. It does not imply a self-degrading dismissal of one's strengths or a self-defeating overvaluation of one's weaknesses. Consider advancing a discussion on embracing a sense of intellectual open-mindedness and tolerance—and consider opposing others' propensity to cling to convenient constructs that rationalize "anything goes" entitlement. After all, such entitlement may be attained through self-bestowed intellectual elitism.

The "Making Up the Rules as You Go Along" Tactic

Perhaps you have, at some point, experienced a fascination with newspaper cartoon sequences. I imagine a sequence published to the tune of "Ring Around the Rosie" that goes something like this:

Explaining Sociopathy in Twenty-four Words

[Adults, join hands and initiate
circular dance.]

Make up the rules as you go along,
Go along, go along!
Make up the rules as you go along,
And blame...other people!

[Adults, release hands, fall down
(giggling optional).]

This folk dance, as I remember it—though with *slightly* different words—often involved young children holding hands and moving in a circular motion, culminating in a fall to the floor after the last line of the stanza. But the real sting of it is—it can be perfectly applicable to describe the malicious intent within the minds of some abusive adult sociopaths. Of course, major skepticism surrounds the premise that this assertion could be proven. For instance, what incentive is there for a potential offender to be forthright enough to admit this line of scheming may accurately reflect an offender's modus operandi? Nonetheless, the rhyme offers us the very plausible reality that "making it out there" may really be this simple for some.

I have this memory as a very young child of being in a footrace with my peer. The terms of the race were rather simple, something to the effect of, "[The] first one to reach the other side of the playground wins the race!" And we were off. At the end, there was a problem. Though my body beat my friend's to the finish line, my friend's mind seemed to beat my body through stating something to the effect of, "Last one there is the winner, not the first one."

Of course, to make up rules as you go along does not necessarily imply sociopathy. For example, anyone can, innocently enough, face the need to modify rules on the spot, especially if you ever had to line up a group of small children to receive ice cream. But if you can get away with making rules up as you go along that negatively affect others, are you so sure you wouldn't?

I hypothesize that making up rules as you go along is an abusive sociopathic behavior utilized by some individuals with antisocial personality disorder rooted in three motives: first, advancing self-interest; second, an authentic disregard for the consideration of other individuals; and third, an attractive, appealing opportunity to exercise control. Self-interest and a disregard for the interests of others seem figuratively two sides of the same coin. Like the races of three- and four-year-old children, even adults in competition may run shortcuts influenced by self-interest as a means to gain an advantage over competitors, a phenomenon exposing self-interest and disregard for others' interests as inextricably linked.

While the preceding sentence sounds just like a description of the nature of "anything goes" competition, a significant question lurks beneath its surface: can "anything goes"—or, in other words, making up the rules as you go along through dirty play—be completely done away with and shut down for business? To the credit of the world, it's not that humanity hasn't tried. But an individual's self-interest can override two critical assumptions that even the best-made set of rules takes for granted: first, everyone wants to accept playing by the same rules; and second, everyone agrees to accept playing by the same rules.

In addition to advancing self-interest, a genuine disregard for considering others is hard to overemphasize. For instance—believe it or not—literally, there are people on this planet who, if such a practice were acceptable, would, with no sense of remorse or injustice, show up to work with an injunction signed by a judge that reads, "This person is now exempt from all organizational rules, policies, procedures, and negative perceptions by superiors, and should be, with all due speed, promoted as quickly as possible above all others because that would appear to be most fair for the individual in question." I imagine, if this were to actually happen for the first time, after the media parade subsided, the employee, feeling entitled to a new lease on life by a judge's signature, would still fail to appreciate the significance of the world bending over to meet his or her interests at the expense of others. But perhaps that's just me. Let's talk about control.

It is worth mentioning—an often overlooked detail, especially by those who are less controlling—some people, perhaps more so than others, desire to control, sometimes with an intensity that appears to rival breathing, which can explain the attractiveness of making up rules. Of course, people might make up rules for any number of reasons. But a lust for power is a need within some individuals that often remains overlooked.

Eventually, when a policy or rule appears to be breached by an individual with enough control, moral and ethical relativism often are utilized to craft loopholes for an individual, or even an entire organization, to escape, if not unscathed, at least undercriticized. Someone with enough power—and by power, in this instance, I mean control—can literally operate above the rules of a system, even a system that should, in theory, prohibit making up rules as you go along. Which also implies that someone with enough power can disavow a less-powerful organizational member making a good-faith effort to operate by the rules of a given system, a critical detail concerning wounding and destroying "empaths."

So in other words, not only can an individual operate above an established set of rules and, if fortunate, escape consequence, but such an individual can wound and destroy a less-powerful individual following established rules for little or no reason at all, even just for fearing another may expose an individual with sociopathic tendencies in an unfavorable light. Research even suggests that psychopaths feel fear, though they may struggle in recognizing the credibility of a particular threat (Pedersen, 2016). This preceding sentiment can serve as the motive for attack when sociopathic abusers perceive a less-powerful organizational member as not only a future, potential competitor for position but as a present threat of "good conscience" who might be willing to disclose how a potentially sociopathic individual may operate outside the parameters of established rules. I—*no, we*—could offer so many examples of how we have observed this phenomenon in our lives, to the point we would have to release multiple volumes of anthologies. Dare I say, there may not be enough trees in the rainforest for the paper we would need to write our grievances.

Action Plan

Earlier, I asked a tough question. If you can get away with making rules up as you go along for your own convenience and potentially at the expense of others, should you? That's all I wanted for you in this action plan: to consider your thoughts on others making up rules as they go along *as you read along*. There's nothing more I can do than what you've already just done yourself.

The Partial Explanation or S'il Vous Plaît: The "Partially True Explanation" Tactic

Hypothesis: some abusive, sociopathic individuals do not feel obligated to reveal the whole truth, nothing but the truth, and often do not. But when pressed, they will reveal the partial truth, to the least minimal degree, in an effort to engage in self-preservation and achieve or retain dominance. The following example illustrates how this might manifest between two partial-truth tacticians.

Sally and Joe dated for two years in their early twenties. After a serious relationship, the couple broke up abruptly on bad terms. Around that time, Joe told his friend Andy that he had to break up with Sally because she is a "stubborn, inconsiderate, self-centered human being bent on her delusional art career." Similarly, around the same time, Sally shared with her friend Emma that she broke up with Joe because he is an "arrogant, insensitive, good-for-nothing, not-ever-going-anywhere, ambitionless loser." Ten years later, Sally and Joe happen to run into each other in a mall.

By chance, both feel comfortable and decide to interact. After the initial pleasantries, the acknowledgement of a past interpersonal relationship verbally surfaces. And Sally proceeds to tell Joe that the reason that she felt they needed to break up was so that she could pursue her educational interest in art history. And Joe tells Sally, "Yeah,

I decided it was the best thing for me to let you go so that you could take that opportunity in that city. It hurt, but I did that for you."

Of course, Joe is lying through his teeth; and unbeknownst to Joe, Sally knows what Joe really told Andy because, over the years, Andy happened to share as much with Sally's friend Emma. Sally decides to call him on it. "But I heard that Andy said you were happy to break up with me because I was inconsiderate and only cared about my dream of being an artist." Joe, caught off guard, doesn't know what to say.

He hesitates. On the one hand, if he flat-out lies and denies talking to Andy, it probably won't sound believable. If he walks away at this moment, word might spread that he had no defense to this particular probing by Sally. So he decides to admit to it, *sort of.* Joe responds, "Yeah, we talked, but that's not what I said to him—honest. I wouldn't have said that."

After an enduring short moment of silence that screams of Sally's skepticism, Joe jumps back in with, "Besides, Andy was sort of a shady person. He probably would say something like that. And I think he may have had feelings for you at the time. It was in his interest to say something like that. I'm shocked. I really am."

In the preceding situation, two potentially sociopathic individuals refused to take ownership for what they had previously said about each other. Both attempted to create an alternate history to mask their own interests, intentions, and images, as well as to throw off each other's efforts to form a negative perception of the other. For the sake of the hypothetical scenario, assume that Joe claimed his part in terminating the relationship was selflessly rooted in letting Sally go to pursue her dreams when, in reality, Joe probably fought tooth and nail with Sally because Sally didn't dream of prioritizing Joe over art. Moreover, Joe's abusiveness includes establishing Andy, not present, as his convenient scapegoat.

Ironically, while both Joe and Sally talked ill of each other to their friends (Andy and Emma respectively), in this situation, it appears that only Sally is aware of Joe's postrelationship commentary. And though Joe shamelessly tries to look like a selfless hero in his less-than-smooth attempt to redefine his past intentions, Sally is not exactly honest herself. Sally, in a self-centered manner, attempts to leverage the information originally disclosed by Joe to Andy—and then transmitted from Andy to Sally, by way of Sally's good friend Emma—passive-aggressively to express contempt for Joe (you could even argue, to take a shot at Joe). And though, in her memory, she knows she has done the same sort of badmouthing against Joe while speaking with Emma, Sally feels no obligation to cast the same judgment on herself that she will direct at Joe during their postrelationship encounter for dominance.

The presence of lying, fabrication, embellishment, or deliberate misrepresentation does not automatically lead to diagnosis of antisocial personality disorder. And this tactic is by no means intended to be all-encompassing for every conceivable situation nor judge people negatively. As stated previously, a fundamental tenet of this writing is not to judge the individual but, if anything, the individual's destructive actions affecting others, as well as him or herself. After all, when you travel, perhaps you have schemed to arrange a neighbor to misrepresent that you are home by collecting your mail left at your front door. And perhaps such intentionally deliberate misrepresentation saved you from attracting the attention of a would-be burglar.

However, deceiving others without remorse or accountability through destructive partial explanations is what is at issue here. Doing so takes advantages of others' emotional health and psychological well-being. In particular, a major negative consequence of the utilization of these misleading partial explanations is that the victims—through being requested to trust others' less-than-altruistic intentions by being asked to believe in and trust what they hear, as well as *whom* they hear it from—are being abused, manipulated, and made to suffer.

Action Plan

One of the most powerful tools you can utilize when individuals attempt to beat around the bush and offer partial explanations is to listen calmly and then ask a direct question, a very direct question, regarding responsibility and liability for the issue at hand. If others insinuate that you are out of line but won't seem to say it with words, they may just be giving themselves up through their actions that, indeed, they are intending to manipulate you by beating around the bush with the deceitful partial truth.

This is a lose-lose scenario. Remain mindful. If you acquiesce to dishonest individuals for the sake of what seems like deescalating a conflict, you, in turn, are teaching individuals that you will tolerate their lack of personal accountability going forward, a destructive proposition for you and your relationship with another—and that is no partial truth.

The "Chameleon" Tactic

One of the talents some skilled sociopaths have in their arsenal is an ability to modify the meaning of past words in the present moment on the spot. The "chameleon" tactic consists of blending in with word or action to adapt, survive, and receive a competitive advantage through deception, manipulation, and false representation. When such an individual becomes aware that he or she has made a contradictory statement or engaged in some sort of action that may be construed as insensitive, politically incorrect, or controversial, he or she enters damage control. Cleverly, the very impulsivity that might have brought forth wrongs may be used to mend them.

Damage control might manifest through a claim that something was said with humor, or perhaps a full-on denial to others of a true, intended meaning. No matter how skilled at recovery from the unintended minor faux pas or even to the major intentional social impropriety, this incurs a certain weakness and vulnerability for the sociopathic abuser. Specifically, the argument can be made that an individual's conscience impairment leads to lacking a conscious awareness of what statements or actions nonsociopaths may deem politically incorrect, offensive, or abusive. Like a chameleon blending in with surroundings, the skilled sociopath identifies an opportunity to modify his or her words or actions to mollify and obtain the approval of others.

Action Plan

The sociopath, in common culture, is notorious for the characteristics of charm, glibness, and ingratiation. Such skills win the day in recovering from even the most blatant solecisms and social blunders. What can you do? Remain equipped with an understanding of what is transpiring. Ask yourself, were two contradictory claims made? What motivation would an individual have to enter into damage control through clarifying, fabricating, or embellishing? Does the person in question possess a certain quality that begs you to see the "best" of that individual?

And what about the potential sociopathic abuser? Remember, abusers don't always know which statements they make that others will construe as offensive or abusive or even why. Put yourself in those shoes for a moment. Learning what is acceptable to say with regard to ethical and cultural norms for a person potentially without a conscience is incredibly difficult. It is probably like learning a foreign language on the job and never knowing what you may be misinterpreting and mispronouncing in real time, quite literally.

Beyond the Charm: The "'It' Factor" Tactic

I t is no *new* news that psychological literature and research describes the sociopath as a master of the skill of charm. However, what is meant by charm may still lack precise clarification. This is how I see it: to be charming, within and of itself, might help an individual come across as pleasant to others. But seeming pleasant to others does not necessarily lead to a charming individual getting his or her way. In regard to those who use charm disingenuously to get their way, something more significant is happening than just the general presence of charm or charisma. There is a certain "it" factor at work—something that accompanies that efficacious charm and does the dirty work. Some people have "it." Some people don't.

Perhaps charm never was the best descriptor because some individuals who are charming are not inherently manipulative. Moreover, individuals who are not conventionally charming can—*through* the "it" factor—manage to influence others into rationalizing their behavior as exceptionally likeable, even harmless. For example, think of a celebrity figure that does something outlandishly irrational, even criminal, and is received as a "cool" or "hip" personality that can do no wrong. So what is that "it"?

Here's what "it" really appears to boil down to: superseding charm, the "it" factor is a tactic used by an individual with sociopathic tendencies, subconsciously or otherwise, to influence others into having a rose-colored interpretation of a manipulator's character or, at least, current intentions. Here is how it works. While assessing another attempting to work you with no shortage of charisma, ask yourself these four questions: "Does this person influence me to always see him or her in the best light? Do I find myself tempted to give this person the benefit of any doubts that I may have concerning him or her? Do I find myself desiring to project positive character attributes onto this person? Do I feel afraid that making a negative assessment will incur the wrath of the individual in question?"

After all, if you find yourself feeling afraid, then the possibility exists that another does not value your emotional well-being or health. And if abusers do not value your sense of psychological security, the possibly exists that, in a destructive manner, they might only value what you can do for them. If you answered yes to any of those four questions, you are likely allowing yourself to succumb to another's "it" factor. And in effect, you may be in a position where you are giving away your power and allowing yourself to be manipulated.

Action Plan

The "it" factor is intangible. And even some people who have "it" may not register as charming at all times. Remember the four questions: "First, does this person influence me to always see him or her in the best light? Second, do I find myself tempted to give this person the benefit of any doubts I may have concerning him or her? Third, do I find myself desiring to project positive character attributes onto this person that might be unwarranted? And fourth, do I feel afraid that not assessing another positively will incur the wrath of the individual in question?"

An affirmative answer to any of these four questions should lead you to think long and hard about the possibility that you are dealing with a sociopathic abuser's "it" factor. After all, if you answered in the affirmative for any one of those questions, then the "it" factor successfully influenced its way into your decision-making, didn't it?

Another way to think about this is while charm may be in the right neighborhood, the "it" factor is more likely the right, specific street address at which the individual with sociopathic tendencies works others' minds for his or her advantage.

Identifying Safe Targets: The "Effective Temper Tantrum" Tactic

When small children and psychologically unhealthy adults alike do not get their way, it is not uncommon to witness a temper tantrum. Why do people perform temper tantrums? Well, for any number of reasons, including but not limited to impulsivity, aggression, vengefulness, irritability, a lack of willingness (or even ability) to control one's behavior, a desire to feel dominant and controlling, a desire to blame others, and a possible inability to care about the feelings and safety of others forced to witness and experience such outbursts. But perhaps, most importantly, more than any other reason, all too often—temper tantrums work.

Sure, not everyone is a very small child who, during a temper tantrum, will be immediately rationalized by others as understandably exhibiting age-appropriate behavior. But believe it or not, some adults never stop throwing temper tantrums. And again, for a specific reason: so often, they work. In six words: insert behavior, get what you want.

Naturally, the question arises: why can they work? While a psychologist could have a field day with the preceding question, three reasons appear demonstrably evident: first, the abuser throwing the tantrum often intimidates victims to repress challenging such outbursts. Such intimidation does not necessarily have to imply a physiological threat but perhaps some sort of leverage or power over the recipient of the tantrum.

Second, tantrums can work because the very victims exposed to and witnessing them may project positive attributes onto offenders. Victims, for example, might rationalize why such behavior, in a given case, classifies as circumstantially acceptable, especially from individuals who are higher ranked in organizational cultures. In such a scenario, the nonsociopath victim may project inaccurate and underserved positive character attributes onto a sociopathic abuser, likely a workplace superior or key organizational leader, rationalizing the offender engaged in a tirade on justifiable, circumstantially acceptable grounds—perhaps due to stressful or extenuating circumstances not privy to lower-level employees.

And a third major reason tantrums work, simply enough, is that they are, in some instances, considered acceptable, and even "ideal," behavior. An allowance for impulsivity and aggression are an attractive proposition for some potential tantrum throwers who might be looking to take shortcuts on the sociopathically adjusted playing field themselves. In effect, if it is understood that throwing a tantrum in a given environment is acceptable—even featuring behavior that directly abuses and violates others—abusers may utilize such a precedent as leverage to allow for and perpetuate an environment of psychologically unhealthy interaction.

Action Plan

A common misperception of tantrums is that they are always by-products of hair-trigger aggression. However, even the most effective adult temper tantrum must remain dormant and passive until two important parameters allow for the onset of aggressive behavior. The first parameter, *when*, deals with the timing concerning the moment a temper tantrum can be effectively thrown; and the second parameter, *who*, deals with an abuser establishing specific victims. In particular, the *who* parameter entails an abuser identifying victims through their perceived and projected inability to subdue an abuser's offensive.

Consider the "identifying safe targets" premise this way: would a physically fit adult who is very angry, valuing his or her health, go into a bar and pick a fight with a group of other physically fit adults all at once? Not unless that individual was ready to go the hospital, or worse. But take that person and put a safe target around him or her, like a small child or even a less-physically-dominant adult. In these sorts of situations, abusive sociopaths are able to identify safe targets and use people like emotional punching bags for any number of self-gratifying motivations. Here are just two: to relieve frustration through impulsively belittling or punishing others for their perceived "inferiority" (possibly to feed the abuser's ego) and to satisfy an internal desire to control others.

Attempting to identify an abuser's incentive or motivation to throw a tantrum may be obfuscated by any number of murky variables. Nonetheless, remember that an abuser's motive might only remain intrinsically rewarding, such as fulfilling a psychological internal desire without any identifiable extrinsic prize. So what can be done to counter the *when* and *who* parameters necessary for abusers to engage in effective temper tantrums?

First, to prevent the *when* component—again concerning the timing of a tirade—please avoid being alone with someone whom you believe might throw a temper tantrum. Remember, not only can such a scenario be unsafe, but also, what actually happens in a person-to-person interaction is different from what a liar might claim happens. Regarding the *who* parameter, preventing an abuser through wishful thinking is not realistic. Nonsociopaths often make the "empathization" mistake of rationalizing that an abuser will not abuse victims who make efforts to treat an abuser particularly well. Toward this goal, for instance, victims might emphatically attempt never to "cross" the abuser.

Furthermore, it is not feasible to assume a potential victim can successfully influence a potential abuser to identify a victim as too innocent, powerful, or risky of a target to be abused. However, if you are able to identify a potential abuser preemptively before a tantrum or, less fortunately, before the next tantrum—you might be in a situation where you can empower yourself and others to take corrective action through identifying a toxic personality, engaging in documentation, communicating through effective channels, and putting in place strategies not only to disempower abusers but to empower victims. As a human being, you do not deserve to feel threatened by another individual who may or may not comprehend or care about the psychological terror he or she creates and imposes on others.

Surrounded But in Control: The "I'm Surrounded, Now Everyone Else Put Your Hands Up!" Tactic

Some people successfully do something most others do not and cannot. It is a rather amazing feat. Some people can insert only people into their lives over whom they have complete control. Imagine that for a minute—you do not, for instance, marry based on who feels right, attraction, or love, but a certain, possibly sadistic, form of compatibility: an ability to control another emotionally. Imagine that you work with and socially interact with only those who do not challenge your sense of dominance. In effect, you can do and say whatever you please and surround yourself with others who accept and even encourage your treatment of them.

Perhaps most people might feel that they could never live that way because they would never have their interpersonal needs met. Think about it—if you managed to surround yourself only with people who submitted to your dominance, you might lose quite a few relationships. You might feel incredibly alone, even depressed.

Not everyone, however, feels, needs, or achieves meaningful emotional connections to or with others. To this end, the American Psychiatric Association—in its alternative model for antisocial personality disorder—even offered an interpretably commensurate term for this concept: "incapacity for mutually intimate relationships"

(2012, 2013a). Am I claiming that sociopaths do not feel meaningful emotional connections to others? Not necessarily, and certainly not every individual is alike. I believe the research is too nascent, especially to make a sweeping generalization.

I am, however, speaking to the lack of need for interpersonal connection within some individuals—an important distinction from a desire for solitude. Certainly, you have met someone who hardly ever chooses to socialize or, in general, communicate with others. But have you ever met someone who did not seem to need *connection* with others?

This provides a fitting opportunity to address a major contemporary misconception circulating among so many. That misconception is as follows: when individuals do not appear to need any acceptance or belonging from others, or interpersonal connection with others, such individuals must be miserable. But perhaps this is best understood as a classic empathization right up there with "Everyone feels guilt."

The argument can be made that due to the ongoing nature of neuroscience research, we cannot implicitly reach summary judgment that those who lack a desire for interpersonal communication or connection are necessarily unhappy or depressed. Thus, we cannot conclude individuals will inherently choose to engage in actions directed toward interpersonal harmony and companionship with others. Moreover, it remains prudent to remember then that an individual who lacks a desire for interpersonal relationships may come across as incredibly skilled at socially interacting with others (see the "it" factor).

I have proposed an assertion that this phenomena of surrounding one's self with others who are controllable while simultaneously lacking a need for interpersonal relationships represents a behavioral characteristic of at least some individuals with antisocial personality disorder, but what makes it a tactic exactly? Chiefly, when individuals do not need any acceptance or belonging from others, or interpersonal connection *with* others, and surround themselves with others who do, they have leverage. Such advantage allows for the possibility of manipulating individuals who do need interpersonal connection.

Action Plan

If you observe someone who appears intentionally "surrounded," realize that your needs, present and future, may lack priority. As touched upon previously, remember that identifying such individuals is not by any means a matter of identifying a recluse, castaway, or even a misanthrope. Rather, such individuals might seem socially ordinary and unexceptional, or even appear remarkably affable—yet personally content with experiencing high-frequency social interaction with negligible interpersonal intimacy.

Be on guard for observing a cutthroat aspect in others' personalities, particularly an individual appearing remorselessly unaffected by cutting ties with a close associate on grounds the associate no longer served some convenient purpose for the abuser. And in addition to the ability of another to disassociate effortlessly from significant interpersonal relationships, pay attention for words or actions that suggest the abuser does not value or need others, no matter how networked and surrounded by others he or she may be. For instance, an abandoner might feel numbness or indifference to the grieving of a victim now pained to be removed from his or her life, even if the victim offered a genuine, healthy friendship and endearing regard toward the abandoner.

Be mindful of those who can throw others out of their lives with ease when their dominance seems challenged, or when the victims they are intentionally surrounded by resist doing their bidding—or simply cease serving some purpose or being of some interest. To that end, you have likely heard from actors, or perhaps in real life, the viscerally painful, stinging phrases, "I don't need you," or "I don't need them anyway." Temporarily resist any filter that urges the perception of the aforementioned sentiments to be interpreted only as indicators of the presence of excessive ego and an intention to hurt another emotionally. And then, as difficult or unpleasant at it may be to ponder, consider that someone who does not need others may simply and directly be speaking such a phrase as honestly as possible—even when such honesty violates the emotional well-being of the message's recipient and, in turn, arguably provides vindicating direct evidence of an abandoner's lack of need *for* others through an exhibited lack of need to treat others with value.

Such individuals may really not need others the way most people do. To such individuals, others may truly be perceived as that expendable—and interpersonal relationships may truly be perceived as that valueless. Again, if such people are possibly born this way, does that inherently make them in possession of destructive character? I would argue not, provided such people do not intentionally abuse, exploit, or manipulate others in order to create an interpersonal social network based not on mutual affinity, respect, goodwill, and consideration, but control designed to reinforce self-interest.

The "'I'm Not Perfect, Neither Are You' Consolation Speech" Tactic

Have you ever called someone out for doing something in his or her own self-interest at the expense of another? Not something small like helping one's self to the last french fry but something like putting another's career in jeopardy for one's own professional benefit? Perhaps you didn't even get a denial; you got an admission, but the truth was served with a little side of, "While we're at it, let's talk about your faults." This phenomenon occurs interpersonally between individuals behind closed doors as well as in group settings, such as during speeches and meetings. It provides a means for the offending party to concede the utilization of dishonesty, deception, and in general, any number of abusive behaviors by mitigating one's own faults through identifying and refocusing upon another's perceived faults as falling short of perfection themselves.

This concept seems very much like ad hominem attacks on another's character, but it's something far simpler than attacking another's character personally. It's simply the impersonal tactic of benchmarking and justifying abusive behavior by setting the bar of what is considered ethical or moral not on a high road but based upon the perceived misdeeds of others. And to the benefit of those who utilize this destructive and abusive sociopathic tactic, there will always appear the perception of misdeeds by others. Translation: some might offer, "We can always argue people do wrong, so we can always use the 'I'm not perfect, neither are you' line of reasoning to do wrong too."

Action Plan

To use a boxing analogy, the "I'm not perfect, neither are you" consolation speech lends one to believe you got another on the ropes. After all, there was an admission of fault! An admission sounds like a breakthrough, and why? Because an admission of fault tempts a nonsociopath to believe that a potential sociopathic abuser is learning to feel responsible and become accountable through the sheer act of not lying to deny his or her questionable behavior. And if you are invested in and love a sociopathic abuser, what could be more promising than a moment like that? So your first initial reaction may be to put on kid gloves, dismiss the misbehavior, and reward the telling of truth.

So subtly, though, with this tactic, the *perception* of your faults—however unwarranted—becomes the focus of the interaction. And then the roles completely reverse: an admission by another turns into an accusation against your character, and the next thing you know, you are on the ropes. What do you do?

First, realize as painful as it is, the teachable moment does not always effectively translate for others. If anything, by allowing yourself, when truly innocent, to be manipulated into thinking you deserve to be attacked and then communicating as much, you are teaching a sociopath abuser that in the event he or she admits fault to you, upon redirecting the perception of fault the other way *toward you*, he or she can resist interacting with you as you desire and ultimately avoid your grievances. So tragically, such unwarranted counteroffensive attacks may come from others with superior leverage, like a toxic personality boss whom one cannot afford to address a grievance with in fear of losing job security. In such situations, a victim might lack the recourse altogether to address the manipulative, unaccountable behavior.

However, when you recognize the tactic and the abuser's motivation to engage in it, you are empowered with an understanding that I believe aids in diminishing its potential for promoting pain. In essence, through seeing it for what it is, a glorified blame game, the attack loses its teeth to address a victim both personally and honestly. And the resultant depersonalization aids a victim in ceasing to internalize the bogus offensive against his or her potentially stellar qualities as an employee or individual in general.

Unfortunately, for some abusers, the truth is, when environments allow for it, however petty, when it comes to self-preservation and self-advancement—what better way to admit dishonesty, deception, and abusive behavior *than* not to take direct ownership for dishonesty, deception, and abusive behavior *through* focusing on the alleged shortcomings and faults *of* others? In the workplace, what can be done is to do your best not to engage in any questionable interaction with others who have no problem pulling this tactic out of the toolbox. When the limelight comes across their calculated misdeeds, rest assured, if they can refocus attention on the perceived faults of others with ease, they can do so just in time to zone in on and even fabricate your perceived "faults" and "misdeeds" as well.

The "Always Deserving to Be the Most Deserving" Tactic

Okay, this definitely will not come as a surprise: some people who have the same jobs work significantly harder than coworkers. Perhaps this will come as a surprise: oftentimes, performance evaluation rubrics cannot accurately distinguish between the two workers. And this, for some, will definitely come as a surprise: some people, *regardless of any circumstance, always* believe they are *the most deserving* to be the most deserving for any reward. For example, a worker may come to work late every single day at an occupation where punctuality particularly matters yet believe he or she single-handedly represents the most deserving candidate for a promotion or increased job security.

Likewise, those who believe themselves most deserving of rewards often reason they are least deserving of punishments. The late worker may be extremely disgruntled and loathe arriving at the job but may reason that the on-time worker is more deserving of being let go during downsizing for something as trivial as "breathing loudly on the job." It sounds like madness, but this phenomenon surrounds us. "Always most deserving for reward, least deserving for punishment" is not merely a mind-set; it manifests through affecting the behavior of an individual vying for "number one" on the sociopathically adjusted playing field.

Okay, maybe that represents an extreme. However, ask yourself the following question: how many people do you know that "mail it in" who would identify with the following sentiment, "I am one of the most deserving for reward, top five—scratch that, top three—and least deserving of punishment"? What is at root of this phenomenon? Arguably egocentrism and a grandiose sense of self-entitlement take center stage.

But perhaps not so far behind their spotlight is an unhealthy sense of delusional thinking and self-deceitfulness. In effect, some individuals, potentially wired to view themselves as superior to others, assume that because they believe they try, they therefore must be trying the hardest. It is as if such individuals take comparative adjectives (e.g., *hard worker*) with which they might truly self-identify and elevate those adjectives to the superlative (e.g., *hardest worker*).

The problem here, especially in some organizational systems, is that some people—through delusional, grandiose thought processes—*truly* discredit the merit-based rewards for which others may prove more deserving. Moreover, the undeserving recipient of reward might, medically speaking, lack remorse for any gain at another's expense. Conversely, many nonsociopathic individuals— even through a sense of guilt to possibly receive another's deserved credit unfairly—may find it particularly difficult to ask or campaign for a personal reward for which they might, in actuality, even prove most deserving. Though, in a healthy manner, such nonsociopathic individuals might like the idea of at least being considered for some sort of recognition.

Nonetheless, many nonsociopathic individuals take ethical issue with, and perhaps lack natural ability for, engaging in unsolicited, self-interest-based personal promotion. Whereas others may feel very comfortable in politicking for their own self-interest. Sadly, in many circumstances, supervisors charged with the task of considering and promoting worthy candidates are subjected to undue influence.

Action Plan

Considering one's self "always the most deserving to be the most deserving" is a mind-set that some people live in, day in and day out. And quite frankly, sometimes it pays off for those with a grandiose sense of entitlement, exponentially. Part of what's underlying the problem is egocentrism. But part of the issue just may be that such individuals struggle to understand that other people are different than themselves.

How so? Well, if you reason that you are always most deserving of reward and least deserving of punishment, it is likely hard to imagine how others are any different than you, always looking out for "number one." To utilize an analogy, for some sociopaths to be asked to believe that not everyone is looking out for number one is a difficult task—like a nonsociopath being asked to believe that not everyone has a conscience and can care about other people. Due to these polarizing extremes of perspective, I refer to this phenomenon as *sociopath inverse image theory.* In essence, one's self-perception might drastically influence his or her understanding concerning others' motivations and thought processes.

It seems something else contributes to the "most deserving" mind-set that warrants acknowledgment. It's difficult to put a finger on, but there seems to be a disconnect within some people's minds between the assigning of reward and punishment and the belief in the legitimacy of a merit-based system. It's sort of like a vote of no confidence for having faith in the beliefs that people *should* credit other people, people credit others fairly, and that people can credit other people genuinely without some sort of strings-attached "What's in it for me to help you?" self-interest. Abusers of merit-based systems are largely responsible for those connotations. And through that light, it can become easy to imagine how someone might destructively reason, "Well, if it's all the same, I might as well get what's in it for me—even if comes at another's expense."

So, realize, any effort on your end to have 100 percent buy-in into a merit-based system may be unrealistic, so plan accordingly. Strive for objectivity. And think about this angle to pick yourself up:

when you are absolutely certain that you worked harder on something than someone else with the same task and received no distinction when another did, you may fail at trying to convince an evaluator not because you do not make a compelling case, but because the evaluator might possess an incapacity to value objective merit-based systems—similar to an undeserving individual who lacks the capacity to cease erroneously believing him or herself as most deserving for reward in any circumstance.

"Why Are You Crying?": The "Empathy Police" Tactic

Perhaps you have pondered questions such as, "Why do some people cry more frequently than others?" or "Is it just as easy for every individual to cry?" Perhaps you have even ruminated upon the very personal question, "Why do I cry?" If your answer is somewhere along the lines of, "Because of how someone else treated me just sort of corresponded with tears coming out of my eyes," I empathize.

Unfortunately, remember tactic 1. In some abusers' perception of reality, *You alone chose to make yourself cry. You alone are responsible for feeling emotion and have no one else to blame. You feel sad? Well you alone did not control how you responded to others pushing your buttons.* Sound abusive much?

Some people can deliver the four-word phrase, "Why are you crying?" with a straight face and a deadpan, emotionless stare—like nothing, as if they are talking to an object before them. And unfortunately, a targeted victim's exhibited emotion may be interpreted by a "Why are you crying?" interrogator not as a justifiable reaction to an external stimulus but as an irrational overreaction. Subsequently, tears may not file a motion for your grievances but rather register within an abuser's mind as reasons to categorize you as "unstable" and "unfit."

In brief, asking another why he or she is exhibiting a particular emotion may be a ploy to get a victim to divulge more information for the ulterior motive of using the disclosure against the victim or others. This tactic involves manipulating and controlling others through targeting and judging victims' alleged emotions or behaviors to be lacking in empathy, on one end of the spectrum, and to be overly emotional on the other.

The "Empathy Police" Tactic Spectrum

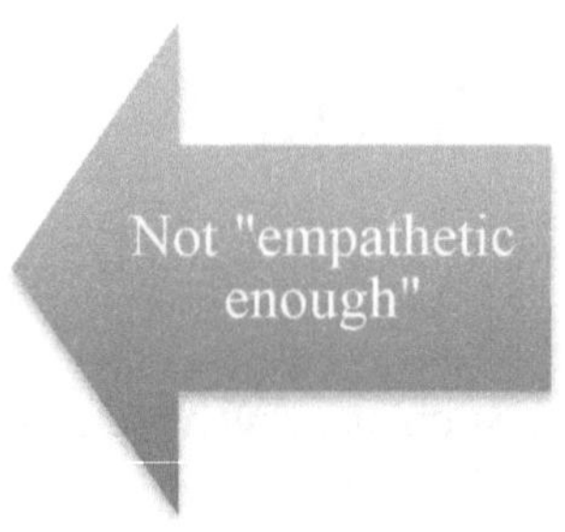

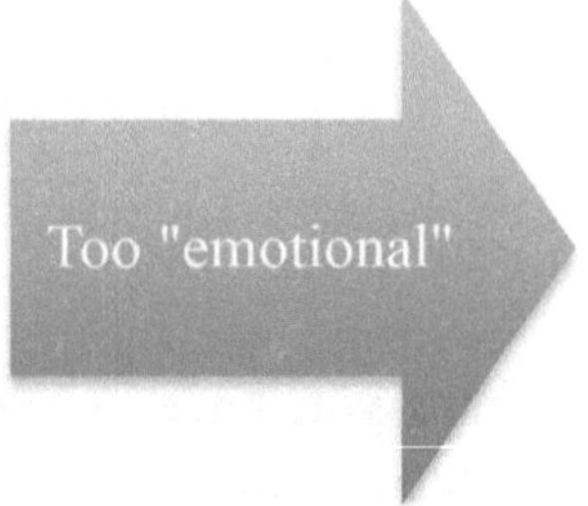

Not "empathetic enough"	Too "emotional"
— Targeting victims to be marketed as antisocial (ironically, often a tactic of hypocrisy)	— Judging others to be "too emotional" or "too sensitive," perhaps at the expense of being more "rational"
— Falsely accusing victims of being callous to others	— Judging others to lack control of themselves (e.g., "Get a hold of yourself!" "Let it go," etc.)
— Falsely accusing victims of being unconcerned for others' welfare	— Judging others to be inferior due to their exhibited emotions and behaviors

Concisely, some abusive individuals manipulate and dominate by judging others' actions to exhibit too much or too little empathy or sympathy—really, whatever arbitrary "amount" is convenient and beneficial for an abuser in a given situation. In the case of crying, an individual can be judged to be exhibiting too much "emotion." And on the other end of the spectrum, abusers can arbitrarily determine who is not exhibiting enough emotion and concern for others.

To illustrate this, take for instance the insensitive, ruthless individual who conveniently slanders a competitor who appears to be showing a negligible amount of empathy for a third party. Of course, the allegation is not necessarily an authentic episode of "Practice what you preach" rooted in concern for an aggrieved victim. But perhaps, rather, a calculated attack on a chosen competitor's character for some tangible benefit, like gaining market share.

Examples abound. Callous people can so coldly accuse for self-serving purposes—ironically exploiting the warmest and most considerate people to fall in line to do their bidding. Remember, on the sociopathically adjusted playing field, demonstrating an "appropriate" amount of empathy for others by an abuser may be more along the lines of going through certain publicly visible motions *designed to create the perception of empathy* rather than a matter of authentic personal investment in another's suffering.

Action Plan

When asked why you are crying, or "Is something wrong?" recognize—*please* recognize—that the question does not imply the asker cares why you may feel what you feel, or for that matter, can care. If you project an ability to care onto someone asking such questions, you may be doing more harm than good. Do not internally translate the attention shown to you through such an inquiry as an admission of genuine concern for you by another. After all, your exhibited vulnerability and emotional expression may be judged as an overreaction by an abuser and thus interpreted so manipulatively as a telltale sign of your "weakness" and "inferiority."

Naturally, this leads to the question, should people just avoid crying so as not to show vulnerability and prevent manipulation in interpersonal situations? In other words, should people just repress emotions? Many researchers have suggested that repressing feelings is not healthy. Moreover, the argument can be made that behaviors and actions, regardless of involuntary feelings, should remain nonabusive toward others.

The human ability to feel emotion involuntarily is remarkable. The argument can be made that the ability of *Homo sapiens* to cry, let alone to express emotion in general, is extraordinary because it represents an intimacy with the human life experience that words fall short of communicating. Further, the argument can be made that while many other organisms involuntarily feel emotion, the human emotional experience is especially unique due to the species' elevated neurological capacity for self-awareness. Though others may wish to dissuade you, consider being proud that you cannot control when you, have in the past or, will in the future involuntarily feel emotion.

If anyone truly looks down upon you for something like crying, there is a chance he or she really cannot relate to what it feels like to weep involuntarily due to an emotional experience. They are not any tougher than you, though so many messages deceptively suggest that is exactly what they are. If you involuntarily cry, and everyone could feel and experience the world like you, quite possibly, *everyone* would be crying.

Don't let others convince you that your ability, which may be foreign to them, is, in fact, a personal limitation. Don't buy into the argument that if you were psychologically healthy and strong, you would know how to be more "numb" at the "right times." No one is entitled to shame you for being in tune with your feelings any more than he or she is entitled to be a manipulative, superficial authority on deciding who is or is not too sensitive or empathetic—when, really, such judgments are all too often merely by-products of an abuser's self-serving motives and agenda—hence, the title of this tactic: the empathy police.

The "Superior Value Proposition" Tactic

Have you ever felt like someone wanted too much credit for a "favor" he or she did for you? Or, perhaps, has someone communicated to you that you owe him or her something significant in the present in return for something minor you received in the past? I theorize that some sociopathic abusers undervalue others' contributions and overvalue their own contributions to others. I cannot prove this theory, but it represents multiple observations. Perhaps what is at the root of this phenomenon is an inability to care about and objectively value others' value propositions—directly resultant from egocentrism, lack of concern for others' feelings, and a willingness to exploit others for personal gain.

What is meant by value proposition? Chiefly, what you give or do for others correlates with an amount of value you place upon your gesture. Here is an example: you buy your friend an expensive meal. That sounds costly but doable, right? Now, contrast that gift to the following: you buy your friend a house. For the sake of the example, assume you are not particularly wealthy. Okay, so the gift of the house equates to far more value than the gift of the meal, right? The measure of value of the gift, in your eyes, is extremely high. Now, to make things interesting, assume your friend feels that you "owe" him or her a house. You might be thinking, *Wait…come again?*

Assume your friend paid several thousand dollars for you to get your car repaired when you really needed to borrow some money, and now that friend feels that he or she is owed a house. It does not add up, does it? While this scenario is extreme and outlandish, it accurately represents the reality of how ridiculous overestimations of value propositions occur in real life. On a much smaller, subtler scale than buying a house for someone undeserving to demand from you such a tremendous financial sacrifice, overestimations of value propositions occur every day.

Here is common-enough example: an individual, say an "old friend" with sociopathic tendencies, personally asks you to take the time to watch an entire television or podcast program in which he or she is featured. Say you make time to do as much even when you are very busy. In the near future, you catch that individual in person and pay him or her an authentic compliment about his or her role in the program you made time to watch. You attempt to arrange a future social interaction with the individual, who proceeds to blow off the opportunity with his or her questionable excuses. Perhaps you remain persistent in attempting to plan a social interaction and receive more excuses.

Clearly, you can directly address the elephant in the room and chance experiencing the individual's wrath (and potential subsequent permanent disregard for your existence), or you can choose not to address the issue and endure the subpar, emotionally abusive treatment you receive moving forward. It is a win-win for your "old friend" who asked you to take your time to watch the program—really to feed his or her ego—because, either way, you deal with the treatment you receive, and your "old friend" still gets rid of you. Even your having to contemplate that conundrum shows evidence of your friend's willingness to disregard your feelings and hints at how manipulating you leaves your friend unaffected. In this example, to your "old friend," the value of your time is worth watching a program in which he or she is featured while, simultaneously, your old friend appraises the value of your time as not worth the value of his or her time for a future social interaction. We can even express this mathematically:

According to the value proposition overestimator (VPO),

your time $\leq$ watching a television program featuring the VPO.

however

your time in the future
+ your acknowledgement to VPO of watching the program
+ your authentic compliment
+ your communicated desire to spend time with VPO
< your VPO's time

where

your time < VPO's time.

Here is a similar example that occurs among "value proposition overestimator" musicians: self-proclaimed higher-profile musicians with sociopathic tendencies quite frequently appraise their brand value higher than other musicians. For instance, even a self-proclaimed "talented" singer, instrumentalist, or songwriter may feel that other musicians are lucky to perform or record with him or her in a group. This may lead to lesser-valued musicians being pushed around in a "my way or the highway" scenario. Such lesser-valued musicians may not be financially compensated but nonetheless remain expected to learn and practice the egotistical, imperious musician's material on their personal time, often receiving absolutely no credit for their sacrifices in the process.

Furthermore, they may lack a chance to have input in decision-making for a music group, decisions that may adversely affect them. Moreover, they may receive inferior interpersonal treatment and incur hostile work environments. In the mind of the self-proclaimed higher-profile musician with sociopathic tendencies, not only does the unilateral decision-making affecting the lower-profile musicians seem fair, the "big deal" musician may feel like the lower-profile musician is more than compensated fairly by simply having an opportunity to play with him or her—for which, according to the sociopathic, self-proclaimed higher-profile musician, the lower-profile musician should be "grateful."

Here is a slightly different example of value proposition abuse: John ran into Allen, whom he knew from first through eighth grade. They seemed to get along and socialize well with each other in elementary and middle school. Allen's family moved away right before he would start high school. Now in their twenties, for the first time in many years, both happen to be at the same location.

John comes up to Allen and enthusiastically asks, "Hi, is your name Allen? My name is John. I think we went to school together!" John sticks out his hand to shake Allen's. Allen remembers John but, with an expressionless face, slowly looks down at John's extended hand and, for a split second, hesitates, feels numbness, and then with visually evident reluctance, agrees to shake John's hand.

John says, "It's great to see you! So what have you been up to?" Allen unenthusiastically replies, "Hi…what's going on, man?" to deflect initiating a conversation for which he appears emotionally unavailable. John then shows an engaging interest in Allen and says, "I heard you played a sport in college!"

Allen's attention now focuses to the conversation since it deals with Allen and, in a serious monotone voice, proceeds to correct John, "I did not play one sport in college, I played two," hinting that John's compliment was somehow beneath Allen. John is taken back by this but manages to finish the conversation with a warm, "Well, it's nice to see you again!" A day or two later, John sends Allen a social media friend request. And several days after that, Allen rejects it.

In the preceding example, Allen exhibits unhealthy egocentrism, self-obsession, and disregard for others. Allen seems to lack an interpersonal awareness of others' feelings and time. Allen overestimated his own value proposition—though, of course, he does not perceive it that way, and moreover, he likely does not care. Specifically, through the action of deleting John's friend request, Allen communicates that he does not value John as worth his time.

Ironically—in a most contradictory manner—Allen, never intending to share his time with John in the future in any capacity, abusively uses John's time in the present to correct John's facts about Allen's grandiose sense of personal achievement! Examples abound. The list could go on and on. Perhaps a similar situation with an individual has crossed your mind from your life experiences as you have been contemplating the previous examples.

Action Plan

The "superior value proposition" complex supersedes its identity as a state of mind and becomes a tactic the moment an attempt at interpersonal manipulation commences. This might manifest through an individual with sociopathic tendencies underestimating others' contributions, overestimating his or her own value proposition, or even attempting to guilt another into engaging in an unmerited action that stands to benefit a manipulator—as in the case of a manipulator callously demanding sacrifices of a victim's time or assets. Or manipulation might manifest through a victim's internal agonizing as he or she deliberates the pros and cons of addressing subpar treatment received from his or her manipulator. Many dysfunctional interpersonal relationships represent derivations of the preceding concept.

In effect, at least one party, treated poorly, perpetually weighs the choice of confronting an abuser or continuing to receive abuse. While, at first glance, which decision to make may seem obvious, the issue remains much more complicated. The victim, especially an empath victim, may feel devastated to lose not only a significant interpersonal relationship, imperfect as it might be, but also may fear the loss of the opportunity to associate with and care for the flawed individual. Moreover, it is not merely a matter of a fear of losing an interpersonal relationship, the empath may fear the tremendous intrapersonal pain that the loss of an individual may bring—not only to the empath victim himself or herself but for others, as in the case of children when an empath may be enduring emotional abuse from his or her abusive spouse and contemplating divorce, for example.

It bears mentioning, people may control their actions and behaviors, but they do not necessarily control what they feel. So to simply dictate that empaths should "override" their feelings of pain represents a gross overgeneralization, often found in contemporary "pop" psychology. In summary, to take action, one must understand the probable futility in attempting to convince a manipulator to reappraise his or her value proposition. Perhaps the strongest angle to accomplish this feat might be attempting to offer an appropriate benchmarking example that provides direct evidence an individual with a comparable value proposition to a given manipulator's *acts, operates,* or *treats others,* in a superior manner.

The "Quantifying the Unquantifiable" Tactic

Are you measurable? Allow me to rephrase: do you feel that you should be measurable? On a scale of 0 to 10, or 0 to 100, do you feel that you can rate intangible aspects of your character—like your level of altruism or degree of "niceness" as a person?

Taking this concept a step further, do you feel comfortable with others rating your intangible qualities, as opposed to you rating yourself? A popular criticism might be, "Sure, it is an imperfect system, but it is a lot better than not rating others." The reality of the situation is that rating others' intangible qualities inundates every aspect of the world around us.

The practice has achieved widespread acceptance, especially in corporate cultures. It incurs imperfection and inaccuracy and, potentially most flagrantly of all, assumes that individuals possess the ability to quantify the value of others' intangible characteristics. I hypothesize that if such a practice were illegal and suddenly became legal, it would face fierce resistance and further be challenged as unethical and off-putting to many.

However, as it stands, the age-old practice is so prevalent, finding the first instance that established a precedent of one individual quantifying another individual's character with a numerical value might truly remain impossible. Wherever you might stand on the issue, with whatever good intention you might possess, understand that in the wrong hands, to rate with subjectivity can be intended to control—and to control can be intended to dominate.

Action Plan

It is not the good-intentioned "rater" assigning a numerical value to another's character that is necessarily at issue. Rather, the danger remains ever present when individuals rating others happen to possess dishonest, deceptive, and disingenuous character themselves. More than simply a disregard for others' feelings, an individual with sociopathic tendencies involved in rating others may engage in a reckless disregard for others' safety.

To illustrate, imagine a highly qualified individual for an employment vacancy being numerically rated inaccurately during an interview for an ulterior motive. Or imagine the competent worker whose boss rips him or her on an annual performance review as a means to engage in an unprovoked personal vendetta, perhaps even for simply "not liking the employee."

It may be a hard pill to swallow, but it appears that numerically "rating" an individual's character attributes equates not only to "controlling" and "dominating" an individual's opportunities but "controlling" and "dominating" the individual through authoring the narrative that inaccurately defines his or her "perceived" identity and limitations. Conversely, it should be noted that the abusive rater with disingenuous character who manipulates a character or competency numerical assessment system can also appraise a "liked" individual with intentional inaccuracy in an undeserved, positive light.

Finally, if you find yourself feeling undervalued or underappreciated by the metrics of others, consider reflecting upon, and even saying aloud, the following sentence: "Just because a system has metrics does not mean it is objective, and just because numbers might be used to describe me does not mean that they can define me; I am a person, not a number." After all, as one sociologist put it, "Not everything that can be counted counts, and not everything that counts can be counted" (Cameron, 1963, p. 13).

The Future Tense of Gaslighting: The "Sabotaging by Convenient Presumption" Tactic

Tactic 50—you made it. You did not croak. Thank you for reading, and analyzing, and considering, and planning for a better world. And, sincerely, thank you for your time. Well, I have some good news and some bad news. The good news is, this tactic deals with abuse specifically going forward into the future—so it is particularly fitting to serve as the last tactic.

However—the bad news is—I saved the longest for last. It was not to be cruel; there just was so much that called for conversation. Culminating all the other sections, this action plan deals with the future *as you prepare* for the future. I hope you might glean something valuable on your journey navigating the sociopathically adjusted playing field from the insights concerning the "distance," "sabotage," and "gaslighting" themes prevalent within this tactic.

According to the *Oxford Dictionary*, gaslighting means to "manipulate (someone) by psychological means into questioning their own sanity" ("Gaslighting," n.d.). There are multiple ways in which gaslighting manifests. Skilled abusers manipulate victims into questioning their perceptions, judgments, recollections, and emotions concerning past situations in hopes that victims misremember experiences that actually transpired, as well as those that never did.

Within and of itself, gaslighting is a tactic skilled manipulators utilize to con and take advantage of others.

Gaslighting deals with intentionally and falsely accusing others of past actions for which they are truly innocent—but what about the future? Specifically, what about falsely accusing others of what they "will do" in the future? Have you ever noticed how people have attempted to accuse you of what "you were going to do anyway"?

Welcome to the future tense of gaslighting—the "sabotaging by convenient presumption" tactic. Why the term *sabotage*? Simply put, the saboteur premeditates the destruction of, well, anything deemed to be undesirable—be that a personal commitment, an interpersonal bond, a victim's *opportunity* for a fair and impartial opportunity, the perception of a victim's truly altruistic intention, or even, most fundamentally of all, the victim him or herself.

It is no surprise that many abusive people have sold others' character short, taken shortcuts to avoid truly knowing others, and have falsely accused others of who they were and are—all for a manipulator's own personal advantage and convenience. But have you ever been in a situation where someone justified hurting you by accusing you of who you will be and what you will do in the future? You know, like someone saying, "Okay, so I lied to you, but you and I both know what you would have done." This train of thought also manifests through, "I betrayed your trust, but you would have done the same thing to me."

The problem here, of course, is that another person does not truly know what you would have done. It creates a convenient loophole in just about any situation for an abuser to justify just about anything. And through making such an assertion, an abuser so subtly attempts to challenge the sanity of a victim, intending to stir up self-doubt within his or her mind.

These gaslighting-into-the-future lines of convenient reasoning do not just occur between people with some degree of familiarity with one another but also with abusers who know nearly nothing about their victims. And to know nearly nothing about others can represent an ideal situation for an abuser. Intentional distance from closeness to victims, like intentional ignorance toward attempting to know a victim's true character, can be an abuser's optimal scenario. And why? Primarily because knowing who a victim truly is makes it far more difficult for an abuser to paint a victim in a certain convenient light. Think of it as an intentional communication breakdown designed by one party. Through this breakdown, an individual avoids any future opportunity for interpersonal connection and potential conflict resolution that might possibly force the abuser's hand into conceding anything to a victim that the abuser has no desire to forgo.

For example, think of the "popular" school-age child who fashions him or herself to be above communicating with a friendly, good-hearted classmate who is unjustly and abusively deemed to be undesirable, awkward, and possibly even unfairly labeled "creepy." This example also extends to the adult sociopathic abuser who labels a coworker—who happens to be nice and friendly to him or her—a "stalker" because the abuser refuses to entertain the possibility of interacting with that individual socially, even in the workplace, as the abuser does not desire to be affable with someone he or she does not want something from.

To this end, there actually exists a term that can describe manipulative, destructive individuals who intentionally and deceptively allege they are being stalked by another: *false victimization syndrome*. Unknown to many false accusers, however, a common difference between legitimate and illegitimate stalking accusations is that, most often, a true stalking victim questions a scenario, searches for alternative explanations, and hesitates to label another individual a stalker; and also of note, in many cases, the false accusation of stalking has been proven to correlate with Cluster B personality disorders (Mohandie, Hatcher, and Raymond as cited in Meloy, 1998).

An individual with false victimization syndrome, lacking empathy or remorse for others, might be quick to injure an unjustly accused victim's reputation. In contrast, many actual stalking victims, through empathizing with their stalking abusers *as human beings*, might be more inclined to hesitate before communicating a potential stalking situation to authorities in fear of negatively impacting another's life or future. In other words, truly being stalked can be so unbearable to accept as a potential reality that many affected individuals search for less-dire explanations for suspicious circumstances. And in the same vein, such individuals remain reluctant, not trigger-happy, to violate another's reputation by labeling him or her a stalker. Nonetheless, for some sociopathic abusers desiring to create and maintain distance in particular interpersonal situations—such as lacking a desire to acknowledge and communicate with a coworker into the future—it truly can remain far easier for the abuser to label another a stalker than to commit to interacting cordially with an individual deemed undesirable.

Distance is a major tool. Have you ever experienced someone who did not like you—really, for no reason—and perhaps even said as much to mutual friends; but no matter how welcoming and honorable you were to him or her, he or she refused to get to know you? Intentional distance from others can be one of an abuser's figurative best friends.

Not only that, abusers can desire intentional emotional distance not only from victims themselves but also from the truth concerning a particular victim's character, perspective, intentions, and circumstances. For example, someone in a position to help a victim may desire to maintain distance and not learn the facts of abusive circumstances affecting a victim—and subsequently engage in the "disingenuous voluntary recusation" tactic—so as not to be forced into taking any corrective action. In essence, through such intentional distance, it is possible for individuals with self-serving agendas to turn a "blind eye" to helping others dependent upon them in their moments of need.

Distance can also be found in the abusive "You and I both know what you would have done anyway" sentiment. In such an instance, the abuser implicitly desires distance from knowing the truth of what the victim would truly do in the future because the truth might contradict a manipulator's destructive course of action in the present. After all, a victim might do something honorable and nonabusive in the future—unlike his or her abuser claims. And if what a saboteur presumes abusively and destructively *in the present* contradicts what a victim would have done nonabusively and constructively *in the future*—the abuser stands to lose ground on legitimizing his or her convenient, self-serving rationalizations.

The distance between who a victim actually is and who a victim can be painted as creates the ideal blank canvas for an abuser to construct who the victim *will be* and what he or she *will do* in the future—for all convenient intents and purposes. And being painted by an abuser's convenient intention is not merely a treatment reserved for those deemed to have crossed an abuser with whom the abuser has some familiarity. To that end, an abusive sociopath might engage in the "sabotage by convenient presumption" tactic with victims he or she knows well, hardly knows, or has never even met. Ergo, it is even possible that an abuser might attempt to sabotage meaningful relationships in the lives of unmet strangers, or even hardly known acquaintances, until they are all but destroyed.

To illustrate this concept, imagine a saboteur in a romantic relationship who selfishly lacks any desire for his or her partner to continue healthy older friendships that predate the romantic relationship. Take, for instance, a hypothetical sociopathic fiancé who does not want his soon-to-be wife's childhood best friends in her life anymore. So the fiancé subtly pushes them out of the life of the romantic partner. Very possibly, these lifelong friends can feel his coldness as well as his unwelcoming disinterest in them. A skilled sociopath can tightrope this line so well that the old friends cannot quite claim an antagonism toward them accompanies the abuser's disinterest in them—thereby making addressing the issue that much more difficult and unlikely.

As time passes by, the friends see less and less of their close friend, his future marriage partner, until one day, such socializations cease altogether. If these companions choose to confront such a situation, the skilled sociopath fiancé can then turn on them and attack them by playing the "victim card" to his romantic partner. He can claim that his partner's friends never liked him, falsely accuse him, and never wanted him in the picture. Of course, this is all a ruse, and he knows what he is doing to fool and influence his romantic partner into severing ties and destroying relationships with them.

Through the preceding example, the fiancé sabotaged by convenient presumption. Not only did he attempt to push others out of the life of his romantic partner, he possessed an internal antagonism toward the older friendships his romantic partner possessed. And then, at an ideal moment, he manufactured an opportune scenario to claim such friendships were, and always will be, unhealthy, against his person, and opposed to his relationship with his fiancé.

It remains important to note that such antagonism within an abuser does not necessarily require animosity, or even hostility, but merely a lack of value for others. For the sake of the example, suppose that the childhood friends have always provided an especially healthy, positive influence in the life of the manipulative fiancé's romantic partner. Nonetheless, they are deemed to pose a threat to the abuser: they represent the opportunity cost of the romantic partner's time that the abuser desires for himself. And also, they represent an identity of his romantic partner that he has no interest in preserving—as he selfishly constructs the identity of who he desires his partner to be going forward.

You might be thinking, *We are all adults here. Come on, how can that really happen? Obviously, a fiancé has a say-so in whom he or she retains as friends. And additionally, since we are adults, most would agree, one's best friends are a part of one's life, and people who love each other will selflessly want their romantic partners to have access to their healthy significant friendships even after they are married.*

If you agreed with the preceding logic, I applaud your devotion to selflessness, but the fact of the matter is that some abusive sociopaths have a very subtle but effective system for seeing sabotage through in real life. And to the credit of a master manipulator, this skill, "the sabotage by convenient presumption" tactic, can require incredible deftness. After all, in line with the preceding example, an abuser would have to fool a significant other into thinking that the abuser truly values his or her partner's past life experiences and meaningful friendships, right?

But regarding those past life experiences, it is necessary at this moment to clear up some confusion. Assume that the manipulative fiancé does authentically desire to form an exclusive, lifelong partnership with the romantic partner. However, simultaneously, the individual abuser in question does not want to embrace his or her romantic partner's past, inclusive of significant friendships and family ties.

This leads to a perplexing question: how can it be that an abuser authentically desires a "happy" lifelong partnership with a romantic partner but also desires to sabotage and subtly aid in severing the ties between that partner and his or her significant, healthy, meaningful interpersonal connections? The answer is rather simple: selfishness, as manifested through egocentrism, and an incapacity to experience remorse for the feelings and needs of those the abuser desires to separate intentionally from the romantic partner.

You just might be pondering, *So a hypothetical saboteur dismisses the romantic partner's needs for belongingness to others, yet that saboteur authentically desires to treat the romantic partner particularly well? That sounds like a contradiction.* Through remembering that not all people experience the same degrees or stages of empathy for others, it becomes rather easy to understand that some individuals who are ruthless and callous to most can be considerate, and even warm, to a select few. Moreover, concerning the thoughts within the mind of the sociopathic abuser, the argument can be made that the empathy experience is not genuinely selfless, chiefly because the individuals receiving special treatment are not necessarily viewed as independent entities but, rather, perceived as extensions of the self by the abuser.

Furthermore, it is easy to become confused about this phenomenon because, as humans, we often perceive self and others through set biological parameters, such as defined bodies that are distinct and separate. In turn, *Homo sapiens* often remain quick to perceive an intended action from one creature that positively affects another independent creature as a gesture of altruism and selflessness. To that end, for example, a psychopath might show incredible compassion for his or her own child, not even because the child symbolizes his or her line of biological survival but simply because the child, within the mind of the parent, may represent "self."

This brings up the question, so are all sociopaths, or psychopaths, actively promoting "self" within their own lives? In effect, are they all looking out for and taking care of "number one," treating the external *who*s and *what*s they perceive as "self" especially well? The answer clearly remains no. Both the *DSM-IV-TR* and *DSM-V* even go so far as to offer that part of the criteria to diagnose antisocial personality disorder can be a "reckless disregard for safety of self" (2000, p. 706; 2013, p. 659).

And that safety does not have to be fast cars racing against oncoming traffic or bungee jumping without a rope, but a reckless disregard for one's own psychological and emotional well-being. And by implication, if an abuser engages in destructiveness and recklessness toward his or her biological self, he or she may engage in destructiveness and recklessness toward others whom the abuser also perceives as "self." Therefore—an abuser does not necessarily treat others perceived as "self" in a healthy manner.

But just because sociopaths might be inclined to mistreat others does not mean that they will. There exists a powerful reason such individuals are not necessarily promoting "self" and willfully living lives of abusing others. Specifically, while some individuals with antisocial personality disorder remain self-destructive to "self," others are intentionally constructive in how they choose to respond to their own condition. For example, an individual struggling with a numbness and apathy for others' feelings and who resists hurting others with every ounce of his or her being arguably lives heroically.

Another common manifestation of the "sabotage by convenient presumption" tactic is the mind-set, "In the future, I don't have to be good or nice to people who I determined have not been good or nice to me." In this instance, the past consists of the perceived shortcomings of others' behavior as interpreted by the abuser while the future is represented by the abuser's justification for yet-to-occur destructive behavior *to be instigated* by the abuser. To attack the logic of such a premise, consider the following.

While, at first glance, "reciprocating niceness to others perceived to exhibit niceness first" may seem to reflect a sense of goodwill and fairness, identify the flawed reasoning that such an assertion exposes. Specifically, if everyone were to operate as their own exclusive and "infallible" judge of what constitutes "nice" treatment by others, there would be tremendous chaos. For example, just imagine how an individual could easily construe an innocent glance from another as admissible proof that someone does not like him or her. Therefore—the premise that "I am only obligated to make an effort with those who I have judged to previously make an effort with me" poses serious problems, thereby promoting toxic interpersonal behavior.

Through utilizing the "sabotage by convenient presumption" tactic, an abuser can justify ceasing to be—of all things—nonabusive to a victim for the indefinite future. However, such an assertion requires an important caveat: specifically, while it is imperative for individuals attempting to maintain and promote healthy interpersonal relationships not to engage in sabotaging others by convenient presumption, it would remain unhealthy to others—as well as unsafe—to presume no one will ever act abusively in the future. For instance, imagine how dangerous it would be to presume all criminals would absolutely never intend to commit future crimes.

In other words, presumption is not inherently unfair, unethical, or abusive. To recall an example offered in the "assume, act, abdicate, and repeat" tactic, if you choose not to walk down a dark alleyway where others are loitering, based on a presumption there might lurk danger, you just might save yourself from being mugged. Therefore, the argument, "If I presume there is a chance that someone will engage in future abusive behavior, I am always acting unfairly, unethically, and abusively" can be easily defeated.

Action Plan

The future tense of gaslighting—the tactic of sabotaging by convenient presumption—demonstrates manipulation, deceitfulness, callousness, and even disinhibition, as exhibited through personal irresponsibility. For instance, through this tactic, an abuser has an avenue to create a justification for any yet-to-occur future abusive behavior, as well as a means to create an easy way out to escape from responsibly honoring commitment. Ironically, through this tactic, a saboteur can renounce a commitment by conveniently and falsely accusing a victim of a breach of contract or character. In effect, through this tactic, an abuser who has engaged in a contractual arrangement can shed out of his or her skin into a new one, so to speak, to nullify current commitments and obligations by blaming others for unlikely yet-to-occur future transgressions.

Pay special attention to the deceitful, disingenuous communications of affirmation and acceptance for others that do not seem to be reflected by an abuser's actions. To illustrate this point, in the preceding example concerning the fiancé, it would not be unrealistic for the abusive fiancé to claim to like the childhood friends of his romantic partner. Imagine the issue coming about: "What do you think about my friends I grew up with, whom I have known for so many years?" The abuser might respond, "They are great! We have got to do more things with them!"

Look out for instances where an individual falsely accuses others of "what they will think" and "what they will do." Such presumptions often seek to serve the accuser's interest. Additionally, look out for presumptions that feature unhealthy amounts of distance between an accuser and an adequate attempt to know the accused's character, feelings, or understanding of a given situation or issue. Remember—the more distant abusers keep you, the easier it is for them to create their own inauthentic perception of your true identity.

Through keeping the victim at a distance, the abuser can enjoy the benefit of remaining ignorant toward learning the character of the abused. In this way, even an individual who may not be diagnosed as having antisocial personality disorder can create a convenient defense mechanism to avoid confronting possible guilt over his or her treatment of others, whereby he or she justifies his or her future abusive behavior toward a victim based on a flawed and inaccurate perception of a victim's imagined character flaws. Some might better term this behavior as a classic example of doing what is easy as opposed to doing what is right.

Also regarding "distance," look for a convenient attitude of, "It is okay to encourage being mean to another—because I never liked him or her anyway. And he or she may not be nice to me even if I tried to get to know him or her—so I am justified." Furthermore, recognize that through this train of thought, an abuser can even lie to him or herself to justify being nasty to a victim through rationalizing that the victim—as perceived by the abuser from a convenient distance—deserves abusive treatment.

To that end, it is worth noting that an abuser erroneously perceiving an individual to "cross" an abuser intentionally is not the only point of origin that may serve as motivation within an abuser to attack a victim through sabotage. Sometimes the abuser intentionally and willfully desires to create the parameters for claiming to be crossed because any reaction by a victim can be used by the abuser against the victim to further, of course, engage in sabotage by convenient presumption. To provide an example, an abuser might not truly feel aggrieved yet proceed dishonestly to gaslight that a victim "crossed" him or her in the past, for the sole purpose of subsequently justifying no longer "playing nice" in the future with a victim—based on dishonest, convenient reasoning that the abuser "already tried" with the victim. And thus, through doing so, the abuser creates an avenue to rationalize and self-justify that the victim does not deserve future consideration for receiving positive behavioral interaction from the abuser. Nonetheless, regardless of an abuser's motivation, recognize that an act of sabotage against a victim does not necessarily concede that a victim truly engaged in any wrongdoing whatsoever.

Unfortunately, there is very little that can be done to safeguard against this tactic, except to protect one's self emotionally from abusers attempting to do this to others. The "sabotage by convenient presumption" tactic might as well be entitled the "guilty until convenient to prove someone innocent" tactic because abusers reserve the right to paint victims as guilty for future transgressions without reasonable proof. This phenomenon presents a lose-lose situation on the sociopathically adjusted playing field. Moreover, trying to talk an abuser out of falsely accusing others in the future for personal gain might prove to be a fruitless endeavor.

Nonetheless, remain cautious of abusers' convenient and flawed reasoning, often exposed through their impulsive quickness in concluding they are exempt from trying to be nonabusive with specific individuals. A significant portion of the action plan strategy for this tactic concerns one of the only plausible defenses to these sorts of infractions: acutely recognizing how this phenomenon may be occurring around you for the benefit of abusers. When you recognize it, be on guard while developing interpersonal trust and emotional intimacy with those who might desire to do this to others because you just might be next.

Part III

Epilogue

Flowers and Weeds

I worried. But then it hit me. The tactics never had to be just right—or, for that matter, perfect. They merely had to catalyze reflection. Reflection becomes identification, which then becomes opportunity. And opportunity provides an avenue for positive impact and betterment. I feel content to catalyze. Many hours spent hoping to encapsulate thoughts with the limitation that is the written word, and it finally occurred: I just needed to get it in the ballpark because reflection advances and does the rest.

The zoo teaches so much about life. Not just lessons regarding the way that species independently behave or even interact with one another, but the zoo also offers insights about human perspective. Merging together at the confines of exotic animals, artificial aestheticism and natural beauty intersect.

For many zoos, the price of admission is determined based on an arbitrary market value. Such a price might be associated with a calculated value representing access to the officially housed biological species, in consideration of maintaining the property, plant, and equipment utilized to provide a means for visitors to move around and experience attractions. But for me, a self-identified recreational aficionado, one particular zoo experience often blurs into the next.

Like déjà vu, the memories just run together. I recall hearing the various species of birds chirping through a zoo's trees. And landing nearby, the pigeon and the crow so subtly urge me to reconsider the world as I know it.

Disconcerted, I restlessly contemplate—what if the common pigeon was the rarest of all birds? Would I still find it so visually unremarkable? Would I appreciate the opportunity to view a pigeon in person and hear its particular vocalizations? Or—would I perceive the bird as I do in my current state, unfazed and uninspired by its presence?

Meanwhile, I envision the squirrels frolicking and scheming nearby. Apathetic, I disregard the impressive fast-twitch muscle movements, followed by frozen, still-frame bouts of paralyzing eye contact. Can the squirrel be searching for meaning as its eyes gaze both outward and into my own? And if the squirrel was of the most uncommon creatures in the world, would I feel particularly appreciative to view one for the first time?

During these blurred-together recollections, my mind races, resolving to find answers immediately. But not just any quick answers, answers that I could live with for a lifetime. And in the distance, I visualize the boundary. Often a chain-link fence covered in weathered fabric, as if to keep a bystander from garnering a free view of the valued spectacle to behold inside.

Of course—from an economics perspective, supply and demand seem to dictate that a rare creature would be of particular financial value to feature on exhibit at a zoo. But it never adds up. It never "feels" more than a meaningless logical rationalization to appreciate the canary more so than the crow. It never brings closure. Not with all the undervalued animal trespassers incapable of being erased from my collective zoo memories, appreciable in their own right.

And then I am forced to ask myself, why do I struggle to appreciate them? Who taught me this? Did I learn this? Or is this how I feel? And if I learned it, can I "unlearn" it?

I visualize the well-manicured landscaping force-feeding repeatable patterns of begonias, impatiens, irises, and Loropetalums *challenging me* as I press onward in mind from one exotic animal's enclosure to the next. All the while, somehow, not even by choice, I remain mindful for the unintended growth of other greenery: the weeds and grass blades teething upward through the pungent mulch, hugging the walkways, intruded upon even further by what else— more crows, pigeons, and squirrels alike.

I struggle to find closure. Searching my feelings, the obsession to manicure nature was not necessarily my identifiable objection. Rather, perhaps it was more along the lines of the obsession to manicure only the flora that was deemed to be of value and worth preservation.

And then it hits: what if I had never seen anything green before? What if the planet on which I resided had only rare patches of plants while primarily being covered in barren rock? In such an event, would I appreciate viewing weeds as an adult—if that, indeed, was the first green growth I ever experienced? Would I find weeds to be "beautiful"?

Many face a similar predicament in contrasting native wild-flowers—not for sale—growing in close proximity to flowered land-scaping projects near roadways. Some find beauty in the wildflowers and perhaps regret not having ever been exposed to their names and known histories. And to the observation of many flower enthusiasts—even the grounds of a nursery that is well-stocked with a vibrant and colorful floral selection can feature wildflowers randomly growing on the very same property.

What should *Homo sapiens* make of this? Functionally, are the flowers that are carefully arranged for sale any more valuable than the wildflowers growing in the crevices of concrete? And in regard to such functionality, would the for-sale flowers have some advantage toward other living organisms—not necessarily as pollinators even but, say, at some other skill set, such as more effectively releasing oxygen for human consumption through photosynthesis?

Assuming they do not, the point is, if there is no authentic reason why some flowers in a respective, given climate are deemed to be of value and others are not—or why some animals are deemed more desirable to be featured in zoos—what should this tell us about people? Sure, some flowers are arbitrarily deemed marketable and attractive, but are they truly any more valuable than wildflowers? And if you saw an image of a pigeon relayed back from a probe orbiting another planet—and it was the first pigeon your mind ever registered—are you so sure that you would fail to find it awe-inspiring and beautiful?

Therefore, remain mindful. No matter how undesirable of a wildflower you are ever appraised to be, never forget an abusive individual does not truly determine your worth. And no matter how nonvaluable of a wildflower anyone might ever deem you, never forget that they do not truly define your beauty. And most importantly of all, never forget that you are, *indeed*, beautiful.

From the Cradle to the Grave

Whenever someone truly attempts to belittle others or, in general, claim they are worthless and incompetent, remember this: everyone, and I mean *everyone*—a multimillionaire executive, a brain surgeon, a rocket scientist, a creator of some unheard of, exponentially profitable technology, similar to a person in a medically induced coma—was at some point dependent on others when they were born. And not just before birth and at birth but *after* birth.

Humans did not simply learn to feed themselves, fend off predators, and create life-saving, habitable dwellings independently of other humans. Nor did any human, in his or her lifetime, achieve modern technological advancement independent of the contributions of his or her predecessors. For example, the invention of the automobile benefitted from advancements in mechanical engineering preceding it since at least the first Industrial Revolution.

Where does this lead us? Today, in the minds of some abusive sociopaths, no one else is needed. From a certain myopic perspective, arguably classifiable as a hero complex teeming with narcissism, abusers perceive and categorize other humans as worthless and valueless.

So selfishly, the present moment for an abuser experiencing a perceived self-sufficient independence from others—who, to him or her, are easily deemed to be irrelevant and expendable—supersedes all other moments of the abuser's own previous "dependence" on anyone. This mind-set is so ingrained into some abusers that victims can literally feel a sense of psychological trauma merely by experiencing an abuser's words and actions. In such cases, victims might experience feeling emasculated, devalued, disenfranchised, dejected, invalidated, "dumb," worthless, or any other number of negative emotions. But just remember: everyone needed someone else.

The unfortunate reality of the situation is that teachable moments do not necessarily translate—no matter how well explained they might be to abusers. Ergo, trying to convince abusers who treat other humans with condescending, patronizing, even mean-spirited attitudes by countering with the principled logic that such abusers once needed others may prove a fruitless endeavor. No matter how cogently even the most intelligent sociopathic abuser may internalize the hypocrisy of his or her actions regarding the preceding sentiment—as the abuser may indeed realize his or her previous dependence on others—he or she will not necessarily abandon a lifestyle of viewing other humans as expendable. The nonsociopath must remember: the abuser does not necessarily have to care, let alone feel confined to live in some moral or ethical framework that may logically defeat any convenient self-centered philosophy justifying abusiveness toward others.

As with the "empathizations" covered in the preceding chapters, a nonsociopath would also do well to remember that logic may fail to change the mind of the abuser and, just as strongly, even fail to influence him or her. In effect, such an empathization may be framed: "If people who are abusive could just see the logic and potential hypocrisy of their actions, then they would care. And subsequently, they would choose to change their behavior."

To counter, some abusers might reason, "So what? I needed somebody to feed me when I was a baby, and now I treat people like they are worthless. I do what I want—so what?" Some might even offer, "Besides, how I devalue people now is further justified because what I do and contribute now far outweighs the contribution someone else might have made to me in the past."

No matter how independent an abuser may be in the present, if he or she lives long enough, at some point, dependency on others will eventually set in. Even if that abuser created an age-defying elixir with some unheard-of technology, somehow or another, a need for others' contributions or assistance ultimately remains inevitable. To illustrate this point, hopefully others never face the following predicament—but if they needed to, could they independently give themselves open-heart surgery?

To some degree, an accompanying helplessness and dependency on others remains ingrained into the human life experience for everyone. Nonetheless, hubris can be manifested through an abuser's perspective that not only is he or she "independent" of the contributions of others, but that others are lucky to be graced by the presence of the abuser and his or her "contributions." In brief, never let an individual convince you that you are without value—especially because an abuser's lack of value *for your value* is ultimately what proves truly worthless.

Looking Backward to Go Forward

Going further back than the individual human experiencing dependency on others after birth, I found myself debating a question regarding ancient history while writing the tactics that initially seemed so easy to answer yet proved so difficult. Namely, did *Homo sapiens* of the past know about sociopathy? Preceding the Geneva Conventions, Johannes Gutenberg's printing press, the Magna Carta, or even the Code of Hammurabi, did they *know* some people might not have consciences or any regard for others' well-being?

The knee-jerk reaction for many may be to assume the term *sociopath* is too recent for past eras to identify, but perhaps—without a readily available word or label, were they thinking it? In other words, were they aware that some people might lie, cheat, steal, or perform any number of cruel or violent acts for no other reason except for the fact they desired to do something, or acquire something, and could not care what happened to others due to their own actions? In contemplation of this question, I found myself weighing the following passage from a very cerebral nineteenth-century novelist Marguerite Gardiner:

> Such were the discussions continually passing between Lady Beauchamp and Mr. Mortimer, discussions in which the pensive widow always suffered the most; for, being of a morbidly sensitive nature, she acutely felt the sarcasms of her brother, whilst he, shielded by his callosity, was proof against her weak reprisals. (1842, p. 53).

When coming across this passage, it occurred to me that long before contemporary mass media; long before the Internet, automobile, or high definition television; long before the color photograph, the satellite, or the airplane; and even before the lines of the telegraph were successfully laid in the ocean, so long ago, real authors—indeed, real people—were acutely aware of sociopathic traits exhibited by others around them. I would even say they were aware of a wordlessness that accompanied certain interpersonally abusive transgressions.

Callosity—an official but antiquated term used by Marguerite Gardiner—seems to sum it up so concisely, as if to convey the abusive sociopath's actions lacking regard for a victim's safety or feelings, a complex thought so impressively offered with only one word. And as evident from such powerful diction, it remains pointless to assume that eras of the past lacked cognizance for the "thing" that was sociopathy or psychopathy—simply because they might have lacked a term for it. Though the case can be made that preceding generations arguably lacked a more formal understanding of mental disability and disorder, concepts that—with good fortune and *good* science—stand to be grasped even more effectively by succeeding generations.

Indeed, throughout the ages, some were acutely tuned-in to a lack of civility among the people with whom they lived. And yet the question remains to this present day—are we more technologically advanced than we are civilized? The microchips and circuit boards that run infrastructures profess an advancement of machinery and technology that laps the substanceless handshake and the superficial, "How are you?" The back dealings, conniving and disingenuous as they are, seem to permeate forward into the twenty-first century.

But the question remains: why? Perhaps the answer lies not in *why* but *why not*. Remember the temper tantrum. Why are they thrown? As was previously offered, because they all too often work.

It is not that those alive today are necessarily any "smarter" than the billions upon billions of *Homo sapiens* who preceded them. While, of course, those at present may be considered the most well educated and perhaps most aware. As Gardiner's quote indicates, some from the past—indeed, many—possessed awareness. But perhaps the difference now is an opportunity to awaken a sleeping giant, well-read and well-abused, to identify and disempower the abusive sociopath's agenda. May the quality of life for every human being be positively affected. Godspeed.

Acknowledgments

With appreciation, I wish to thank the Rice University Fondren Library resource and archiving staff, the University of Texas at Austin, Perry-Castañeda Library resource and archiving staff, the American Psychiatric Association staff for tracking down and confirming a source of questionable origin for me, as well as Trevor and Mark and the team at Page Publishing. I would also like to thank the following individuals for their time and/or their words of support: CLC, RMC, Norman Ley, P. McClurg, Trey Pharis, Erick Pharis, David A., C.W. Cox, NGB, JWF, AMN, DJB, DJS, NDB, RLP, the late Mike Anderson, A. Alexakis, Jennifer Edmiston, Claudia Jones, Robin Williamson, J. Butler, Nicole Casarez, T. Rebard, Nancy Liscum, Tommy Damora, Joan Connor, RPR, JCS, and BR. I am indebted to you for your actions of empathy.

Notes

American Psychiatric Association. 1952. *Diagnostic and Statistical Manual [of] Mental Disorders*. Washington, DC: Author.

American Psychiatric Association. 1968. *Diagnostic and Statistical Manual of Mental Disorders*, 2nd ed. Washington, DC: Author.

American Psychiatric Association. 2000. *Diagnostic and Statistical Manual of Mental Disorders*, 4th ed., text revised. Washington, DC: Author.

American Psychiatric Association. 2012. *DSM-IV and DSM-V Criteria for the Personality Disorders*. [PDF document of a preliminary *DSM-V* draft] Retrieved from http://www.psi.uba.ar/academica/carrerasdegrado/psicologia/sitios_catedras/practicas_profesionales/820_clinica_tr_personalidad_psicosis/material/dsm.pdf.

American Psychiatric Association. 2013a. *Diagnostic and Statistical Manual of Mental Disorders*, 5th ed. Washington, DC: Author.

American Psychiatric Association. 2013b. *The Principles of Medical Ethics with Annotations Especially Applicable to Psychiatry*. Arlington, VA: Author.

American Psychological Association. 2015. *APA Dictionary of Psychology*, 2nd ed. VandenBos, G. R. (Ed.). Washington, DC: Author.

Anderson, M. and W. March. 1985. *Bad Seed: The Dramatization of William March's Novel "The Bad Seed"*. New York, NY: Dodd, Mead & Company. (Original work published 1955).

Berger, F.K., D. Zieve, and I. Ogilvie, eds. 2014. National Institute of Mental Health. Retrieved from https://medlineplus.gov/ency/article/000921.htm.

Bianconi, E., A. Piovesan, F. Facchin, A. Beraudi, R. Casadei, F. Frabetti,… S. Canaider. 2013. "An Estimation of the Number of Cells in the Human Body." *Annal of Human Biology* 40(6): 463–471. doi:10.3109/03014460.2013.807878.

Bonn, S. 2014. "How to Tell a Sociopath from a Psychopath." *Psychology Today*. Retrieved from https://www.psychologytoday.com/blog/wicked-deeds/201401/how-tell-sociopath-psychopath.

Bruni, L., and P. L. Porta, eds. 2016. *Handbook of Research Methods and Applications in Happiness and Quality of Life*. Cheltenham, Gloucestershire, England: Edward Elgar.

Burton, N. 2015. "Empathy vs Sympathy." *Psychology Today*. Retrieved from https://www.psychologytoday.com/blog/hide-and-seek/201505/empathy-vs-sympathy.

Cameron, W. B. 1963. *Informal Sociology: A Casual Introduction to Sociological Thinking*. New York, NY: Random House.

Center for Building a Culture of Empathy. n.d. *Culture of Empathy Builder: Mark Davis*. Retrieved from http://cultureofempathy.com/references/Experts/Mark- Davis.htm.

Cleckley, H. M. 1941. *The Mask of Sanity: An Attempt to Reinterpret the So-Called Psychopathic Personality*. St. Louis: The C.V. Mosby Company.

Cleckley, H. M. 2016. *The Mask of Sanity: An Attempt to Clarify Some Issues About the So-Called Psychopathic Personality*, 3rd ed. Pickle Partners Publishing. (Original work published 1955).

Conlon, P. M. 2012. "Conflict of Employee–Employer Interest: Introducing an Optimal Work Happiness Framework." Retrieved from https://scholarship.rice.edu/handle/1911/77668.

Cox, T. 2011. "Brain Maturity Extends Well Beyond Teen Years [Interview]." *National Public Radio*. Retrieved from http://www.npr.org/templates/transcript/transcript.php?storyId=141164708.

Davis, M. H. 1983. "Measuring Individual Differences in Empathy: Evidence for a Multidimensional Approach." *Journal of Personality and Social Psychology* 44: 113–126.

de Waal, F. 2014. "Ethics without God? The Evolution of Morality and Empathy in the Primates." Lecture presented at the Houston Museum of Natural Science, Houston, TX.

Decety, J., and P. L. Jackson. 2004. "The Functional Architecture of Human Empathy." *Behavioral and Cognitive Neuroscience Reviews* 3: 71–100.

Decety, J., and M. Meyer. 2008. "From Emotion Resonance to Empathic Understanding: A Social Developmental Neuroscience Account." *Development and Psychopathology* 20(4): 1053–1080.

Diener, E., and E. M. Suh, eds. 2000. *Culture and Subjective Well-Being.* Cambridge, Mass: MIT Press.

Fisher, A. 2015. "How Microaggressions Can Wreck Your Business." *Fortune.* Retrieved from http://fortune.com/2015/11/19/microaggressions-talent-business/.

Ferguson, C. J. 2010. "Genetic Contributions to Antisocial Personality and Behavior: A Meta-Analytic Review from an Evolutionary Perspective." *The Journal of Social Psychology* 150(2): 160–180. doi:10.1080/00224540903366503.

Gardiner, M. 1842. *The Lottery of Life.* Retrieved from https://play.google.com/books/reader?id=0VhcmLhxPi4C&printsec=frontcover&output=reader&hl=en&pg=GBS.PP9.

Gardner, H. E. 1983. *Frames of Mind: The Theory of Multiple Intelligences.* New York, NY: Basic.

Golman, D. 1996. "Forget Money; Nothing Can Buy Happiness, Some Researchers Say." *The New York Times.* Retrieved from http://www.nytimes.com/1996/07/16/science/forget-money-nothing-can-buy-happiness-some-researchers- say.html?_r=0.

Grohol, J. M. 2015. "Differences Between a Psychopath vs Sociopath." *PsychCentral.* Retrieved from http://psychcentral.com/blog/archives/2015/02/12/differences-between-a-psychopath-vs-sociopath/.

Hanson, R. 2010. "How Did Humans Become Empathic? Empathy Is Unusual in the Animal Kingdom." *Psychology Today.* Retrieved from https://www.psychologytoday.com/blog/your-wise-brain/201003/how-did-humans-become-empathic.

Hare, R. D. 1999. *Without Conscience: The Disturbing World of the Psychopaths Among Us.* New York, NY: The Guilford Press. (Original work published 1993).

Hare, R. D. 2003. *Manual for the Revised Psychopathy Checklist*, 2nd ed. Toronto, Ontario, Canada: Multi-Health Systems.

Headey, B., and A. J. Wearing. 1992. *Understanding Happiness: A Theory of Subjective Well-Being.* Melbourne, Victoria, Australia: Longman Cheshire.

ICD Codes. 2015. "What is ICD (International Classification of Diseases)?" Retrieved from https://icd.codes/articles/what-is-icd.

Kiehl, K. A. 2006. "A Cognitive Neuroscience Perspective on Psychopathy: Evidence for Paralimbic System Dysfunction." *Psychiatry Research* 142(2–3): 107–128. Retrieved from https://www.ncbi.nlm.nih.gov/pmc/articles/PMC2765815/pdf/nihms-151746.pdf.

Kiehl, K. A., and M. B. Hoffman. 2011. "The Criminal Psychopath: History, Neuroscience, Treatment, and Economics." *Jurimetrics* 51: 355–397.

Kiehl, K. A., and W. P. Sinnott-Armstrong, eds. 2013. *Handbook on Psychopathy and Law.* Oxford: Oxford University Press.

Kusy, M., and E. Holloway. 2009. *Toxic Workplace!: Managing Toxic Personalities and Their Systems of Power*, 1st ed. San Francisco: Jossey-Bass.

Lee, J. L. 2013. "Is My Child a Sociopath? An Elephant in the Room Parents Can't Afford to Ignore." *Psychology Today.* Retrieved from https://www.psychologytoday.com/blog/your-home-is-not-democracy/201306/is-my-child-sociopath.

Lenzenweger, M. F., M. C. Lane, A. W. Loranger, and R. C. Kessler. 2007. "DSM-IV Personality Disorders in the National Comorbidity Survey Replication." *Biological Psychiatry* 62(6): 553–564. doi:10.1016/j.biopsych.2006.09.019.

Lipman, V. 2013. "The Disturbing Link Between Psychopathy and Leadership." *Forbes.* Retrieved from http://www.forbes.com/sites/victorlipman/2013/04/25/the-disturbing-link-between-psychopathy-and-leadership/#60a828d12740.

Lykken, D., and A. Tellegen. 1996. "Happiness Is a Stochastic Phenomenon." *Psychological Science* 7(3): 186–189. doi:10.1111/j.1467-9280.1996.tb00355.x.

Lyubomirsky, S., and K. Layous. 2013. "How Do Simple Positive Activities Increase Well-Being?" *Current Directions in Psychological Science* 22(1): 57–62. doi:10.1177/0963721412469809.

Lyubomirsky, S., K. M. Sheldon, and D. Schkade. 2005. "Pursuing Happiness: The Architecture of Sustainable Change." *Review of General Psychology* 9(2): 111–131. doi:10.1037/1089-2680.9.2.111.

March, W. 1997. *The Bad Seed: A Novel by William March*. New York, NY: HarperCollins. (Original work published 1954).

Martin, S. 2009. "Improving Diagnosis Worldwide: Major Changes Are Ahead for the World's Disease Classification System, and Psychologists' Input Is Crucial to Getting It Right." *Monitor on Psychology* 40(9). Retrieved from http://www.apa.org/monitor/2009/10/diagnosis.aspx.

Maslow, A. H. 1943. "A Theory of Human Motivation." *Psychological Review* 50(4): 370–396.

Meloy, J. R., ed. 1998. *The Psychology of Stalking: Clinical and Forensic Perspectives*. San Diego: Academic Press.

Merriam-Webster Dictionary. n.d. "Antisocial." Retrieved from http://www.merriam-webster.com/dictionary/antisocial.

Merriam-Webster Dictionary. n.d. "Antisocial Personality Disorder." Retrieved from http://www.merriam-webster.com/dictionary/antisocial personality disorder.

Merriam-Webster Dictionary. n.d. "Psychopath." Retrieved from http://www.merriam-webster.com/dictionary/psychopath.

Merriam-Webster Dictionary. n.d. "Sociopath." Retrieved from http://www.merriam-webster.com/dictionary/sociopath.

Merriam-Webster Medical Dictionary. n.d. "Empath." Retrieved from http://www.merriam-webster.com/dictionary/empathy#medicalDictionary.

Merriam-Webster Medical Dictionary. n.d. "Sociopath." Retrieved from http://www.merriam-webster.com/dictionary/sociopath#medicalDictionary.

Meyers, S. 2013. "Understanding the Sociopath: Cause, Motivation, Relationship." *Psychology Today*. Retrieved from https://www.psychologytoday.com/blog/insight-is-2020/201304/understanding-the-sociopath-cause-motivation-relationship.

Nauert, R. 2015. "The Anatomy of a Psychopath." *Psych Central*. Retrieved from http://psychcentral.com/news/2009/08/05/the-anatomy-of-a-psychopath/7559.html.

O'Malley, K. J., K. F. Cook, M. D. Price, K. R. Wildes, J. F. Hurdle, and C. M. Ashton. 2005. "Measuring Diagnoses: ICD Code Accuracy." *Health Services Research* 40(5p2), 1620–1639. http://doi.org/10.1111/j.1475-6773.2005.00444.x.

Oxford English Dictionary, 2nd ed. n.d. "Empath." Retrieved from http://www.oxforddictionaries.com/us/definition/american_english/empath.

Oxford English Dictionary, 2nd ed. n.d. "Gaslighting." Retrieved from http://www.oxforddictionaries.com/us/definition/american_english/gaslight.

Pedersen, T. 2016. "Psychopaths Feel Fear but Have Difficulty Detecting Threats." *Psych Central*. Retrieved from http://psychcentral.com/news/2016/08/31/psychopaths-feel-fear-but-have-difficulty-detecting-threats/109290.html.

Pettigrew, T. 2013. "Why We Should Forget Einstein's Tree-Climbing Fish." *Maclean's*. Retrieved from http://www.macleans.ca/education/uniandcollege/why-we-should-forget-einsteins-tree-climbing-fish/.

Riggio, R. E. 2011. "Are You Empathic? 3 Types of Empathy and What They Mean: When Is Empathy a Good Thing, and When Is It a Bad Thing?" *Psychology Today*. Retrieved from https://www.psychologytoday.com/blog/cutting-edge-leadership/201108/are-you-empathic-3-types-empathy-and-what-they-mean.

Robinson, K. M. n.d. "Sociopath vs. Psychopath: What's the Difference?" *WebMD Mental Health Feature Stories*. Retrieved from http://www.webmd.com/mental-health/features/sociopath-psychopath-difference.

Seabrook, J. 2008. "Sufferings Souls: The Search for the Roots of Psychopathy." *New Yorker*. Retrieved from http://www.newyorker.com/magazine/2008/11/10/suffering-souls.

Songer, J. 2011. "New Words and Slang Submission Archives." *Merriam-Webster Open Dictionary*. Retrieved from http://nws.merriam-webster.com/opendictionary/newword_search.php.

Stout, M. 2005. *The Sociopath Next Door: The Ruthless Versus the Rest of Us*. New York, NY: Broadway Books.

Taylor, S. 2016. "Negative Empathy." *Psychology Today*. Retrieved from https://www.psychologytoday.com/blog/out-the-darkness/201605/negative-empathy.

Time. 1937. "Medicine: Pedophilia." *Time* 30(8): 42–44.

Van Luling, T. 2015. "Here's One Thing You've Never Noticed about Disney Parks." *The Huffington Post*. Retrieved from http://www.huffingtonpost.com/entry/two-finger-disney-point-_us/_55a3f000e4b0b8145f731d99.

Viding, E., R. J. Blair, T. E. Moffitt, and R. Plomin. 2005. "Evidence for Substantial Genetic Risk for Psychopathy in 7-year-olds." *Journal of Child Psychology and Psychiatry* 46(6): 592–597. doi:10.1111/j.14697610.2004.00393.x.

Viding, E., A. P. Jones, J. F. Paul, T. E. Moffitt, and R. Plomin. 2008. "Heritability of Antisocial Behaviour at 9: Do Callous-Unemotional Traits Matter?" *Developmental Science* 11(1): 17–22. doi:10.1111/j.1467-7687.2007.00648.x.

Warren, J. I., M. L. Burnette, S. C. South, P. Chauhan, and R. Bale, R. Friend, and I. Van Patten. 2003. "Psychopathy in Women: Structural Modeling and Comorbidity." *International Journal of Law and Psychiatry* 26(3): 223–242. doi:10.1016/s0160-2527(03)00034-7.

World Health Organization. 1992. "The *ICD-10* Classification of Mental and Behavioural Disorders: Clinical Descriptions and Diagnostic Guidelines." Geneva: Author.

Wynn, R., Høiseth, and G. Pettersen. 2012. "Psychopathy in Women: Theoretical and Clinical Perspectives." *International Journal of Women's Health* 257. doi:10.2147/ijwh.s25518.

About the Author

Paul M. Conlon, MBA, has worn many hats, having worked in business consulting as well as education. Conlon's *Optimal Work Happiness Model*, published in 2012, offers a novel approach to perceiving and striving for worker happiness. In addition to sociopathy, his research interests include organizational behavior, astrophysics, and musicology. An alumnus of the University of St. Thomas in Houston, Conlon holds graduate degrees from the University of Houston-Victoria and Rice University. The native Houstonian also composes orchestral music, most notably writing the "L'inizio di un Viaggio" overture while a graduate student at Rice University. Conlon enjoys watching and participating in America's pastime, and has received five at-bats at Fenway Park during an adult recreational baseball tournament. He struck out twice and hit a single.